PIVOTAL
MOMENTS
in Nursing

Leaders Who Changed the Path of a Profession

VOLUME I

BOOKS PUBLISHED BY THE HONOR SOCIETY OF NURSING, SIGMA THETA TAU INTERNATIONAL

Being Present: A Nurse's Resource for End-of-Life Care, Schaffer and Norlander, 2009.

Why Retire? Career Strategies for Third Age Nurses, Bower and Sadler, 2009.

B Is for Balance: A Nurse's Guide for Enjoying Life at Work and at Home, Weinstein, 2008.

To Comfort Always: A Nurse's Guide to End-of-Life Care, Norlander, 2008.

Ready, Set, Go Lead! A Primer for Emerging Health Care Leaders, Dickenson-Hazard, 2008.

Words of Wisdom From Pivotal Nurse Leaders, Houser and Player, 2008.

Tales From the Pager Chronicles, Rancour, 2008.

The Nurse's Etiquette Advantage, Pagana, 2008.

NURSE: A World of Care, Jaret, 2008. Published by Emory University and distributed by the Honor Society of Nursing, Sigma Theta Tau International.

Nursing Without Borders: Values, Wisdom, Success Markers, Weinstein and Brooks, 2007.

Synergy: The Unique Relationship Between Nurses and Patients, Curley, 2007.

Conversations With Leaders: Frank Talk From Nurses (and Others) on the Front Lines of Leadership, Hansen-Turton, Sherman, and Ferguson, 2007.

Pivotal Moments in Nursing: Leaders Who Changed the Path of a Profession, Houser and Player, 2004 (Volume I) and 2007 (Volume II).

Daily Miracles: Stories and Practices of Humanity and Excellence in Health Care, Briskin and Boller, 2006.

A Daybook for Nurse Leaders and Mentors. Sigma Theta Tau International, 2006.

The HeART of Nursing: Expressions of Creative Art in Nursing, Second Edition, Wendler, 2005.

Making a Difference: Stories from the Point of Care, Volumes I and II, Hudacek, 2005.

A Daybook for Nurses: Making a Difference Each Day, Hudacek, 2004.

For more information and to order these books from the Honor Society of Nursing, Sigma Theta Tau International, visit the honor society's website at www.nursingsociety.org/publications, or go to www.nursingknowledge.org/stti/books, the website of Nursing Knowledge International, the honor society's sales and distribution division. Or, call 1.888.NKI.4.YOU (US and Canada) or +1.317.634.8171 (Outside US and Canada).

PIVOTAL
MOMENTS
in Nursing

Leaders Who Changed the Path of a Profession

BETH P. HOUSER, DNSc, FNP, NEA-BC
KATHY N. PLAYER, EdD, RN, MS-N, MBA

VOLUME I

Sigma Theta Tau International
Honor Society of Nursing®

Sigma Theta Tau International

Publisher: Jeff Burnham
Acquisitions Editor: Fay L. Bower, DNSc, FAAN
Development Editor: Carla Hall
Proofreader: Linda Canter
Indexer: Angie Bess, RN
Graphic Designer: Graphic World, Inc.
Cover Designer: Rebecca Harmon

Printed in the United States of America

Printing and Binding by Edwards Brothers, Inc.
Composition and Interior Design by Graphic World, Inc.

Sigma Theta Tau International
550 West North Street
Indianapolis, IN 46202

Visit our Web site at www.nursingsociety.org for more information on our books and other publications.

ISBN: 978-1-930538-11-5

Library of Congress Cataloging-in-Publication Data

Houser, Beth, 1957-
    Pivotal moments in nursing : leaders who changed the path of a profession / by Beth Houser and Kathy Player.
        p. ; cm.
Includes bibliographical references and index.
ISBN 1-930538-11-1
    1. Nurses—United States—Biography. 2. Nursing—United States—History. [DNLM: 1. History of Nursing—United States. 2. Nurses—United States—Biography. 3. Leadership—United States—Biography. WZ 112.5.N8 H842p 2004]
I. Player, Kathy, 1962- II. Sigma Theta Tau International. III. Title.
RT34.H68 2004
610'.92'2—dc22
    2004005624

Fifth Printing, 2009

Dedication

This book is dedicated to nurses worldwide
who are the true leaders of healthcare.

Save one life,

and you are a hero.

Save one hundred lives,

and you are a nurse.

—by Chuck Stepanek

Acknowledgements

FROM THE AUTHORS

Heartfelt thanks go out from the authors to the 12 nurse leaders. You so graciously accepted our requests for interviews and then submitted to the subsequent journalizing of your lives. Your dedication to this project has been at a level none less than ours. You embraced the concept of what we were striving to achieve. In return, we know that the lives of those who read your pages will be all the more enriched for the legacy you continue to leave to the nursing profession.

We would also like to express our gratitude for the support of the Robert Wood Johnson Foundation and the Robert Wood Johnson Executive Nurse Fellows Program. The Robert Wood Johnson Foundation has been visionary in its support of healthcare and nursing, and this book is but one example of its generosity.

We would also like to thank Sigma Theta Tau International and its professional staff for a job well done. A special thanks to Carla and Fay who moved us through the process in expert style.

BETH HOUSER

I would like to thank the John C. Lincoln (JCL) Health Network and, specifically, Sue Hanauer for overwhelming support, trust, and professionalism. To my JCL nursing colleagues—you define leadership excellence!

My life has brought me many gifts, but none as great as my soul mate, Bob, who has taught me how to perform at a higher level and demanded that I follow my dreams. I thank you for your patience, intelligence, and willingness to read every word I wrote. I love you.

I would also like to thank my mother, who taught me that anything was possible if I worked hard enough, and my dad who made me believe in myself. Dad, I can see the twinkle in your eye and your gleaming grin, even from heaven. Billy and Sandy, you are my heroes, and life is certainly made richer by your character, integrity and values.

I need to thank my remarkable mentors—Sylvia Root, Barbara Durand, Sue Donaldson, and Lee Ford—who have patiently and persistently pushed, pulled, and cajoled me to the next level of thinking. I thank you for your vision when I could not see.

The rare gift of unconditional friendship has graced my life thanks to Susie Johns, Linda Kerley, and Melanie Brewer. You have shared with me in great abundance laughter, kindness, and caring. You have made me a better person in every way.

This project would never have come to completion without my partner Kathy Player. She is a professional in every sense of the word. It is an honor and pleasure to collaborate with someone who produces such a quality product.

Last but certainly not least, I want to thank my children—Jess, Rob, and JJ— you have been my loudest cheerleaders. The sacrifices you have endured for my dreams have left me speechless. Your leadership is what keeps me going! I am counting on you, and I love you to the moon and back again.

KATHY PLAYER

I would like to thank my colleagues in the College of Nursing and the College of Business and Professional Studies at Grand Canyon University for their support, specifically, Dr. David Braaten. You have provided me the freedom to pursue these human stories profiled here, and the journey has been most memorable.

Of course I would like to thank my supportive friends and colleagues—Marla Weston, Anne McNamara, Carolyn Hinderliter, Kim Coffman, Arlene Boucher, Teri Britt, and Kay Moroz, along with my RWJ Fellows cohorts for always asking how this book was coming along and for inspiring me to keep typing. In the midst of daunting task, you helped me to laugh and yet still remain focused on striving to reach my goal. Thanks for always creating a sense of balance with your guidance and friendship.

One of the most important lessons I am constantly reminded of is that no success of mine could be achieved without the patience and devotion of my wonderful spouse. Ken, for your unconditional love and support throughout my life, I love and thank you.

For two of the best parents placed on this earth, Adam and Mary Nosal, I offer thanks to both of you for always being in my corner and inspiring me to stretch beyond my imagination. Mom, as a retired nurse from an earlier generation, I dedicate this book to you.

And to my partner in this book, Beth: Thanks for allowing me to share in this experience. It has been an incredible ride for which I am most grateful.

About the Authors

BETH P. HOUSER, RN, DNSc, FNP, NEA-BC

Dr. Beth Houser is Chief Nursing Officer of Baylor Regional Medical Center at Grapevine in Texas. Her previous leadership roles included Director of Critical Care and Telemetry at Scottsdale Healthcare (2005-2008) and Director of Nursing Research and the Magnet Project for John C. Lincoln-North Mountain (2002-2005) in Arizona. Since 2002, she has been a Magnet appraiser for the American Nurses Credentialing Center and has been involved in all aspects of the application process and program evolution. She is a Robert Wood Johnson Executive Nurse Fellow (2002 cohort) and coauthored, with Dr. Kathy Player, *Pivotal Moments in Nursing: Leaders Who Changed the Path of a Profession,* volumes I and II, as partial fulfillment of the Fellowship.

Dr. Houser graduated from the University of Arizona in 1978 with her Bachelor of Science in Nursing. Twenty years later, she completed her Master of Science degree from Arizona State University as a family nurse practitioner. In August, 2004, Beth completed her doctoral dissertation, titled "Nursing Staffing Levels and Patient Outcomes," at Johns Hopkins University School of Nursing. The Johns Hopkins University program of study was devoted to educating nurse scientists to use large databases to answer global healthcare questions. Her career interests include patient safety and nurse-sensitive quality indicators, excellence in professional nursing practice, interdisciplinary team building, and creating a Magnet-like work environment.

She has guest lectured at many schools of nursing, presented Magnet information at national conferences, and published extensively on both leadership and Magnet topics. She is an active member of the American Nurses Association, Sigma Theta Tau International, American Organization of Nurse Executives, and the American Academy of Nurse Practitioners.

Dr. Houser can be reached via e-mail at Beth.Houser@Baylorhealth.edu or via telephone at 817-329-2508.

KATHY NOSAL PLAYER, RN, EdD

Dr. Kathy Player is President of Grand Canyon University. She joined Grand Canyon in 1998 and served in several leadership roles prior to being appointed President. Most recently, she served as Provost and Chief Academic Officer. Prior to that, she was Dean of the Ken Blanchard College of Business. She has published widely, including *Words of Wisdom from Pivotal Nurse Leaders, Pivotal Moments in Nursing: Leaders Who Changed the Path of a Profession,* volumes I and II, and a chapter titled *Legal Accountability and Responsibility in Nursing Fundamentals* (2009).

Dr. Player serves as a board member for St. Luke's Behavioral Health Hospital. She was the second Vice President for the American Nurses Association (2006-2007), and served as a board member of the American Nurses' Credentialing Center (2006-2007), Arizona Nurses' Foundation (2006-present), and was past president of the Arizona Nurses' Association (2001-2005). She was a participant in a Healthcare Leadership Exchange in Cuba, meeting with leaders from the Ministry of Health and sharing ideas and solutions on US/Cuban healthcare, sponsored through the University of California San Francisco and Medical Education Cooperation with Cuba (MEDICC). Additionally, she volunteered for a healthcare mission to Trang, Thailand, to teach both nursing faculty and students in a baccalaureate college. She volunteers with community and professional organizations, including lobbying on behalf of nursing issues at both the state and national level for the past six years. She was awarded the Robert Wood Johnson Executive Nursing Fellowship in Leadership (2002-2005) and is an invited member of the Global Nursing Exchange. Dr. Player is past Vice President of Nu Upsilon chapter and is a current member of the Beta Mu chapter of Sigma Theta Tau International.

She holds a Doctorate of Education in Counseling Psychology from Argosy University (formerly the University of Sarasota in Florida); an MBA from Grand Canyon University; a Master of Science in Nursing from Grand Canyon University; a Master of Science in Counseling from Nova Southeastern University in Florida; and a Bachelor of Science in Nursing from St. Joseph's College in Maine.

Dr. Player can be reached via e-mail at kplayer@gcu.edu or at Grand Canyon University, 3300 W. Camelback Road, Phoenix, AZ 85017.

Table of Contents

Prologue xiv

Preface xvi

Foreword by Dr. Dan Pesut xvii

Chapter 1 Loretta C. Ford 1

Chapter 2 Shirley Sears Chater 23

Chapter 3 Joyce C. Clifford 45

Chapter 4 Luther Christman 67

Chapter 5 Vernice D. Ferguson 89

Chapter 6 Ada Sue Hinshaw 105

Chapter 7 Faye Glenn Abdellah 129

Chapter 8 Sue Karen Donaldson 147

Chapter 9 Margretta "Gretta" Madden Styles 169

Chapter 10 Rheba de Tornyay 187

Chapter 11 Claire Fagin 205

Chapter 12 Linda H. Aiken 225

Appendix A Leadership Challenges 249

Appendix B Biographical Summaries 259

Appendix C Resources 275

Index 277

Prologue

In the spring of 1996, Loretta Ford, the birth mother of the nurse practitioner movement, was the featured keynote speaker at Arizona State University. What happened next was the genesis of this book. Loretta filled the room with passion, professionalism, and a resounding call to leadership. This remarkable nurse leader stood before a group of hundreds of nursing colleagues and directed them to "get to the table and be a player." The only reason they were all gathered in that very conference room was because Loretta had been a formidable player who had produced an astounding ripple throughout the world of healthcare.

It was this seed that germinated this book. We felt that these nursing leadership stories simply had to be told. We feel that the future of nursing depends on our ability to understand the past through the profound leadership lessons we can learn from those who have gone before us. We wanted to share how these leaders were ordinary people who had accomplished extraordinary outcomes in their careers, and in turn, we hope to inspire future leaders to envision their own leadership capacities through a richer understanding of these leaders and how their respective journeys evolved—warts and all.

In strategizing how this dream could become a reality, we determined that the leaders selected for this book should represent a broad array of domains within nursing—academics, acute care, public policy, research, and so on. We knew that the leadership of these individuals had to be pivotal in the advancement of the profession and that the selected leaders had to be living so the stories could be told with the leader's voice in the forefront. Moreover, we determined that the writing style should be easy to read, inviting, and relevant to practicing nurses at all levels.

A hypothetical list of 12 leaders who met the criteria and were universally recognized as legends was selected. We hoped that at least half of these leaders would consent to a book written by unknown authors who had yet to secure a publisher. We were astounded when every single leader responded to the invitation with resounding enthusiasm and appreciation for the project. These leaders opened their hearts, souls, and minds to share the archives of their journey with the "up and coming" leadership with the hopes that you, the mysterious reader, may improve on their work. In their eyes, this book represented a passing of the leadership torch.

As the project progressed, themes of leadership emerged among all the selected leaders that clearly defined the fundamentals for their success. Without question, each leader was scholarly, committed, responsive, thoughtful, humble, innovative, creative, courageous, resilient, and visionary. How these qualities were expressed in their individual journeys are the pearls of wisdom within each chapter. We hope these pearls will assist you in developing your own unique brand of leadership.

This book has only scratched the surface of those nurse leaders who deserve recognition. There are many more worthy stories to tell, and we plan to bring this history to you in future volumes so that, as nurses, we may all be more effective and efficient "players" at the healthcare table.

Sit back and relax as you gain a greater understanding of leadership from the masters of our profession. Picture how each journey may lend itself to your opportunities. Let your story be the next leadership victory worthy of a place in history.

Preface

This book was initially envisioned as a document for inspiring and encouraging nurses to "take the lead" in nursing, like the people highlighted in this book. Lessons learned through the rich experiences of others are the most valuable educational tools for illustrating both what works and what doesn't work. To experience the full appreciation of successful risk taking in leadership, one must acknowledge that the same amount of energy and passion can bring setbacks or failures in pursuit of a goal. It is the fear of failure that prompts some to choose to disembark on their journey, while the leader will hunker down and come back stronger.

The stories told in this book do not represent the only leaders in nursing. As the authors soon realized, the list of qualified nurse leaders is quite extensive. However, the 12 individuals described in this book represent various aspects of nursing and a diversity of accomplishments, and all have international recognition. Again, this book does not include a finite list of qualified candidates, but it is a great start in an exploration of the leadership lessons that are there to be learned. If the interest of you—the reader—allows, we look forward to future volumes that reflect on the lives of many more great leaders. These 12 nurse leaders have honestly addressed their trials and tribulations in pursuing their vision of change and the advancement of the profession. Not one of these leaders woke up one morning and had a career handed to her or him. It was the result of much perseverance and clever strategies; some of them did not work initially. While this book was envisioned to be an inspiration for others to pursue the same kind of endeavor, it was concluded as a labor of love for the body of knowledge it provides for the generations of nurses to come. Read on and discover the power available to all nurses to impact change if they are willing to take the challenge.

Forward

THE SPIRIT OF LEADERSHIP

This book is about the spirit of leadership. Harrison Owen (1999) believes there are five functions of leadership: To evoke spirit through vision, to grow spirit through collective storytelling, to sustain spirit through structure, to comfort spirit when things fall apart, and to raise spirit to enable renewal.

A careful read of each chapter in this book provides insights and lessons into how individual nursing leaders represent and embody the spirit of leadership. Each of the nurse leaders profiled in this book has had an incredible impact on the world of nursing and healthcare in general. Each leader had a strong set of personal values and beliefs she or he transformed into professional influence. Each is guided by values and beliefs about the greater good that nursing contributes to the social fabric of healthcare.

In every story, the five functions of leadership are evident. Each evoked spirit with vision. Each tells stories that inspire and reveal the spirit of leadership lessons. Each had opportunities to structure situations in strategic ways in order to realize the outcomes they desired. Each shares trials and tribulations that required the comforting of self and others when things seemed to fall apart. Each is a source of inspiration that sustains the spirit of leadership and provides that spark of creativity and renewal that individuals, groups, communities, and organizations need in order to keep visions alive.

The spirit of leadership is communicated in the stories contained in this book. I believe that as you read, study, and share these stories with others you are growing the spirit of leadership in nursing. On behalf of nurses around the world, I am grateful that Beth Houser and Kathy Player had the vision to capture and record these stories and reflections from nursing leaders about the spirit of leadership. I expect the stories contained in this book will contribute to the development of your own leadership skill set and be a source of inspiration and renewal for you.

Daniel J. Pesut, PhD, RN, APRN, BC, FAAN
President, Sigma Theta Tau International 2003-2005
January 1, 2004

Owen, H. (1999). *The spirit of leadership.* San Francisco, Berrett-Koehler.

CHAPTER 1

Loretta C. Ford

Loretta Ford, RN, EdD, PNP, FAAN, FAANP, is a nurse leader who transformed the nursing profession by initiating a movement that changed the delivery of healthcare, so much so that the words "nurse practitioner" are nearly synonymous with the name Loretta Ford. In 1965, Loretta and Henry Silver, a pediatrician, pioneered the first Pediatric Nurse Practitioner role at the University of Colorado. It was a period of political and social unrest in nursing and medicine that provided an opportunity for the expansion of the role of nursing. Loretta seized the moment.

The nurse practitioner movement has been a leadership journey that began with one courageous public health nurse in Denver, Colorado. Thirty nine years later there are more than 106,000 nurse practitioners around the globe.

Loretta's accomplishments have exemplified three precepts that have driven her career and the nurse practitioner movement.

1. Crisis invites opportunity. (Loretta points out that the Chinese symbol for crisis and opportunity are one and the same.)
2. Get to the table and be a player or someone who does not understand nursing, will do that for you.
3. Be in a hurry; there is not a moment to waste.

One should never be fooled by Loretta's petite frame. She is a giant in nursing. On occasion, she has been known to delight conference attendees by taking the podium wearing her "Super Nurse" costume, complete with red tights, a flowing red cape, and the large red "S" across her chest. Those who know her well would agree that the large red "S" represents scholarly, salient, self confident, sharp, speedy, savvy, and special.

Super Nurse Loretta Ford with Linda Pearson, editor-in-chief of Nurse Practitioner Journal, *and Loretta's daughter Valerie Monrad.*

One of Loretta's favorite quotes comes from the anthropologist Margaret Mead: "Never doubt that a small group of thoughtful, committed citizens can change the world; indeed, it is the only thing that ever has." Replace the word "citizens" with "nurses" and that is precisely what Loretta accomplished.

She believes that the credit for the nurse practitioner movement belongs "to the small band of nurse pioneers willing to take the risk," which is true, but she was the force behind making the vision a reality.

EARLY INFLUENCES

Loretta Cecelia Pfingstel Ford was born December 28, 1920 in Bronx, New York. She was named after a favorite aunt, but as a child she never really liked the name and her family and friends nicknamed her Dolly. When she turned 18 years old, Loretta decided that Dolly did not sound serious enough, so she unofficially changed her name to Lee. Recent colleagues call her Loretta, which has become her professional designation; however, she recognizes the era of the relationship by the name.

Loretta was the fourth in a line of seven children. It was a house full of very strong personalities who ultimately all grew to be leaders in their own right. Her father was a master lithographer who frequently found himself on union strike, sometimes for as long as a year. During these periods of unemployment, her mother "would manage the children" while her father went fishing and hunting.

One summer, when finances were tight, Loretta recalls the family moved to the mountains of New Jersey, where they lived in a tent by a creek. She describes this as a wonderful family adventure and perhaps her first experience of "crisis invites opportunity." They lived off the land and learned to appreciate the wildlife, terrain, and the peace of living outdoors.

Some of Loretta's earliest influences came from teachers. She still remembers her first grade teacher, Miss Reed, who recognized her academic abilities and moved her forward in her studies. Once Loretta's myopia was corrected at age nine, she sailed through school, skipping the third and sixth grades. She was a voracious reader, and dreamed of being a teacher.

It was a great disappointment to her when she was unable to afford the tuition at a teacher's college. But her sister in-law, who was also one of her high school teachers, suggested she consider nursing school.

She was not particularly interested in nursing, but she was motivated to get an education, and so she enrolled in the nursing program at Middlesex General Hospital in New Brunswick, New Jersey, because it was an affordable alternative.

Her father borrowed $100 dollars to cover tuition, and Loretta worked as a nurse's aide at Middlesex General Hospital and lived with the nursing students while she waited for her 18th birthday—the minimum age for entry into the program. By the time of entry in 1939, Loretta had read all the nursing books and so started ahead of her class. She describes her nursing school instructors as "very militant and very starched," and there was "no fooling around."

After graduation in1941, Loretta went to work for the local Visiting Nurse Service in New Brunswick. She also had plans to marry a Navy pharmacist mate. However, in 1942 she was notified that her fiancée had died when his ship went down during a World War II battle.

Grieving over the loss, Loretta decided she was going to make a contribution to the war effort in his honor, so she joined the United States Army Air Force. She became a first lieutenant and found the experience to be highly rewarding. Loretta was stationed for the majority of her military service in Miami, Florida, where she cared for servicemen who suffered from post-combat psychoneurosis. Her military duty gave her ample opportunity to provide leadership to the corpsmen with whom she worked, and she feels her military experience infused a strong sense of discipline and teamwork which served her well throughout her career.

NURSING AND FAMILY

In 1946, upon completing her tour of duty, Loretta took advantage of the GI Bill and went to the University of Colorado at Boulder to pursue a baccalaureate degree in nursing. Having spent her life on the east coast, Loretta had decided that it was time to feed her adventurous spirit and head west to parts unknown. Moreover, the University of Colorado at Boulder was one of the schools that offered a certificate in public health nursing at the baccalaureate level. By this time, Loretta had come to recognize that nursing was her calling, and she was particularly interested in the prevention of illness embodied in the public health model. While working part-time and going to school, she managed to meet her soul mate—Bill Ford. Loretta entered marriage believing Bill was a terrific person, but she was taking no chances. She opened a savings account where she deposited $250, which was the cost of a divorce, as a "just in case" fund. This was one account that has never been touched in almost 60 years of marriage.

In 1995, when the University of Rochester dedicated an endowed chair in Loretta's name, she insisted it be called the William J. Ford and Loretta C. Ford Chair in honor of his contribution to her professional success. She admits, without hesitation, that her professional accomplishments would have been impossible without the support of her family.

Her only child, Valerie Ford Monrad, born in 1952, is Loretta's most ardent cheerleader, calling her mother a remarkable visionary. Valerie believes that the gift of her mother's vision included being able "to hang on to the saddle because it was a ride worth taking" when most had given up.

The Ford house was filled with culture and love. According to Valerie, their home resembled a mini-United Nations, with visitors from around the world sharing their customs. Loretta blended family and career with such grace that Valerie often boasts about their charmed life.

In 1949, Loretta entered the Master of Science in nursing (MSN) program at the University of Colorado at Boulder and focused on public health. It was during her graduate education that Loretta felt she began to expand intellectually. She began to see the nurse as a knowledge worker rather than a performer of tasks.

While in the MSN program, she had the opportunity to work with some extraordinary mentors and "challengers," such as Pearl Parvin Coulter who provided a philosophical orientation to the public health nurse role; Katherine Kelly who infused the research component and scholarship to the profession; Henrietta Loughran who demonstrated patience, precision, and strategy to manipulate the environment in order to promote fundamental change; and Irene Murchison who specialized in the legal aspects of nursing practice. In their own way they were all extremely powerful people in Loretta's socialization as a professional. Pearl Coulter, through her power of persuasion, talked Loretta into accepting a position as a public health nurse for Boulder County, Colorado. Henrietta Loughran prompted Loretta to fill out her doctoral application telling her it was time to take the next step. Henrietta was also instrumental in helping Loretta obtain a scholarship making it impossible to turn her back on doctoral studies.

COMING OF AGE AS A YOUNG NURSE LEADER

Loretta Ford spent 12 years as a public health nurse, supervisor, and director. She learned early on that the health of the residents in some Colorado communities depended upon competent public health nurses.

There were two kinds of well-child clinics in rural Colorado: One was a well-child health operation that was physician attended and the other was an intermittent well-child health nursing clinic run by nurses without physicians in attendance.

It was because of the nurses' abilities to run these clinics that Loretta concluded nurses were being under utilized. If they could run clinics, their knowledge, skills, and competencies were logically much broader than was allowed in practice. The ideas for how nurses could become integral to healthcare solutions began to percolate for Loretta.

According to Linda Pearson, an early nurse practitioner pioneer and editor-in-chief of *The Nurse Practitioner Journal*, it was Loretta Ford who moved the nurse practitioner role idea forward, which energized many in the world of nursing. Says Linda, "[we saw that] of course this was what we should be doing, and it made so much sense that thousands of rebel nurses rallied to the cause."

CRISIS INVITES OPPORTUNITY

The early 1960s in the United States were a time of political and social unrest. The Vietnam War was on-going, and the nation's fabric was being torn by the extensive loss of life and diversion of U.S. dollars to a war that appeared to many to be hopeless.

Poverty was a major social issue, and access to healthcare services was a significant concern for many people. Educational preparation and distribution of physicians was heavily weighted toward specialty care, creating a shortage of generalists who were needed to meet community demands.

World War II had demonstrated the value of nurses to the world, and the nurses themselves now sought autonomy and independence in practice. Education was the key to social mobility, and nurses recognized this. Healthcare in America was experiencing a crisis that presented an opportunity to introduce an expanded role for nurses.

Loretta is very clear that the nurse practitioner movement was *not* created to meet a deficit of physician services. She visibly bristles at the very suggestion. "That is a myth. There was no reason in the world that I, as a nurse educator, should make up for medical deficiencies. That is the physician's responsibility, not nursing's." However, the physician shortage did create an optimal environment for change in nursing.

As healthcare and nursing opportunities evolved, Loretta had three assets in her possession that allowed her to begin to implement her vision of the nurse practitioner role. She had:

1. Extensive public health nursing experience, during which she had witnessed the impact public health nurses had on communities as champions for prevention and promotion of health via nurse-

focused teaching and counseling. She believed that with additional training nurses could identify deviations from wellness and direct the care accordingly.

2. Involvement in exploring advanced practice nursing roles for the Western Interstate Commission for Higher Education in Nursing (WCHEN).

3. Dr. Henry Kempe. Henry Kempe was a pediatrician who had gained international fame for the identification and development of the Battered Child Syndrome, as well as for directing global initiatives to eradicate small pox.

While co-serving on the dean search committee for the school of nursing at the University of Colorado Medical Center in Denver, Colorado, Loretta and Henry Kempe began a running dialogue about "advancing the practice of public health nurses for the pediatric population." Maternal child health promotion was a large part of Loretta's practice as a public health nurse, and Henry Kempe was the chairman of the pediatric department at the university.

Kempe suggested Loretta contact a pediatrician colleague named Henry K. Silver, MD, who was Kempe's second-in-command and a well-respected pediatrician in Denver. Ironically, Silver had just returned from a conference on community childcare where he had received many complaints from public health nurses about inadequate pediatric services in rural communities.

Loretta Ford in 1965.

BUILDING THE CONCEPT

Given their experiences and their interest in providing services to the rural areas, Loretta and Henry Silver, after months of discussion, collaboratively fashioned the pediatric nurse practitioner model. The model was designed so that nurses could be extensions of the patient, not physicians. It was designed as a different kind of service driven by the nursing process from a holistic perspective.

Loretta applied nurse theorist Virginia Henderson's definition of nursing to the nurse practitioner role: The job of the nurse was to do for the patient what the patient would do for him- or herself if he or she had the knowledge, will, and skill.

According to Loretta, Virginia Henderson believed nurses are an "extension of the patient—the eyes of the newly blind, the legs of a new amputee, and the confidence of a new mother." Pediatric nurse practitioners were to monitor pediatric growth and development, promote optimal health, provide anticipatory guidance for parents, and facilitate self care by the child, whenever possible, in order to maintain wellness.

Loretta Ford and Henry Silver surveyed rural public health nurses to determine what they needed to know in order to perform in an advanced practice role. Nurses were saying that the advanced practice nurse should be clinically competent, capable of practicing independently and autonomously in any setting, and able to work as a partner with physicians.

She knew that nurses could make competent and confident patient-care decisions. "I always thought it was ludicrous that hospital nurses could make clinical decisions at 3 AM that they couldn't make at 3 PM," said Loretta.

Moreover, public health nurses were already running unsupervised well-child clinics, school immunization programs, disabled-child services, and other healthcare offerings, irrespective of the time of day. Many of the processes for nurse-driven care were in place. Loretta simply needed to formalize and augment them.

The role was initially restricted to public health nurses and was originally named the Public Health Nurse Pediatric Nurse Practitioner. Later the name was shortened to Pediatric Nurse Practitioner (PNP) for simplicity purposes.

The pediatric focus created some credibility issues for Loretta. She was viewed as a public health nurse, not a pediatric nurse, which posed a perception issue that only time and her achievements were able to erase.

She was tempted to think big and include family care early on, but was concerned that she was setting the project up for failure by thinking too big. Properly framing the scope of a project is a leadership decision, and Loretta intuitively opted for a manageable scope that could be expanded later.

BUILDING A PROGAM

Loretta and Henry Silver decided to pursue a demonstration project to test the viability of the Pediatric Nurse Practitioner model. The program was to be taught by physicians and nurses with an intensive four month theory and practice classroom component followed by an eight month supervised practice clinical rotation.

The PNP program had three stated goals:

1. Prepare academically qualified and experienced public health nurses to provide comprehensive well-child care and study the Pediatric Nurse Practitioner model and role;
2. Prepare the nurses for emergencies that might occur in the community;
3. Integrate the program into graduate curricula.

In 1965, Loretta and Henry Silver procured a small grant from the University of Colorado School of Medicine for approximately $7,000 dollars to begin the Pediatric Nurse Practitioner project. They decided to test their model with one nurse, Sue Stearly, an experienced public health nurse with a master's degree.

Beginning with only one student had its advantages. It allowed Loretta and Henry to adjust the curriculum as needed. According to Loretta, Sue performed beautifully in the expanded role of the pediatric nurse practitioner.

Loretta was concerned about creating a curriculum that would meet academic standards in order that the graduates could be credentialed. Loretta was also adamant that the nurses not be exploited. Therefore, if the students were going to take the risk with this new expanded role, Loretta

Dr. Henry Silver, Loretta (to Dr. Silver's right), and Sue Stearly (to Loretta's right) with a group of nursing students in 1967.

was going to assure the validity of the education by upholding admission standards, academic requirements, and accreditation criteria. Henry Silver, on the other hand, was less concerned about accreditation and more concerned that the nursing practitioners receive the skills needed to practice. Both concerns were met.

The demonstration project was a success. The model had been tested and was believed, from the data collected, to be valid. Now came the time to integrate the advanced practice curriculum into the nursing school. While they could have pursued this direction, Loretta and Henry opted to extend the project by four years to gather the necessary data to evaluate the model on a larger scale. The initial funding of the four-year extension came from the Commonwealth Fund, the Robert Wood Johnson Foundation, and the United States Department of Health and Human Services, in that order.

TAKING THE RISK—THE PAIN OF CHANGE

In 1966, the first class of nurse practitioner students included five or six students. While they all did not have a master's degree, they were all academically and experientially qualified for graduate school.

Loretta felt it was her duty to create life-long knowledge workers rather than technicians. She believed it was important to create critical thinkers who could determine and solve the problems inherent in providing quality care in the ever-changing healthcare systems. This meant teaching students how to learn, how to evaluate, and how to process.

As the notoriety of the program increased, so, too, did the challenges. Unexpected resistance to change factors began to plague Loretta. "Everyone is interested in change as long as it does not affect or threaten them," says Loretta. She was a new faculty member who was naïve to the micropolitics of the faculty power structure. She had not anticipated that her own faculty colleagues would be among her greatest detractors.

She remembers feeling very conflicted by the paradox of the academic environment. While academe reputedly encouraged faculty to push the envelope and seek new knowledge, at the same time there were sanctions for those who were not in line with traditional thinking or the conservatism of the faculty. She felt that she was treated like a pariah by her colleagues.

The nurse practitioner program had gone against the grain of the School of Nursing faculty at the University of Colorado, and Loretta paid a leadership price as she became a "persona non grata." There were three distinct concerns associated with the nurse practitioner movement from the faculty perspective.

1. Public health education was not a valued program.
2. The concept of the nurse practitioner threatened the skill level of many of the faculty who had little or no experience in public health settings, much less the newly created advanced practice role.
3. The faculty believed Loretta, and thus nursing, was selling out to medicine. Some faculty even went so far as to dub Loretta as a traitor to the profession of nursing.

Loretta struggled to convince her nurse colleagues that the use of stethoscopes, otoscopes, ophthalmoscopes, and critical thinking did not erase the nursing perspective.

She was also struggling with other external concerns that ranged from the extravagant to the practical. One such concern was the horrified feelings of many within nursing regarding the fact that physicians were teaching nurses, which was unthinkable to most. There was also the companion fear that physicians would begin to dominate nursing education once they got a foothold with the pediatric nurse practitioner program. At the same time, she was finding it very difficult to secure clinical sites for the students. Those who ran the clinics did not understand the intended functions of the nurse practitioners and so they shied away from allowing them to practice in their clinics.

At a time when others were turning their backs to the program, the Denver VNS opened their doors and provided the nurse practitioner students with an opportunity to test their newly acquired skills and knowledge. "I have to give the leadership of the Denver VNS a lot of credit because they provided us with a testing ground, and thus the data, to adapt the model and advance the pediatric nurse practitioner movement," said Loretta. At the time, Margaret Lewis, RN, PhD, was the director, and Dorothy Gerrard was the associate director of the Denver VNS site. They were quite forward thinking in their approach to healthcare and understood that the challenges facing nursing and healthcare in general required innovative and creative solutions. In a classic you-scratch-my-back-I-scratch-your-back approach, the Denver VNS gave the PNPs an opportunity to hone their skills, and the nurse practitioners gave the Denver VNS an out of the box method of healthcare delivery.

One early conflict between the student nurse practitioners and the Denver VNS helped to define the role identity of the practitioners. Interestingly, it was clothes that helped to define them. The nurse practitioner students un-

Loretta (2ⁿᵈ from right), pediatrician Dr. Duke Duncan (4ᵗʰ from left), Madeleine Nichols (3ʳᵈ from left) and a group of NPs (in white coats) at the University of Colorado Medical Center in 1969.

understood they needed to differentiate not only their practice but their professional appearance. Meanwhile, the Denver VNS was adamant that the nurse practitioner students wear the traditional nurse uniform. The students approached Loretta with the dilemma, and she advised professional behavior while maintaining autonomy and control. The students chose to wear professional street clothes, showing up that way one day at the Denver VNS. They believed the negotiations had failed, and action was now called for. They were questioned by Denver VNS management, who, upon hearing the students' defense of their clothing choice, elected not to re-act—a victory for professional differentiation by the students.

Loretta was impressed with their courage and determination, and even picked up some leadership tips that day from the students. Loretta believes it is possible to learn leadership skills from anyone, if only you're wise enough to see the lessons. She freely acknowledges her students were terrific teachers of courage, enthusiasm, and persistence.

GROWING PAINS

Henry Silver had encouraged Loretta to publish the concepts and findings, and within months she was traveling the nation disseminating the nurse practitioner message. Loretta discovered that the nurse practitioner movement was being embraced by the military, Veterans Administration, and even physicians; however, nurses, nurse faculty, and nursing organizations were slow to even acknowledge the new advanced practice role. Many nurses across the country were verbalizing their beliefs that the nurse practitioner movement had been co-opted by medicine, and further, they believed that these nurses were not providing nursing care. It took a long time for nurses in all capacities to accept the role as a nursing role. It wasn't until the role was accepted into academics that the nurse practitioners were recognized by many of their nursing colleagues.

Concurrently, the Physician Assistant (PA) role was being developed by the military and physicians in an attempt to improve access to healthcare services. Both the PA and NP programs progressed side by side without competition because the need for care for the public superseded territorial domains; however, there was considerable confusion regarding the differences of the roles and scope of practice. It was organized medicine that first credentialed pediatric nurse practitioners via the American Academy of Pediatrics under the National Association of Pediatric Nurse Associates/ Practitioners. It wasn't until later, as the number of nurse practitioners grew, that organized medicine began to erect barriers to the NP position.

Organized nursing had waited too long to step in to manage the credentialing of nurse practitioners and lost control. Nurse practitioners had wanted the ANA to develop a nurse practitioner council. From Loretta's perspective, the ANA simply stalled these efforts, which pushed nurse practitioners into creating their own specialty organizations, further fracturing the power base of organized nursing. The rapid uncontrolled growth of the nurse practitioner movement almost led to its demise.

There was a surge of nurse practitioner programs with dubious quality control that left the movement open to criticism. Nonetheless, study after study supported the legitimacy of the role, providing further evidence that the Ford and Silver NP demonstration project was not a fluke.

The early years of nurse practitioner leadership were a difficult period for Loretta. She was isolated by criticism and mired in uncertainty of how the practitioners would perform long term with expansion. It would have been easy to give up because the scope of the project seemed daunting and the barriers to success felt oppressive.

As Loretta reflects on this leadership journey, four things kept her leadership fire burning:

1. She was committed to improving the care of patients;

2. The NP students were so enthusiastic and courageous;
3. Public healthcare nurse colleagues across the nation were enormously supportive and applauded the intervention; and
4. She had the support of her family.

GET TO THE TABLE AND BE A PLAYER

According to Loretta, as the nurse practitioner movement gained momentum, so did the scrutiny. Everyone had an opinion. As the controversy began to grow, Loretta's leadership cry became: "Get to the table and be a player or someone who doesn't understand nursing will do it for you."

Being at the table meant bringing valued data and leadership to the discussion, and Loretta often led the charge. She helped to motivate, organize, and maintain the focus of the nurse practitioner movement through some very difficult leadership moments.

Neither Loretta Ford nor Henry Silver anticipated the kind of resistance to change the nurse practitioner role would exert on the healthcare system. Early on, they had recognized the need for expert advice in the change process. They consulted with a social scientist, Robert Hunter, from the University of Colorado at Boulder to better understand the strategies, logistics, and tactics for surviving social change imposed by the nurse practitioner movement.

Hunter helped provide a proactive rather than reactive response to the social implications of the NP movement. Bringing the intellectual perspective of a social change theory into the nurse practitioner movement was a pivotal point for Loretta.

The structure of a theory applied as a blueprint changed the situation for her. The emotional roller coaster was replaced by a chess game of social change. Loretta recalls that this one simple resource reduced the frustration significantly and allowed both her and Henry to begin to gain control of the situation and enjoy the process. In this situation, getting to the table and being a player meant getting the proper resources in place. This was a leadership lesson in knowing what you do not know.

RIDING OUT THE STORM

The list of concerns that grew out of the NP movement cast a broad social and political net, which created real practical implications. There were questions of legality and fear of legal retribution with legitimate concerns of nurse practitioners going to jail while performing their duties. The legislation in most states prohibited nurses from making diagnoses and from writing prescriptions. Michael Carter, a nurse and an early NP pioneer, paints a vivid picture of the times, saying: "Only if you were willing to stare down a bull elephant in full charge were you able to be a nurse practitioner" in the early years. A vocal minority expressed outrage at the changes wrought by the NP movement.

Loretta never dreamed that doing a physical exam would create such a turf war. It was fine when nurses were using the stethoscope to take a blood pressure reading, but when the nurses moved that same stethoscope to the left chest area in order to assess heart tones, it stirred up the world of organized medicine. She was now staring in the eyes of not only nursing faculty but also the American Medical Association (AMA), neither group was happy. "The AMA was not against nurse practitioners as long as physicians could control them as they did the PAs" states Loretta. She also indicates that it was organized medicine, not the individual physicians, who exacted an "unnecessary emotional quotient that wasted a great deal of money and time."

There was also the unknown of how the public would accept the concept of the nurse practitioner. Physicians had always been near perfect in the eyes of the public. Would the public ever accept an alternative form of healthcare? Would they trust nurse practitioners as they had physicians? The NP initiative was a huge unknown and a considerable risk.

There were also concerns about who would be responsible and accountable for the care provided by nurse practitioners. Would organized medicine prevent individual physicians from collaborating with nurse practitioners?

Commonly, the questions of competence, confidence, and judgment were framed around location. Mystically, if located in rural, underserved communities, the nurse practitioners were touted as very capable and trusted providers; however, nurse practitioners practicing in a competitive market drew endless scrutiny.

There were legislative battles that waged for years, fueled by the AMA, over the scope of practice and prescriptive authority of nurse practitioners. Each state initiated different legislation with varying practice authority across states. Loretta was adamantly opposed to a second license through legislation. She believed that the nurse practitioners should be certified for expanded scope of practice similar to other healthcare disciplines.

The nurse practitioners had to organize and fight for each small gain over the decades. Michael Carter feels strongly that the "blood of many paved the road for nurse practitioners of today."

An example of the challenges of the nurse practitioner movement was a nationally profiled case in Missouri. In 1985, several Missouri physicians brought charges of illegal practice of medicine against two nurse practitioners who had been providing healthcare services to low-income women in Flat Valley, Missouri. It was an economically challenging time for physicians, which was further exacerbated by the growing strength of the number of certified nurse practitioners—a number which had grown to 20,000 strong. Nurse practitioners were becoming increasingly more visible in healthcare delivery.

This legal case became high profile as it made its way to the Missouri Supreme Court. Dr. James Keyhoe, one of the physicians who filed the charges in this case, announced on national television that nurse practitioners were breaking Missouri law. However, as his discussion continued the argument became distilled down to a very simple message—this legal battle was about parity and professional turf. Said Keyhoe, "I think the issue that has come about now is that nurses want parity with physicians. It's the idea of someone encroaching on your territory without paying the dues, if you want to get right down to it."

The elephants were charging, and Loretta grabbed her weapons. She appeared on national television to debate the Missouri case with the president of the American Academy of Family Physicians—Gerald Gehringer. Gehringer spoke first and admitted that nurse practitioners had a track record of providing good care. He reported that the only problem organized medicine had with the movement was when nurse practitioners attempted to "practice *medicine* independently when they don't have the education and experience to do so." Again, the issue of control of practice had reared its ugly head.

Loretta's response was articulate, concise, and professional. She had only a few moments to send the message, and she did so in a collegial and collaborative manner. She told the nation that "patients receive better care when nurses and physicians collaborate, that nurses are not a substitute for physicians and physicians are not a substitute for nurses, that medicine wants to claim all of healthcare without recognizing the contribution of other disciplines, and the charges of illegally practicing medicine were financially motivated."

When Gehringer was asked about the national implications if the case were decided in favor of the nurses, he indicated, after a noticeable pause, there would have to be recognition of another level of healthcare provider in the United States.

Loretta had gotten to the table and was a formidable player because she stayed with her message and delivered it with polish and poise. The case was ultimately decided in favor of the nurses with, according to Loretta, "the judge defining beautifully the role of the nurse practitioner."

Loretta's weapons in defense of the nurse practitioner role were the evidence and data that had been collected that supported the successes of the nurses. Nurse practitioners became the most studied profession in the history of healthcare as a result of the AMA resistance. In the first 20 years, there were more than 1,000 publications by a variety of researchers, many of them physicians, supporting positive nurse practitioner outcomes including the fact that patients love the nurse practitioner model of care.

Loretta, center, with Linda Pearson (L) and Michael Carter (R). Linda and Michael are each NP pioneers in their own right.

MOVING ON TO THE NEXT CHALLENGE

After 12 years at the University of Colorado Medical Center, Loretta recognized her career had reached a stalemate, and she decided to take on a different leadership role.

By 1972, the nurse practitioner movement was well on its way, with numerous specialties and strong leadership across the nation. Loretta had a larger vision of unifying practice, research, and education, and she felt she could do so as the founding dean of the School of Nursing at the University of Rochester. She believed it was "essential to change systems or there would be no future for nursing." She believed the University of Rochester had made a commitment to the preparation of nurse practitioners and nurses. Additionally, the University of Rochester had the potential for advancing nursing research and a commitment of merging practice, education, and research to prove it. She believed it was an excellent opportunity to advance the profession. Her expertise and experience would be needed there.

Loretta's leadership skills were tested in many ways in her new role. She learned to think quickly on her feet and to understand when to take a stand and how to gain support even if it means doing something she does not completely agree with. She recalls a particular University of Rochester Medical Center board meeting, while acting as both the dean for the School of Nursing and chief nursing officer (CNO) for the hospital, where there was to be a vote for hospital reorganization that was considered highly controversial for nursing.

She was the only woman and the only voting nurse in a group of 25 to 30 people, including the hospital chief executive officer and the University of Rochester president.

The vote was a secret ballot, and Loretta knew the board would question both her vote and her level of support. This was a moment she could not afford to waste.

She turned to her colleague on her right and strategically showed him that she had voted in favor of the proposed reorganization. She did not believe nursing would benefit greatly from the reorganization, but she knew the battle was lost and it was time to cut potential losses. She felt it was essential to make friends rather than enemies going into the change, because when the going got tough she would need the support of friends.

When the votes were publicly counted, there were two votes against the proposed reorganization and the remainder for. Loretta knew a leadership moment had arrived. She addressed the all-male board and informed them that she had voted for the reorganization. Moreover, she planned to fully support the initiative.

As she left the meeting and was nearly to her office, she heard her name being called. She turned to see the president of the university chasing after her. When he reached her, he extended his hand and said "Lee, never worry. I assure you the school of nursing will receive every consideration."

Loretta was the only nurse at the table and had the courage and vision to play her cards in the most effective manner for the future of the profession. She had bitten her tongue and swallowed a bit of blood that day, but there was not a drop of blood on the floor when she departed. Her leadership choices assured that nursing would win the war, irrespective of losing a battle.

BE IN A HURRY: THERE IS NOT A MOMENT TO WASTE

Ford is the first to acknowledge that everything she does is fast. She says, "I walk fast, talk fast, and think fast." Ford chuckles as she shares that she is "able to make mistakes and fix them before they are even noticed." Moreover, she recounts there are advantages to being in a hurry—"it is hard to hit a moving target and most people are poor shots anyway." Ford also believes she is the definition of impatience. Her speedy pace and inherent impatience has forced her to be strategic.

Loretta is also in a hurry to be the best she can be. She works daily on perfecting her skills. Even at age 83, she is seeking methods of improvement. Recently, she enlisted the advice of a drama coach to improve her speaking skills. She was initially surprised when the coach made the observation that she pointed her finger when she spoke. She is now committed to changing this habit but is sure there will be times that will call for just such emphasis.

She has never taken herself too seriously. Humor has often been her secret weapon, and she uses it frequently. She is a master collaborator and takes responsibility for being prepared, professional, and polished, irrespective of age. According to Loretta, every day should be devoted to improving oneself in every way possible. Her creed of "be in a hurry, there is not a moment to waste" is a leadership cry she applies first to herself and then to those around her.

Loretta leads by example. One of the major influences in her life has been her love for work. From the time she was 12 years old, she has worked to support herself. She remembers selling salve or other products door-to-door and "learning the value of the dollar and the responsibility of handling finances."

In 1990 Loretta was awarded the prestigious Gustav O. Lienhard Award, an award given to individuals for outstanding achievement in improving health care services in the United States, with a focus on creative or pioneering efforts that have appreciably improved personal health services. Dr. Louis W. Sullivan, the 17th Secretary of the Department of Health and Human Services, is to her left.

The emotional and intellectual rewards of work often outweighed the financial rewards, and she discovered that work was actually therapeutic when life became stressful. While holding dual roles at the University of Rochester as CNO at the hospital and dean for the School of Nursing, Loretta would sometimes work 60-80 hour weeks and never gave it a thought. "I have never worked to retire from anything," but rather "used my work mainly to try and help others."

Valerie, Loretta's daughter, remembers her mother visiting the nurses on the hospital units each Christmas Eve and Christmas morning to thank them for their service. According to Valerie, her mother "never had work commitments" but rather "commitments to people," which was a lesson that earned Loretta her daughter's profound respect.

RETIRED LEADER

Loretta retired from the University of Rochester School of Nursing deanship in 1986, and, predictably, has never been busier. She remarks that she needs to retire from retirement but doesn't have the time to write the resignation letter. She travels around the world speaking on the nurse practitioner journey, contemporary healthcare issues, and the role nurses must play in the future.

Loretta has mentees from several generations that she corresponds with on a regular basis. She actively raises funds for nursing education and universities. She has continued to publish, to participate in national think tanks on healthcare issues, and to consult in the public policy arena. She's also still not afraid of a debate with the AMA.

In September, 2003, Loretta was awarded the Elizabeth Blackwell Award by the Hobart and William Smith Colleges. The Elizabeth Blackwell Award is given to "A woman whose life exemplifies outstanding service to humanity." Loretta embodies the values and principles of a leader who exemplifies outstanding service to humanity and to the profession of nursing. Loretta C. Ford, like Blackwell, was a woman ahead of her time.

Loretta is known to frequently end speeches with a quote from Aristotle that she feels should be uppermost in our minds: "Where your talents and the world's needs cross, there lies your vocation."

The remarkable reflection of this quote is that *Ford* helped create and sustain, through leadership and courage, the professional opportunity for all NPs who chose to meet the world's needs.

She had the courage to stand her ground while being viewed as a pariah by her colleagues, and still remain intensely focused on the mission of taking care of patients.

Loretta's contributions to nursing through her devotion to practice, education, research, and expanding the scope of nursing practice by the creation of the nurse practitioner role is of historic proportions.

According to Michael Carter, "Loretta Ford didn't have the intention of being the birth mother of the nurse practitioner movement" but the world today agrees with the clarity of her vision. Her leadership, without a doubt, changed the path of a profession.

CHAPTER 2

[handwritten in margin: cooperative leadership & teamwork social sec. Admin]

Shirley Sears Chater

Shirley Sears Chater, RN, PhD, FAAN, grew up in a small town in eastern Pennsylvania that was filled with the deeply conservative Amish culture and influences that so often instill strong values and a deep sense of community into those raised there. These strong influences have been Shirley's beacon throughout her leadership career. She was a first: the first woman assistant vice chancellor at the University of California, San Francisco; the first nurse president at Texas Woman's University; and the first woman nurse commissioner of the Social Security Administration for the United States with responsibility for 62,000 employees. However, she never lost sight of those simple values of cooperative leadership and respect for others.

THE EARLY YEARS

Even though her family was not Amish, Shirley loved the close-knit Amish community where she grew up and where she worshipped. Her aspirations, however, were not for settling down in her hometown. She knew that someday she wanted to leave and experience the rest of the world. This desire became more pressing after her family attended a Mennonite worship service when she was very young where the women were segregated from the men, with the women on one side of the church and the men on the other side. Not only was she upset that the family could not sit together, but the purpose of the segregation did not make sense to her—perhaps the roots of her sense of injustice were fed there, as later, important aspects of her career would be dedicated to serving women and minorities.

Shirley was the firstborn of three and at an early age demonstrated the leadership traits typical of a firstborn child, such as being the first to respond, the first to step forward, and the one who set the standards for the siblings. For example, at a very young age on the playground she frequently took charge by organizing groups and games.

Her family lived a humble existence. Her father was a blue-collar worker, and her mother was a homemaker. Neither parent had more than an eighth-grade education. However, they were very supportive of Shirley's aspirations. So, while she did not grow up with college-educated role models, she did recognize early on that education was her ticket out of town. Because her parents did not have the financial means for a college education, she had to find a way to make it happen, which she did.

NURSING SCHOOL

It was one summer job in particular that guided Shirley Chater's career into nursing. During high school she worked in a local family physician's office. While the doctor saw patients, Shirley watched and learned various treatments. There she discovered she wanted to become a nurse.

When Shirley was a senior in high school, she applied to eight colleges, all in Pennsylvania, as she knew her parents would not allow her to go too far from home. In her applications, she informed the schools that she had a 4.0 grade point average, wanted to be a nurse, but had no money and would need a full scholarship.

It was not long before she received the first response from the University of Pennsylvania Hospital School of Nursing. She was offered a full scholarship and an opportunity to live in Philadelphia. Convincing her parents that Philadelphia was *not* too large a city nor too far away was a difficult task, but she was relentless and ultimately was successful.

Shirley had always been a good student, so she did not struggle to succeed in the three-year diploma program. In fact, she earned the Florence Nightingale award, an award that clearly indicated her outstanding qualities as a nurse and future potential within the profession. Upon graduation, Shirley was offered a full-time teaching position that enabled her to complete a Bachelor of Science (nursing) at the University of Pennsylvania.

Upon finishing the baccalaureate degree, she applied to and was accepted by the American Nurses Association to participate in an international exchange program. She chose to go to London, England, for one year, with all expenses paid.

Shirley Chater as a student nurse at the University of Pennsylvania Hospital School of Nursing in 1953.

Surprisingly, for a woman of 20 who had seldom been out of Pennsylvania her entire life, Shirley was not terrified by the adventure that lay ahead, but instead had a sense of courage and determination. She ended up working at St. Bartholomew's Hospital in England, which had been founded in 1123. She recalls the most memorable part of the experience was the fact that the nurses were in charge of the patients at St. Bartholomew's. "They shut the doors to the ward, only opening them when they were ready for the doctors to make rounds." She also recalls a significant difference in the bedside care provided in England where they used few IVs for patients. Instead the nurses would pull up a chair and sit at the bedside and feed the patients cups of tea by the spoonfuls. "It was a striking contrast between the two kinds of nursing," remembers Shirley.

GRADUATE NURSING SCHOOL

Shirley Chater came back to the United States and worked for a year or two as a faculty member in order to earn enough money to get a master's degree. Theresa Lynch, who was the director of the Hospital School of Nursing at the University of Pennsylvania took Shirley aside one day and suggested she consider pursuing an advanced degree. Theresa Lynch was one of the few nurses with a doctoral degree at the time, and she made a major impact on Shirley. When Shirley shared with Dr. Lynch that she wanted to continue at the University of Pennsylvania, Dr. Lynch discouraged that direction and encouraged her instead to get a different perspective by experiencing a different culture in a different state. Being an adventurer and trusting Dr. Lynch's advice, Shirley did exactly what was suggested.

She had heard that the University of California at San Francisco (UCSF), under the deanship of Dr. Helen Nahm, was developing a department of social and behavioral sciences, which coincided with her interest. Again, Shirley had to convince her parents, who could not understand her drive for yet another degree, that this move was a necessity. She then persuaded a group of her roommates to go to California for a vacation, which in turn gave her the transportation that she needed.

Unfortunately, this time good fortune did not come so easily to her. Shortly after submitting an application to UCSF, she was declined admission with the stated reason being that she did not meet the qualifications for admission to the master's program in nursing. There was no further explanation. The rejection letter may have surprised her, but it did not deter her from packing her bags and going out west to the campus, determined to get into UCSF. With what would strike most people as an indomitable spirit, she packed two suitcases with everything she owned and was dropped off by her roommates at the University of California at the Berkeley Women's Club.

On arrival at the campus, Shirley went directly to the admissions office, where she learned she had been declined admission because she had taken most of her undergraduate courses in an order that was not acceptable to UCSF. They did not approve of the fact that she had taken advanced psychology before psychology I, physiology before anatomy, and so on. Because she had completed course work in the BS program while teaching at the University of Pennsylvania, she had simply taken classes when she could get them to fit her working schedule, but not necessarily in a traditional order.

With persistence, she finally got the admissions advisor to admit there was a university policy that would allow students to obtain "credit-by-exam" for courses that would not transfer. She agreed to the plan and proceeded to study for approximately seven courses.

With her typical perseverance, she met with every professor to obtain the textbook and to talk about the exam. Over the course of several weeks, she successfully passed all but the physics exam. In the end, her determination and focus prevailed. She was admitted as a special status student (a category that allowed a student to take a course without admission into the university with a declared major) so she could complete the physics course. Luckily, she did not have to work full time while pursuing graduate school because of a traineeship she had received. (Most of the nurses in master and doctoral programs during those years were the recipients of United States Public Health Service (USPHS) traineeships, which allowed them to devote full concentration on their studies.)

Soon her life would take a new turn as she met and married her husband Norman Chater, a fifth-year neurosurgery resident. The ironic thing about this new relationship was that for the first few weeks of dating, neither knew the other was a health-science professional.

Shirley and Norm were married during the middle of her master program. One year later Shirley had a baby girl, Cris. Interestingly, when Shirley was pregnant with Cris during her master program, she was told by the administrator that she could no longer remain in the program and was invited to take a leave of absence. Because Shirley wanted to finish with the rest of her class, she challenged the old rules and was able to persuade the university to change the policy.

Shirley and Norm had two children—Cris and a son named Geoffrey, who was on the way within 18 months of Cris. And while she had a husband who had a successful career, she never gave up her own career. Her husband worked his schedule around hers as much as possible. Other support came from a caregiver who served as a babysitter/housekeeper for 15 years.

While the children were small, Shirley worked part time doing private-duty nursing and teaching. She accepted a full-time faculty position when the children went to school all day. She was also pursuing doctoral studies and recalls, "It was not easy and there were times when it was very difficult to go to work and pursue doctoral studies, particularly if the children were sick and I wanted desperately to stay home with them." But the juggling of schedules and the demands on her time paid off when she graduated in 1964, as the 64th nurse in the United States with a doctoral degree.

In those days, nurses who had completed a doctoral program were highly sought after. However, Shirley did not believe she could realistically leave San Francisco due to her husband's medical practice and the two small children. She did, though, accept an assistant professor position at UCSF's School of Nursing.

Quickly, she made the climb to associate professor, then full professor, then head of a department called the Functional Division (similar to department chair in today's terminology). Ironically, it was the same school that originally would not accept her as a graduate student that was now promoting her into an administrative role.

ADMINISTRATIVE LEADERSHIP

During Shirley's professorial years, she had the opportunity to work with and be mentored by Dean Helen Nahm, the creator of the first Department of Social and Behavioral Sciences at UCSF School of Nursing. Shirley describes Dr. Nahm as the "steel hand in a velvet glove" type, who, during an early nursing shortage, called the faculty together and asked them to consider reducing the length of their master programs to one year in length. At that time, graduate nursing programs had grown to be two-to-three years long. This reduction in length became a model for graduate nursing education as other programs did the same thing. Quality did not suffer, which was validation that length was not the best indicator of quality.

In the '70s, when colleges and universities were required to write affirmative action plans, a position for assistant vice chancellor was created at the UCSF campus. The job description for this position included writing and developing an affirmative action plan to be implemented by the faculty at UCSF. Shirley was nominated and awarded the position. When pushed, she humbly claims no one else wanted the job.

As assistant vice chancellor, Shirley was able to work in academic affairs, which meant working with faculty and faculty governance. Her affirmative action plan was so well received that not only was it implemented at UCSF, but in fact, was then used as a model for the other eight campuses in the University of California system. As a direct result of this affirmative action plan, more women and minorities were hired for faculty positions on campus. As the assistant vice chancellor for academic affairs, Shirley had academic planning responsibilities for all of the schools on the campus, which included the schools of medicine, dentistry, nursing, and pharmacy, and the graduate school.

A few years later, when the position for vice chancellor opened up, Shirley was nominated by several of her female colleagues on campus who were very interested in seeing women reach that level of administration. Shirley did receive the promotion and became the highest-ranking woman on any of the nine University of California campuses. Reflecting upon her time as vice chancellor, Shirley says she "had the privilege and opportunity to make the medical-centered campus much more of a health science campus."

Shirley admits she learned much from her mentors during her rise in leadership. Besides working with Dr. Lynch (former director of the Hospital School of Nursing at the University of Pennsylvania) and Dean Nahm, one of her strongest mentor relationships was with the chancellor at UCSF, Frank Sooy. He was a physician and had been named chancellor a few years before he hired her. He was a delegator and trusted Shirley to carry out her responsibilities. "He gave me a wide scope of opportunities with lots of latitude to do what I wanted to do, and he was extremely good at interpersonal relationships."

Through Dr. Sooy, Shirley learned how to manage with respect and how to terminate someone without taking away his or her dignity along with the job. He also taught her the fine art of dealing with uncomfortable situations in leadership. One of the key lessons she learned during those years from him was active listening, a skill that Shirley successfully developed in her own career.

Five years after Shirley started as vice chancellor, Dr. Sooy left his position and a search committee was formed to appoint a new chancellor. "I was nominated by my peers on the campus as a potential candidate for this position," said Shirley. "I knew that it was not likely that I would be chosen. The campus has been there since the 1800s, and never had anyone been in the chancellor position other than a physician. It was and still is primarily a medical center. Having a chancellor who was a nurse and also a woman would not have occurred."

When Shirley learned she was one of the final candidates, she withdrew her name. "I did not want to go through the interviews in the final stage because it was not the right time or place for me." It was disappointing for Shirley as she knew the culture would not accept a campus leader with her background, but for her, it was one of those motivating times that prompted personal change.

Shirley did change. The new chancellor asked her to remain in her position, but she declined and took advantage of the sabbatical leave she had never used. She took her sabbatical in Washington, D.C. to work with the American Council on Education (ACE). She wanted to expand her view of higher education in general and examine other institutions of learning. In the past, she had been on several of the ACE commissions, so she was eagerly accepted. Not only did she have one year working in Washington, D.C. but she extended her leave of absence from the university in order to serve another year with the council. During this time, Shirley commuted between San Francisco and Washington, D.C. every other week. With the children both away at college, she and her husband were able to work their schedules so both could benefit.

PRESIDENT OF TEXAS WOMAN'S UNIVERSITY

It was during her second year in Washington, D.C. when Shirley learned she had been nominated for the presidency of Texas Woman's University (TWU). Initially, she declined the offer because her husband, as a physician, would have to take new state exams, and she did not consider that fair to him. Still, she did not withdraw her name from the committee, and they went together to be interviewed during the final stages of the search.

It turned out the opportunities at Texas Woman's University were so great, with so many challenges, that it was an offer too good for Shirley to refuse. With 50% of TWU's programs in the health sciences, including a large nursing program, she believed the fit was very good. Finally, the fact that the Board of Regents was particularly supportive and persuasive in its

Shirley Chater while president of Texas Woman's University (1986-1993).

recruitment efforts made her decision that much easier. Shirley was offered the presidency position in July of 1986 but did not begin until October of 1986 because she had prior commitments. "Between the time I accepted this position and the time I arrived at TWU," she related, "the legislature of Texas had formed a commission on higher education to study the entire higher education system of the state."

Between July and October, the commission decided there were too many public universities in the state of Texas (37 total), so they considered merging some institutions with others. TWU was to be merged with another institution of higher education, the University of North Texas, which was relatively close.

When Shirley arrived on the campus, her first job was to go to the commission on October 2, 1986, and present testimony about why TWU should not be merged with another university. She knew the magnitude and timing of this situation were critical in terms of how her leadership would be perceived. She testified that one major aspect of TWU was that it was the only public university in the country primarily for women. She continued with the supporting argument that women who graduate from single-sex institutions develop more intellectual self-esteem. The merger issue was not resolved until two months later in December 1986, when the commission voted to cancel the suggested merger between TWU and North Texas on the basis that there was not enough evidence to support a merger of the two institutions. In retrospect, not only had she gained the support of the faculty, students, and alumni, but also the support of the community and the entire city, because TWU was one of the largest employers in the area.

Even though Shirley found herself thrust into the middle of an unexpected leadership crisis, she used this crisis to rally faculty, staff, and students to move forward. Neither TWU nor North Texas closed, but the logic of merging schools within close proximity that offered duplications of some degree programs provided an opportunity for dialogue between the two university presidents.

She had won the merger battle but knew there was merit in downsizing and restructuring TWU in response to the legislative request. She also realized that the strategic plan would have to streamline TWU to make it more efficient, while working with fewer resources. She knew tough decisions about reorganization lay ahead, which led to tremendous pressure on her during the first year from both inside and outside the walls of the institution, as everyone in town knew the business of the university.

She dealt with the pressure by ensuring good communication and seeing that the correct message was being delivered. Shirley made speech after speech focusing on the goals and purpose of the university. In typical Chater fashion, her strategic process allowed faculty and staff participation so ideas could be generated at all levels. She knew radical change could not occur without ownership and buy-in from employees. As a result of her grassroots leadership, the system of 11 colleges was reduced to eight through a consolidation of some and a renaming of others to better reflect the innovations that had been made over time. In this instance, Shirley was able to use a crisis situation to organize a vision, a mission, and a set of objectives in order to guide the organization into the future, while still ensuring support from the employees.

Shirley envisioned opportunities for expansion and growth at TWU, and accomplished this through a number of new start-up programs. Increasing diversity on campus was an important area of focus. "We worked very hard to put into place not just a recruitment process that would bring minority women to the campus, but we also worked hard to create a climate for success on the campus."

It was not just enough to get minorities into TWU—Shirley wanted them to graduate as well. She selected a strong team who put several programs in place to honor different ethnic groups. For instance, TWU instituted tutorial systems, whereby students had extra faculty attention if needed. Pre-registration was done before students arrived on campus to allow for a smooth transition back to campus, and university-wide programs were offered to include both students and their families. In addition, young girls were encouraged to become interested in math and science through the use of summer camps sponsored by TWU. Another program enabled single mothers to bring their children to live on campus for four to five years; while the mothers worked part-time jobs and held scholarships through school, the campus became the home for them and their children. The single mothers' program became so popular that even today there is a waiting list.

De Madras De Madras, from mother to mother, is another thriving program that Shirley is most proud of. This program was offered through the School of Nursing Houston Center. It enabled pregnant Hispanic women to receive prenatal care from other Hispanic women who had gone through an educational program supervised by the School of Nursing. Eventually, this program grew to be so large a separate house was purchased and its own board of directors was formed. "Being president of a very special university was the highlight of my career. ...It was an honor and a privilege to work with a superb and supportive Board of Regents, as well as a talented faculty and staff eager for future-oriented leadership."

It would be difficult to get Shirley to admit to her quiet prowess, as she steers most of the credit for her success to the people surrounding her, and to the husband who provided her with all the support that she needed. (During the first year at TWU, Shirley's husband commuted between San Francisco and Texas. However, he eventually cut back his neurosurgery practice to part-time so he could reside primarily in Texas with his wife.)

COMMISSIONER OF THE SOCIAL SECURITY ADMINISTRATION

Shirley would likely still be at TWU if she had not been called to an interview in Washington, D.C. for the position of commissioner for the Social Security Administration (SSA). How she came to be picked as a candidate is a leadership lesson for history, as Shirley did not have connections in Washington at that particular time. Eventually she pieced together the events that led up to the offer of an interview. It appeared the first piece of the puzzle was the American Nurses Association (ANA), which was very interested in having nurses in high-level governmental positions. The ANA lobbied hard for nurses in select positions in the Clinton administration. As President Clinton's mother was a nurse, he did not have to be persuaded about the value of nursing, and he did listen to the ANA, so the ground was prepared. Secondly, unbeknownst to Shirley, Ann Richards, then governor of Texas, sent a letter to President Clinton recommending President Chater as a talented executive-level leader. Richards included Shirley's résumé, and this act put her résumé in the files of the White House Office of Personnel. Third, Donna Shalala, the secretary of Health and Human Services, had hired a former chancellor from UCSF to come to Washington as her assistant secretary for Health and Human Services. His name was Dr. Phillip Lee. He had been the chancellor at UCSF when Shirley took her first faculty position there, and he provided a verbal recommendation and strong support for Shirley.

The lessons here are clear and serve as a reminder of how important it is to maintain strong professional relationships. Shirley had no in-depth knowledge of social security, a point she made clear during the interviewing process. But what the administration was seeking was leadership, which she had amply proven. On October 8, 1993, Shirley, upon confir-

Shirley Chater and President Bill Clinton in the Oval Office.

mation by the U.S. Senate, did become commissioner of the Social Security Administration.

In 1993 when President Clinton took office, his initiative was to have a government that worked better and cost less. The SSA volunteered to become part of that initiative. "To put customers first, that was our theme, our mission, our goal, and the idea around which we made all decisions," said Shirley.

After many of the operations of the Social Security Administration were redesigned under Shirley's direction, and with much hard work from the staff, the Social Security Administration was voted number one in customer service in an independent survey that compared the SSA with such customer-service giants as the Disney Corporation and L.L. Bean.

The major leadership lesson Shirley highlights with the restructuring efforts within the SSA is that creativity is key. "You can have improved results, without having the results cost more. The focus is on the word 'different' and on *not* doing more of the same. You really have to be creative in finding new and different ways to cause an improved result."

CHALLENGES OF A NEW WORK ENVIRONMENT

While at TWU, Shirley, together with the Board of Regents, set priorities. In the Social Security Administration, she had to adapt to a world where priorities were established by the president, the vice president, the secretary of Health and Human Services, and various congressional committees. To carry out the president's mission of creating a government that worked better and cost less, approximately eight areas were designated as vanguard departments. These agencies would be expected to change for the better in terms of efficiency and service while spending less money than was previously spent. The Social Security Administration was one of the eight selected agencies.

Shirley acknowledges she walked into a very different culture and environment in Washington, D.C., but she kept her leadership style participatory. She worked to create an environment of teamwork and collective decision making. Typically, Washington is a command and control style environment. In other words, the commissioner was expected to tell the employees what to do and they would do it.

"But I cannot work that way," says Shirley. "I have always surrounded myself with the best people to do their jobs, because I do not want to learn what they already know better than I do."

One of the first things Shirley did to turn around the command and control culture within the agency was to no longer meet with executives individually, with the exception of the initial session. She brought them together as a team because their work and decisions impacted other areas. Relationships needed to be cultivated.

Shirley had made a four-year commitment to herself and her family regarding this position. Four years is a very short time to create any kind of cultural change and make it stick, but having the time frame turned out to be significant, as it forced her to move a little faster. She tackled things in the beginning much like she had at TWU, providing lots of examples, being consistent, and being persuasive. "Saying the same thing over and over and over again, and reminding employees constantly that it is our mission to put customers first and to do things differently in order to save money and time" was the tactic she took. "We were compelled to make decisions

Shirley Chater and Vice President Al Gore at the Social Security Administration.

in concert with each other. We could not allow the luxury of duplication of efforts." Further, "The number of constituencies for whom one feels responsible is exceedingly broad in government compared to an academic setting."

There were many customers to please. In addition to a client base of 44 million social security beneficiaries, there are many advocacy groups interested in the social security program. One challenge for Shirley was that it took so long in government to get things done, as the legality of everything had to be confirmed first. And if the change wasn't allowed by law, "you have to go back to the legislature and have the law changed; it can take such a long time."

During Shirley's first year in Washington, D.C., she reported to the Department of Health and Human Services secretary Donna Shalala. During this time, Congress voted to make the SSA an independent agency, the largest in the government. Interestingly, President Clinton signed the bill on August 16, 1994, using the same pen that Franklin D. Roosevelt used to enact social security in 1935.

The challenge for Shirley was to create an independent agency and to make the conversion from governmental department to independent agency appear seamless to beneficiaries. The transition was made in 1994 with few people even aware of it. One of the biggest changes for Shirley was that she would attend presidential cabinet meetings. "This was always an extraordinary experience participating with a team of experts providing counsel to the president of our country."

At SSA, Shirley had 62,000 employees working for her, and she worked and studied harder during these years than she did at any other time in her life. "I never pretended to know more than they did. I depended enormously on the competence of the employees in the Social Security Administration who were extremely dedicated, and so loyal."

On April 19, 1995, Shirley was thrust into a crisis situation that was both monumental and devastating when the Murrah Federal Building in Oklahoma City was bombed. One hundred forty-nine adults and 19 children were killed; 16 of the adult fatalities were SSA employees. Shirley was asked not to go to Oklahoma, but within two days, she made plans to go in order to provide comfort and support.

Her situation in Oklahoma City was a case in which she did not have the answers, but she found her nursing experience directed her actions. She spent time visiting families of employees who had died, visiting employees who were in hospitals, attending funerals, and offering support to

Shirley Chater with Bill and Hillary Clinton.

survivors, all the while providing leadership to staff and reorganizing a new office.

Within 24 hours of her arrival, a temporary office was set up for the employees. The degree of survivors' guilt and the level of mourning were tremendous for the employees. "What I did not anticipate was the reaction of the people who were alive, because they were not at work when they might have been."

Shirley heard stories of an employee who had been late to work that day and, while driving on the freeway, saw the building explode. One woman, Shirley remembers, "had a doctor's appointment in the morning and while returning to work heard the news on her car radio." And then there was the woman who survived because a week earlier she had agreed to change office desks with someone who was killed.

Through the chaos, Shirley listened to the employees' reactions and the expressed needs they had for a new office space to be anything but a high-rise building, with as much light and sense of security as could be found. Very quickly, she had a functioning office in a strip-mall storefront with many windows and much light. She supported the staff in every way possible and made sure they understood they were going to be taken care of, both them and the families of lost colleagues. "This incident was the most moving experience of my career. My role was to establish the fact, very forcefully, that leadership from the top was present and doing something about the situation, and most importantly, making sure the families were being cared for—not just in the nursing sense, but overall."

CHANGING CLIMATE

During the first two years of her term, the White House and the congressional majority were both of the same political party, allowing for an atmosphere of advocacy and support. Two years later, that all changed when the congressional majority represented a different party than the White House. Shirley describes the new relationship as more adversarial than before, making testimony to congressional committees more difficult. "It was not unusual to be asked questions about the social security program that I should not answer, not that I COULD not answer but because the administration did not necessarily want the information to be discussed at a particular time. I was, after all, a presidential appointee, representing the White House whenever I spoke. Many times I was pushed by congressional committees to give my personal opinion about an issue, but it was not my role to present my personal views in those situations. I always worried that my children might be watching television, wondering why I could not, *would not*, answer questions." Nevertheless, Shirley gained an important new perspective during her days of testifying:

"I learned that it was not me, Shirley Chater, being quizzed. I simply represented an issue, or an idea, that the committee members wanted to probe because I was the commissioner and I represented the president as a presidential appointee. That insight helped me to take the questions less personally."

However, as much as she enjoyed her work, there were other issues to consider when she was asked to stay another term. Her husband had retired from his practice and had moved to be with her in Washington, D.C., where they had bought a house. Very soon after that he died suddenly, and Shirley chose to deal with her grief by working extra hard and extra-long hours.

By this point in her career, she was ready to return to the San Francisco Bay area to be close to her grown children and grandchildren. Despite the excitement of meeting with the president and others in the oval office, flying on Air Force One, and attending Christmas White House parties, working four years day and night, with numerous evening activities, proved enough for her. Shirley returned to the West Coast where UCSF honored her with a prestigious Regents Professorship and the University Medal, the highest award given by the University of California.

THE LATER YEARS IN NURSING

Shirley has cut back her hours from those she was keeping during her SSA days but is not anywhere near retired. She has promoted nursing by being in positions outside the nursing box and is a superb role model for other nurses. Most of her career has been a juggling act. She says, "You can think of balancing your life in two ways: One I call *both/and*, while the other is *either/or*. A lot of people think they can either go the professional route or choose to be a wife and mother. I like the both/and approach. ... You can have both and do both. You can enjoy a family life while leading a professional life. I really believe I am one of those people who had it all. While it was not always easy, the support services I established and the friendship of my colleagues made it possible."

Shirley has always remained passionate about improving the nursing profession and believes the current health care workplace is not an attrac-

Shirley Chater (left) with Dr. Fay Bower at the 1995 Sigma Theta Tau International Biennial Convention.

tive place to work. As nurses, she believes "we need to be relieved periodically from stressful workplace situations in order to become refreshed or we become victims, and that is discouraging. Perhaps this new nursing shortage issue will motivate the profession to find ways to deal with the workplace culture and to encourage nurses to take on more personal responsibility for how they feel and act." Shirley views the health care system as broken and confused, in need of new visions and strategies that will make order out of chaos. She further believes these new visions and strategies should come from nursing leadership.

Shirley is the chair of the National Advisory Committee for the Robert Wood Johnson Executive Nurse Leadership Program, which allows top nurse executives an opportunity to gain advanced leadership training in order to lead and shape the United States health care system of the future. Based on the high quality of fellows in the program and the excellent projects they complete, she is optimistic that positive change is happening.

She travels around the world as a consultant in various capacities. She also serves as the co-chair of the advisory committee for the UCSF/John A. Hartford Center of Geriatric Nursing Excellence, whose mission it is to prepare an exceptional cadre of nurse scientists who will provide the critically necessary academic leadership in teaching, research, and practice in geriatric nursing.

Yet, with the numerous honorary doctoral degrees and awards, coupled with all the high-profile positions Shirley has held throughout her career, at the end of the day when she is asked what her greatest accomplishment to date has been, she smiles widely and responds, "Without question, my greatest accomplishment is raising two very talented and respected children. They, by far, bring me the greatest joy and are that of which I am the most proud."

Shirley's family: Husband Norman Chater, MD, daughter Cris, and son Geoffrey, relaxing together in 1986 at Texas Woman's University.

CHAPTER 3

Her leadership
Her leaders.
Built leaders.

Joyce Clifford

Joyce Clifford, RN, PhD, FAAN, is credited with developing the Professional Practice Model while serving as vice president for nursing and nurse-in-chief for Beth Israel Hospital in Boston, Massachusetts.

Her leadership took nursing to the edge where she took intuitive leaps that permitted the nursing profession to reach new heights. When Joyce Clifford arrived at Beth Israel Hospital in 1973, the annual nurse turnover rate was approximately 70%, and within five years there was a waiting list for nurses seeking a position.

For nearly 25 years the Beth Israel leadership experience was Camelot. Over time, all the pieces fell into place and patient, nurse, and organizational outcomes soared. Joyce quite simply built leaders, and the leaders created excellence.

Joyce and her management team amassed a long list of professional firsts for nursing because they dared to dream what could be and what should be in hospital nursing care.

She has been involved in the design and delivery of nursing care for nearly 50 years, and yet she still becomes visibly choked up as she speaks of the privilege of taking care of people. "I become overwhelmed with emotion when I think of quality patient care, and I am passionate about the nurse's role in this outcome."

At times in her career, quality patient care has required a Herculean effort under extreme conditions. To achieve this goal, she became a health-care visionary who dared to make a difference by creating pathways that never existed. Joyce never encountered a challenge she did not try to overcome.

THE EARLY YEARS

Joyce Catherine Hoyt Clifford was born September 12, 1935, sporting the same flaming red hair as her mother. This distinguishing feature became a trademark

Joyce inherited a love for books and education, an analytical mind, and a strong work ethic from her father, Raymond Martin Hoyt. Although educated only to the 10th grade, her father instilled in her and her sisters that education was everything. Raymond was a self made man who told it straight and ended everything with "kid."

Joyce spent her childhood in a homogenous neighborhood of West Haven, Connecticut. She was interested in a career, and her sisters wanted to get married. They wanted to clean house, and she wanted to read the Cherry Ames nursing stories.

On her 16th birthday, Joyce went to the Social Security office to obtain her Social Security card and work permit, and then proceeded directly to St. Raphael's Hospital to apply for a nurse's aide position. She was hired by Sister Catherine Anne to work on a medical surgical ward for 35 cents an hour. She loved this job.

She tells poignantly of the Christmas Eve she chose to stay with a young nun who was dying. Her father was furious that she wasn't with her family, but her heart was filled by the privilege of taking care of people. This was her passion, and she knew it at age 16.

NURSING SCHOOL

Upon graduating from West Haven High School, Joyce applied and was accepted to the University of Connecticut School of Nursing. She remembers her father sitting her down and saying "now here's the scoop, kid. I have enough money to get you through one semester at the University of Connecticut or three years at St. Raphael's Hospital School of Nursing program. I don't know what will happen after one semester, but I will try. What do you want to do, kid?" She chose St. Raphael's, but always knew that she would get a bachelor's degree. Joyce wanted to graduate from college, which was something no one in her family had ever accomplished.

She began at St. Raphael's in 1953. Nursing school was an exciting time, but Joyce earned a reputation for being a troublemaker for silly things like leaving newly polished white shoes on the windowsill to dry. This resulted in fireside chats with the director of nursing. Undoubtedly this is why Joyce developed a respect for troublemakers whom she believed could provide an honest perspective on processes.

After graduation from St. Raphael's, Joyce worked for a year to save enough money to attend St. Anselms College in Manchester, New Hampshire. For her, the most stressful part of college was the required public speaking class. Speaking in front of large groups terrified her. Her knees would knock, her face would turn as red as her hair, and she often felt physically ill.

Miraculously, Joyce managed to negotiate her way out of the public speaking class by agreeing to take an extra class. She had delayed the public speaking experience, for the time being, and in 1959 she was awarded a bachelor of science in nursing (BSN) degree.

Her parents attended her graduation and beamed with pride. Shortly after graduation, she returned to West Haven and it wasn't long before the St. Raphael nuns contacted her to teach in their hospital diploma program. Joyce accepted the position.

Hospital diploma programs were desperate for faculty members with bachelor degrees, and Joyce was determined to overcome her fear of public speaking. Giving book reports or presentations in school was painful, and now the St. Raphael nuns were asking her to teach microbiology, anatomy, physiology, and chemistry! It was the chemistry that stopped her in her tracks. Joyce exclaimed, "Sister, I earned a D in chemistry." The Sister responded that it wasn't a problem. She could help in the lab. In reality, the thought of teaching any of these subjects terrified her, but chemistry put her over the top.

Joyce remembers teaching her first lecture in anatomy and physiology on the cardiovascular system. She had read everything ever written on the subject and amassed note cards that stood more than a foot tall. She had practiced her lecture for hours. The day arrived, and she entered the classroom scared to death.

She stood before her 60 students silently praying, with knees knocking, face reddened, mouth dry, and feeling like she would burst into tears at any moment. She mustered her courage and presented her three-hour lecture in less than 45 minutes, having moved through the hundreds of note cards at lightening speed. She looked at the class, which collectively appeared somewhat dazed, and blurted out "OK, you can leave now."

Ultimately, she had to repeat this lecture, the second time at a normal pace, but she had taken the first step in conquering her fear. She had given her first lecture—twice—but it was a good start. St. Raphael had managed to help make a public speaker out of her. Today, her Curriculum Vitae lists more than 150 keynote presentations to some of the most prestigious healthcare forums around the world.

CROSSING THE BRIDGE TO PROFESSIONALISM

Joyce's faculty role at St. Raphael's was a time of personal and professional growth. It changed her career trajectory. There were moments of opportunity that serendipitously opened doors that she never anticipated. It was the director of nursing at St. Raphael, Evelyn Kennelly, who bridged these opportunities, literally and figuratively.

Evelyn Kennelly became the first lay person to be appointed as the director of nursing at St. Raphael's. Prior to Kennelly's arrival in 1960, St. Raphael's School of Nursing had been run by the nuns. With the proposed National League of Nursing (NLN) accreditation changes, St. Raphael nuns believed Evelyn Kennelly, with a master's degree from Columbia Teacher's College, would provide the knowledge and expertise to make the changes. Evelyn was creative, bright, and aggressive, and she became a very influential figure in Joyce's professional development. Amazingly, it was fear that brought them together.

Evelyn Kennelly would often go to New York to collaborate with her Columbia colleagues, but she had one major problem—bridges. She had a paralyzing fear of driving over bridges. Thus, she would come to the St. Raphael faculty meetings and ask if anyone would be interested in going to New York with her. Joyce was amazed that no one raised their hand, so she volunteered. Soon she became Evelyn's regular driver, and, much to her delight, was exposed to some extraordinary professional experiences.

Through this fortuitous circumstance, Joyce became a student of nurse leaders such as Mildred Montague, whose dissertation is the basis for the development of associate degree nursing programs in the U.S. and Katherine Nelson who taught at Columbia University Teacher's College and was considered an expert in cancer nursing. Joyce believes that she got a degree without getting a degree, simply by sitting in the corner and absorbing the discussion.

She was privy to remarkable discussions that helped shape her professional growth, and she learned a valuable leadership lesson—take advantage of opportunities because you never know where they might take you. Driving Evelyn opened up an entire new world for Joyce, and she advises her mentees to, likewise, keep their eyes and ears open and seize the opportunities that come along.

As a result of her chauffeur experience, Joyce developed a close personal relationship with Evelyn Kennelly. She became a strong mentor for

1967 at Maxwell Air Force Base. Joyce Clifford (nee Hoyt), on the right, with LPN Mrs. Bonner, center, and Lt. Colonel Dodson, on the left.

Joyce and was determined to develop Joyce's potential to the fullest. As a result of Evelyn's prodding, Joyce encountered three influential nurse leaders who shaped her thinking: Lydia Hall, Frances Reiter, and Jean Barrett. Joyce was in her early twenties and was very open to the futuristic thoughts offered by these nurse leaders.

Lydia Hall

Evelyn Kennelly was committed to moving Joyce beyond her shy tendencies. She forced Joyce to become involved in professional organizations. At one point, Joyce found herself on seven different professional committees, all at the same time, thanks to Evelyn. She was co-chairing a committee with Evelyn when she experienced a "pivotal time" in her life. They were setting up a program, and Evelyn directed Joyce to contact Lydia Hall as a potential speaker. Hall was a very important woman who had left her teaching practice at Columbia to open the Loeb's Center for Nursing Rehabilitation Center at the Montefior Hospital in New York City. The center was completely nurse run and was a model for empowering nurses. In the early 1960s, Lydia was beginning to develop the professional practice model at the center.

When Joyce finally gathered the courage to call Lydia, she received an extended philosophical lecture about nursing from Lydia's unique perspective. When she finished, Lydia asked if Joyce still wanted her to speak knowing what she was going to say. Joyce wasted no time in telling her "absolutely... now more than ever."

Lydia Hall agreed to the speaking engagement, but on the condition that Joyce visit the center to see it firsthand before the program. Joyce made two or three trips to the center and received an individual tutorial from Lydia which shaped Joyce's views on continuity of care, direct services to patients and family, and the autonomy of decision making by nurses. Joyce also gained insight into the educational requirements needed to support an autonomous practice. As a result, the thoroughness of entry-level education became a professional torch that Joyce would carry throughout her career.

A later direct outcome of Joyce's exposure to Lydia was a program Joyce initiated at Beth Israel called "Seminars in Nursing." Seminars in Nursing provided an opportunity for staff nurses to contact nurse leaders across the country to speak at Beth Israel. The nurses were responsible for designing the program, contacting the speaker, creating the budget, making the public introductions, and providing speaker hospitality.

Frances Reiter

Around the same period, Joyce was exposed to a second influence, Frances Reiter, whose work contributed significantly to expanding nursing roles. Frances Reiter was the first nurse to initiate the clinical nurse specialist and nurse clinician role. Joyce had been awarded a federal traineeship to attend a three-week seminar conducted by Frances on rehabilitation nursing. Because of this program, Joyce was exposed to Frances' radical thinking—things such as offering graduate nursing degrees to other professional groups, moving faculty from the classroom to the practice setting, and promoting advanced nursing practice roles. Says Joyce, "all the things that the Institute of Medicine report is saying right now, Frances Reiter was doing four decades ago." The three mesmerizing weeks Joyce spent with Frances had a major impact on her perspective on the scope of nursing practice.

Jean Barrett

Evelyn Kennelly encouraged Joyce to attend a lecture given by Jean Barrett who had just written her book entitled *The Head Nurse*. Jean presented a model of a head nurse who was developing her staff and working and interacting with them, as well as with the patients. It was a completely different model of nursing leadership than was practiced at that time. Before Jean's changes, head nurse roles had been completely administrative in nature. They made assignments, ordered supplies, and counted narcotics but seldom developed the staff nurse to improve patient outcomes.

Next Steps

All three influences—Lydia Hall, Frances Reiter, and Jean Barrett—seemed to be lending themselves to models of nursing care that were cutting edge. The seeds had been planted, and by 1964 Joyce was becoming restless to return to school. She and Carole Boehle had gone to nursing school and college together, and they worked together for several years when they decided that it was time to experience life beyond West Haven.

Joyce applied to New York University's (NYU) School of Nursing master program and Carole joined PAVLA—The Pope's Appeal for Volunteers in Latin America. Joyce had mentioned her NYU plan to another friend, Eleanor Carey, who was also a St. Raphael Air Force recruiter. Eleanor suggested Joyce consider the military. After a bit of convincing, Joyce agreed to apply to both, with the deciding factor being whichever acceptance letter she received first she would pursue. If it was NYU, she would go there, and likewise for the Air Force.

Eleanor worked diligently to move Joyce's application through the military process, and the Air Force letter arrived one day before the NYU letter. Joyce could not believe that she was headed to the Air Force. She remembers being a little concerned that she didn't know how to salute, and, she laughs, that she really didn't want to.

Moreover, how could she become an Air Force officer if she had not ever been on a plane? Joyce took immediate steps to correct this deficiency by booking a trip to Puerto Rico to visit her friend Carole Boehle. Joyce was about to find adventure as an Air Force Captain.

LEADERSHIP IS NOT A POSITION, BUT AN ACTION

Joyce entered the Air Force a little unsure of what to expect or even what it meant that she would be in the military. One of the first impressions the military made on Joyce was the idea of diversity. Not ethnic diversity, but diversity of thought and action. Her life experiences consisted of her isolated and homogenous West Haven, Connecticut experience.

The military allowed her to work with superb nurses and physicians who came from areas across the U. S. with very diverse educational preparation. She learned there was more than one right way to do something. She found that in dealing with others in her team, there was an immediate and overwhelming recognition that "you were right and I was right." This lesson taught her to listen to ideas that were different than her own.

Joyce also learned the value of team work. There were numerous people on the team and learning how to create efficiency was at times quite challenging. She learned the "rank on your shoulder means nothing" if the people you work with do not respect you and want to work with you. She remembers working with airmen who were "just kids," some who were just a few steps away from the brig (military prison) at any given time. They were commonly in trouble, but she loved working with them because they knew how to get the job done.

On weekends, these airmen would spend all night drinking and then show up to work "hung over" the next day. Joyce would say, "OK guys, I know you are tired and that you want to sleep, but you have some work to do first, and then you can sleep."

She would give them their list of duties and then give her permission for them to sleep. If she allowed them to sleep, she at least knew where they were when she needed them.

Over the years, Joyce developed the highest regard for the work that the airmen provided for patients and appreciated the value they brought to the team. She got done what needed to be done, and they worked very hard to please her because she showed them compassion and respect.

Joyce also learned that in the military 'giving it to them straight without beating around the bush' worked well. She has found that people in positional leadership are often not expressive enough about what they want done, or what they expect. She believes that explicit instructions will set the tone for expectations.

According to Joyce, the primary role of leaders is to give responsibility to others in order to develop their leadership qualities. She is adamant that it is "not about my leadership, it is how much I can develop your leadership that is important."

Joyce believes that everybody has the potential to be a leader, and therefore she ingrained in her team that "if you are going to call yourself a professional, then you must call yourself a leader." The leader must motivate, nurture, support, and develop the team so that each member develops a unique leadership style. She continues with that line of thinking, saying that the "most important thing for those in hierarchical positions is to fade into the background and let the others shine." Many of these leadership lessons were learned in the Air Force and practiced throughout her career.

The military also taught Joyce how to follow even when you don't want to. She learned the fine art of compromise, and when it was important to wage war. Joyce acknowledges that most things could and should be solved by compromise, but there are issues of professional integrity that call for holding your ground. One such example involved the performance review of a nurse who Joyce firmly believed was performing at a substandard level. It was well known in the military that performance reviews were "generous." When it came time to complete her review, the highest rating Joyce could give the nurse was average. The chief nurse, a superior officer to Joyce, paid an unexpected visit to her office and asked her to consider changing the evaluation at the request of the commander of the hospital. Joyce took a deep breath and said, "Colonel, if the Commander wants this done, he is going to have to do it himself or get somebody else to do it."

Joyce was willing to risk reassignment for the sake of her professional integrity. The chief nurse stood for a moment in deep thought and then shook Joyce's hand and picked up the phone and called the commander of the hospital to report that Joyce Clifford was going to stick by her evaluation. The underperforming nurse was transferred from Joyce's unit. Ultimately, this nurse experienced performance problems in other environments. Joyce's intuition had been on target, and she learned to trust it.

Joyce left the U.S Air Force – she was a reservist by that time – after 7 years. She had made some remarkable friendships, and she bonded not only with individuals but with the military itself. To this day, Joyce still feels an immediate kinship for those in uniform. She says that there is a "sense of loyalty and camaraderie that is second to none." As military members "we learned to work together with scarce resources to create miracles."

Joyce discovered that the diversity of the military environment taught her the fundamentals of leadership. Moreover, it was while she was in the Air Force that she met her husband, Larry Clifford.

In 1967, she married Larry in Montgomery, Alabama, and when she completed her tour of duty they moved to Birmingham so he could pursue a master's degree in psychology at the University of Alabama. Joyce accepted a head nurse position of a 37-bed medical surgical unit at the University of Alabama Hospital. She believed this position would be an easy one, given her Air Force responsibilities of a 105 bed unit. Lesson learned—numbers can be deceiving.

A YANKEE LEADER COMES OF AGE IN THE SOUTH

In December 1967, Joyce began her new position at the University of Alabama Hospital and discovered that this unit cared for a "very sick population of people." During the first 18 days of her employment, there were 21 cardiac arrests on her unit; these intubated patients remained on her unit, which did not have one registered nurse on staff.

Joyce's staff consisted of licensed practical nurses (LPNs), nursing assistants and non-licensed graduate nurses. The non-licensed nurses had attended nursing school and either did not pass the state exam or attended a non-accredited nursing school and therefore were not allowed to sit for the state exam. Joyce was stunned to discover she was in a clinical war zone without properly trained troops. The military hospital now looked like a vacation.

She quickly learned that the general consensus around the hospital was that 'this was the unit that you had to be well enough to sign for your autopsy but sick enough to need one.' She also discovered that her staff didn't leave the unit for breaks because they didn't want to hear all their friends talk about how terrible it was to work there.

Prior to Joyce, there had been a long string of head nurses who had short tenures. Within the first few weeks, she announced "I have a sense you are all waiting until I just give up. I have news for you, I don't give up, and I am going to be here long after you are." With this, she immediately became an agent for change.

Soon, she was dubbed the "Red Head" by her staff, the "Yankee Missionary" by the physicians, and the "Damn Yankee" by a few from other departments. Joyce, new to the South, had no idea what each of these titles meant, but she was about to find out.

Joyce shortly after arriving at Beth Israel Hospital in 1973.

The Red Head

The unit staff watched as the Red Head began to clean the environment. A pivotal moment occurred when Joyce received notice that her order for hooks to hang clipboards on the unit had been "refused at this time" by the maintenance department. Outraged, she bounded down 11 flights of stairs to *chat* with one of the hospital administrators who could assist her unit—Mr. Ron Hendricks. She burst through the administration doors, short of breath but not lacking in energy, and asked if Ron had a moment to talk with her.

She spent the next hour sharing in detail with Ron the supply and environmental deficiencies of her unit. Joyce questioned why he had not made rounds on her unit so that he could make informed decisions about her unit's requests.

As he had promised during this discussion, Ron visited her unit and discovered the floors, walls, and lights were black with filth. Soon, the staff watched in amazement as workers scrubbed, repaired, and painted nearly every inch of the unit. The clipboard hooks were installed, and, to everyone's amazement, she had managed to secure Kleenex, which had been exclusive to private patients, for all patients. The Red Head became the talk of the hospital, and her staff began to take breaks to boast of the changes on their unit.

The Yankee Missionary

As Joyce picked her battles, she remained focused on her mission of providing quality patient care. It was through this patient-care focus that she built strong relationships with physicians.

Joyce began patient rounds with the physicians and had the honor of collaborating with Dr. Tinsley Harrison who was famous for *Harrison's Principles of Internal Medicine*. Dr. Harrison could not believe a head nurse was out working with the patients. This level of commitment to patients earned her the Yankee Missionary title. Physicians, administrators, and staff were learning that Joyce was about one mission—quality patient care—and look out if something stood in the way. Joyce modeled her leadership style after Jean Barrett's writings because it made sense to her. She was determined to take care of her patients and do what she needed to do to build her nursing staff.

Joyce's leadership predictably included developing her staff. She encouraged those who had failed the state exam to study and retake the exam. Nurse graduates of non-accredited programs were encouraged to return to school so they could become licensed. She worked with the local community college to get the LPNs enrolled in the nursing school and fought for a tuition reimbursement program to be implemented at the hospital. Joyce even returned to school herself, earning a master of nursing science (MSN) degree in 1969 from the University of Alabama.

Joyce was surprised that nursing students from the University of Alabama were not doing rotations at the hospital, so she befriended the dean of the nursing school and began to build relationships to encourage students to consider working at the University of Alabama Hospital.

Joyce even managed to organize nursing students on their days off to provide babysitting services for registered nurses who could staff her unit but needed help with childcare. Joyce was forced to think outside of the box, and that is exactly what she did. She could not run that high acuity unit without a professional staff, so she grew her own professional nursing staff and over time they were becoming leaders.

The Damn Yankee

Joyce began to raise the bar on expectations, but it wasn't without making a few blunders. (She would never call these mistakes or failures because "as long as there is learning and forward progress these are growth opportunities, not failures.")

As she reflects on a 'moment of forward progress,' Joyce recounts that one of the most important considerations is that "you better know what you are doing before you make any changes."

Joyce thought she knew what she was doing when she confronted the hospital food service situation. According to her, the food was literally slopped together on the plate. She thought the kitchen staff were being negligent in how the food was presented and instructed them to separate the meal portions so that is was more appealing.

The next morning, the trays arrived arranged just as she had instructed, with each item neatly separated. Joyce was so pleased to see the kitchen staff had been so careful and felt sure this would improve patient satisfaction. As she strolled through the unit puffed up with pride, she witnessed each and every patient dumping the portions into one large heap on their plate resembling "the slop" that Joyce had just corrected. She had made a change without understanding the culture. This was how the people in this area preferred their food, and the kitchen staff understood the culture, but she had not.

This "Ah-Ha" moment was one she never forgot and has forced her to pause and ask the question "do I know what I am doing? If not, who would know better than I?"

It was these moments that earned her the "Damn Yankee" title. The kitchen delighted in her blunder, and Joyce learned a great deal about the power of culture and creating change consistent with the culture.

In 1971, Joyce left the University of Alabama because her husband was relocating to Indiana for doctoral studies. She owes a great debt to her Alabama experience as it taught her much about herself and overcoming adversity, as well as how to lead with confidence, creativity, and credibility. Says Joyce, "Alabama was probably one of the most useful experiences of my career."

BUILDING THE VISION—A LONG LIST OF PROFESSIONAL FIRSTS

Joyce accepted an associate professor position with the School of Nursing at Indiana University to teach nursing administration in the graduate program. She soon discovered that she had transitioned from a crisis management existence to deciding if she would give a student an A or B. After being in the Alabama 'war zone,' she found this to be "deadly dull"; however, the academic setting exposed her to the scholarly side of the profession.

She found herself immersed in the nursing management and leadership literature. Joyce was retrospectively discovering what she wished she had known prior to tackling Alabama. Nonetheless, she was relieved to find she had not been too far off track in her decision-making.

Another valuable experience while working at Indiana University was her role as the coordinator for student placement, which would provide Joyce with an introduction to the art of building relationships between universities and hospitals. By the time her husband was finishing up his degree, Joyce was ready for a new challenge.

A colleague, Ann Black, mentioned to Joyce that there was a chief nursing officer position opening at Children's Hospital in Boston. Ann had recommended that Joyce take a look at the advertisement in the *Journal of Nursing Administration* (JONA) where she also found an ad for an opening as the chief nursing officer at Beth Israel Hospital in Boston. When she saw the Beth Israel advertisement, she actually laughed because she had worked there for six months in 1960, and it was such a bad experience that she never listed it on her résumé.

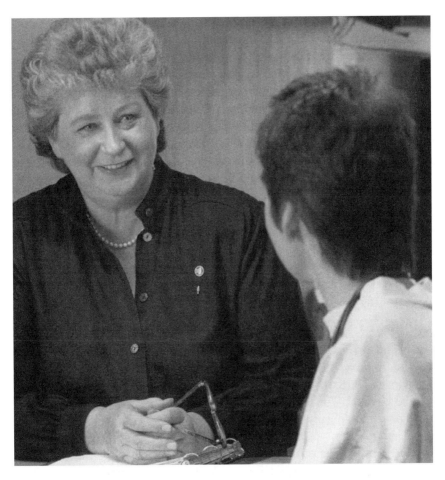

Joyce at Beth Israel Hospital talking with a clinical nurse in 1990.

On a whim, Joyce decided to send her resume to both hospitals. Afterward, the Beth Israel name kept popping up through headhunters, colleagues, and professional contacts, and her interest moved from icy to lukewarm. It was the call from Dr. Mitch Rabkin, who was the chief executive officer for Beth Israel that piqued her interest.

Dr. Rabkin was a 44 year old *wunderkind* who had recently received national acclaim for authoring the Patient Bill of Rights. One phone conversation convinced Joyce that Dr. Rabkin was a visionary. She detected an immediate synergy of goals. She learned that Beth Israel didn't need to be convinced that quality was important; they just didn't know how to get there.

At this same time, the University of Alabama administration was asking her to return in the newly created role of chief nursing officer, a position that she had tried to persuade them to create during her years there. But her interests lay elsewhere at this time.

In May 1973, Joyce decided to interview with Beth Israel. She met with the clinical chiefs and Dr. Rabkin and learned first hand of their commitment to quality. Before agreeing to employment terms, Joyce negotiated only one point with Dr. Rabkin—a seat on the medical staff committee. Intuitively, she knew that she must have a relationship with the clinical chiefs. A nurse had never held a seat on this small but powerful committee. Nevertheless, he agreed.

On August 1, 1973, she accepted the Beth Israel job without even discussing a salary. This is not a strategy she would recommend, but it reflected her faith in Rabkin. When Rabkin offered her $27,000, after her acceptance, which was equivalent to other executive leaders, he validated her value to the process.

CHANGING THE WORLD AT BETH ISRAEL

When she arrived at Beth Israel, her mission for the department of nursing was to improve patient care, optimize the nurses' abilities to use the knowledge and skills they possessed, and to do this in a cost effective way for the hospital. The focus was the rights of the patient, nurse, and hospital. The message was simple and repeated often.

This mission was first challenged by a glaring nurse staffing crisis. Staffing was the infrastructure necessary to achieve the mission, and it was reeling from a nurse turnover rate of 65-70%. A common tenure was three months. Initially, Joyce simply wanted to retain staff nurses for nine months, and she would be satisfied.

There were approximately 80 authorized full-time equivalent (FTEs) positions that were vacant when she took over. Let there be no doubt things were chaotic. Joyce had to stabilize the staffing, stabilize the schedule, and stabilize staff nurse assignments. She believed if she could do so then there was an opportunity to create an environment focused on quality patient care with a philosophy of professional growth and development.

Joyce had been warned that there were pockets of troublemakers on her staff, and she had concluded that she needed the troublemakers to get the hospital out of trouble. She decided to call a meeting with some of these informal leaders and acknowledge she needed their help. She challenged them and empowered them to become a part of the solution. Over the years, many of those same troublemakers became leaders at Beth Israel and elsewhere, assuming director and manager roles.

Joyce also created a recruitment committee of staff nurses, much to the chagrin of human resources, and they began to contact faculty and colleagues, broadcasting to all who would listen that Beth Israel was going to change the world. The energy was palpable.

Beth Israel was undergoing a cultural evolution under Joyce and Dr. Rabkin's leadership. Joyce hired Trish Gibbons in 1974, and she became instrumental to the team on the operational side while Joyce paved the way at the organizational level.

Every Friday afternoon Joyce would meet with four or five nurse leaders for "popcorn time" to discuss what they had accomplished that week at the unit and organizational levels to improve the nurse-patient relationship and patient care quality.

The nursing leadership team was drawn to primary nursing as a model of care, which meant moving to an all baccalaureate nursing staff. On February 17, 1975, Trish Gibbons and the head nurse for the chosen unit, Ellen Liston, began primary nursing on the first demonstration unit. Joyce was very purposeful with her language. She called this a demonstration unit because it was meant to *demonstrate* to the other units how primary nursing was going to function. According to Joyce, to call this a "pilot test

1992. Joyce, 2nd from left, and Dr. Mitch Rabkin, center, with Dr. Maureen McCausland, Associate Vice President of Nursing, far left, with international visitors.

unit" was sending the wrong message that primary nursing was being tested or was optional—this could not have been further from Joyce's intent. The importance of language has played a prominent role in Joyce's leadership, and this is just one example of attention to detail.

Ellen Liston's unit adopted a no floating policy, which was unheard of at that time. The next six hires were placed on this demonstration unit, and it was expected that this unit would be self-supporting for staffing. Roles were clearly defined in order to differentiate practice and to enhance professional accountability. Processes for communication were simplified, and the authority was given to the person with the greatest knowledge for the situation, which, according to Joyce, was commonly the staff nurse.

This was a groundbreaking method of practice. Joyce had begun to build a professional practice model that was focused on building the clinical nurse as the central role for quality patient care.

Colleagues report that as the professional practice model unfolded, the nurse manager became the single most important role in the hospital. It was at this level that the mission of providing quality patient care was fully actualized.

Joyce spent a great deal of time working with nurse managers to lay the foundation for professional practice which included teaching, professional development, and collegiality. She was a highly visible leader who was also known to be accessible. Employees had to pass Joyce's office on the way to and from their cars, and she made it clear that her door was open.

She began to instill the values and principles of mutual respect and recognition among the staff. It was an environment built on sharing the diversity of talent, much as she had learned in the Air Force.

Joyce began setting this standard in orientation by asking newly hired nurses to look around the room at the talent surrounding them and to capitalize on this collective knowledge to improve their own practice. She also began to raise the education bar. Joyce believed professional practice was seeded in professional preparation. At Beth Israel, nurse managers were eventually required to have master's degrees, and the culture was so strong that nurses would not stay if they did not accept and assimilate the values and standards being set.

By 1976, all new hires were required to have a baccalaureate degree. When Joyce arrived at Beth Israel there were few BSN nurses, and within ten years the staff was 94% baccalaureate prepared. She never fired anyone for lack of a degree, but all new staff members were hired to the higher standard. The LPNs that were at Beth Israel before the rule changes went into effect were encouraged to continue their education. Ultimately, LPNs were phased out.

As the nursing staff became clinically stronger, they began to question orders and collaborate with physicians rather than simply executing physician orders. Joyce prepared and guided the physicians for the changes in professional nursing practice, framing this change around the predicted positive patient outcomes. Her intuitive request for a seat on the medical staff committee gave her this physician forum to facilitate the cultural change that was now impacting their medical practice.

From the beginning, Joyce went out on a limb and began to empower nurse managers. The Chief Financial Officer became crazed when Joyce asked for ledgers for the nurse managers to create their own budgets. *Nurses did not do that.*

The Human Resource Director was apoplectic that Joyce wanted the nurse managers to conduct the hiring and firing of nursing staff. *Nurses were not trained for this.*

Years later, after persistently planting the seeds of professionalism at Beth Israel, Joyce produced a seismic shift when she sought to have registered nurses salaried. *Nurses had never been salaried.*

The success of the salary initiative, after a few failed previous attempts by nursing management, was achieved when they convened the proper team including nurse managers, clinical nurses, and members from the accounting and human resources departments who had the proper knowledge. This group got it right.

LEGACY

In 1996, the Beth Israel Hospital merged with the Deaconess Hospital to become the Beth Israel Deaconess Medical Center. The Beth Israel Deaconess Medical Center is one of five Boston-area hospitals in the larger corporation of the Care Group. Joyce became a Senior Vice President of Nursing for the Care Group until 1999 at which point she established the Institute for Nursing Healthcare Leadership in Boston, Massachusetts. The mission for the institute is to promote nurses in leadership in healthcare services. Once again, Joyce found herself grooming new leaders, but this time she was mentoring nurses from around the world.

As Joyce reflects on her leadership journey, she believes that she blazed these professional firsts because it "seemed like the right thing to do."

Joyce speaking at a farewell reception for Peggy Reiley, left, associate vice president at Beth Israel, upon Peggy's move to Scottsdale Health as vice president and chief clinical officer.

She empowered nurses, capitalized on knowledge, applied accountability to practice, and developed leaders, even with the staff nurse team, and was a leader herself within five to six years of her arrival. Beth Israel became recognized as a national example of nursing excellence because of Joyce.

Joyce built a career by empowering nurses, capitalizing on knowledge, applying accountability to clinical practice, and developing leaders at all levels. Beth Israel became recognized as a national example of nursing excellence because of Joyce's commitment to principles that became the professional practice model.

Joyce's influence extended well beyond Beth Israel. She was president of the American Organization of Nurse Executives (AONE) from 1983-85. (AONE facilitated the dissemination of the professional practice model across the nation.) She also advocated for baccalaureate education as an entry-level requirement. She did not win all the battles on entry-level education, but she believes she raised the consciousness of numerous hospital administrators across the country.

While president of AONE she had an opportunity to work with the then president of the American Hospital Association, Alex McMahon, who agreed to include the term nurse administrators whenever he spoke of executive leadership. This was a major victory for nursing.

One of Joyce's great talents is her ability to mentor nurses. She knows how to get the very best from her staff. Peggy Reiley, a member of the Beth Israel nursing staff, was mentored by Joyce for nearly 25 years. Peggy believes that she learned from the master and marvels at the relationship that Joyce developed with her staff. It was a special connection that was created by Joyce's remarkable listening skills. According to Peggy, the staff felt very valued because Joyce showed the "utmost respect for what staff nurses do each day." Peggy further suggests Joyce's profound leadership was about setting standards and expectations and then allowing others to create the outcome. Joyce was gifted at being able to present the vision and then get out of the way and let those with the most knowledge create the reality.

Joyce Clifford delighted in the recognition of her staff. And when she was nominated for the National League of Nursing's Mary Edding Nutting Award, she told the committee that they were nominating the wrong person—it should be her management team. The nomination was changed, and Joyce states this was a "most rewarding moment" because "the right people were recognized." Joyce is quick to acknowledge that she was able to shine because she worked with the best. This included Rabkin who she identifies as essential to her success.

Joyce says, "he didn't always know what I was all about, but he trusted me, and we trusted each other" and the end product was 25 years of outcomes that changed how healthcare professionals viewed the profession of nursing through the development of the professional practice model.

Joyce Clifford is without a doubt a gifted leader who followed her own vision in a career filled with trailblazing professional firsts.

She always remained focused on the mission and had the intelligence to incorporate leadership lessons and influences along the way. When she was once asked to identify her best asset she replied "I am a people person—I am just very good with people."

Fortunately, she has devoted her people skills to the privilege of taking care of people. Eleanor Roosevelt once suggested that "one's philosophy is not best expressed in words; it is expressed in the choices one makes." Joyce Clifford chose to build leaders, and her devotion has resulted in an internationally recognized standard of nursing excellence—the professional practice model.

CHAPTER 4

Luther Christman

A man in female world = a vision
Nurse education @ higher level

Luther Christman, RN, PhD, FAAN, is one of most well-known and respected leaders in nursing. He says that this is because he is a minority in a predominantly female profession, but in reality it is because he is a leader with a vision that is matched by few in the profession.

Luther remains one of the most controversial leaders in nursing because of an inability to keep his viewpoints to himself. His passionate spirit for the nursing profession cannot be contained, despite those throughout his career who have tried. He is a man revered by many within nursing. (Although he believes he was probably disliked by many more.) Regardless of his notoriety, no one can dispute his genius.

With a characteristic twinkle in his eye, he is a man ready to battle wits with anyone willing to engage him in a conversation about the future of the profession. Whether speaking individually or to a room filled with nurses, Luther enjoys "dropping bombs" during speaking engagements just to see who is up for the challenge of a hearty discussion.

He was the first male dean of nursing in the United States, introduced the physician-nurse team approach to patient care, and stressed the importance of using nursing faculty comprised of expert clinical nurses. To teach in a Luther Christman-run nursing school, faculty could expect to spend two-thirds of their time in a clinician role and one-third in a classroom role.

A man ahead of his time, he could never just blend in with his colleagues and, more importantly, he never wanted to if it meant holding back the profession. Being idealistic, his rugged individualism made him stand out as destined to be both enterprising and successful. As Luther says, "my so-called icon status came after I retired, when I was no longer a perceived threat to the women in nursing." Bombs away!

THE EARLY YEARS

Luther Christman was born in 1915, and his siblings included two sisters and a brother. He grew up in the small town of Summit Hill, Pennsylvania (pop.5200). Growing up in the Christman household was not peaceful by any standards, as his parents were complete opposites. Luther admired and respected his father, but feared his mother.

There were many personal hardships for Christman, including being enrolled in first grade at age four (so that he could go to work by the age of 16), being pushed academically throughout his school years, and, later, having the money that he had saved for college taken from him for use for household expenses.

One of the brightest moments in life for Luther, however, was an accidental meeting with a woman by the name of Dorothy Mary Black in 1932, when he was 17. They met by chance, even though they were in the same town, but he knew after their first date they would be inseparable—that was over 70 years ago

As a young man contemplating college and looking into future career options, Luther only considered offers that included his high school sweetheart. Unfortunately, they graduated from high school during the depths of the economic depression at a time when choices for their future were limited.

His friend, a minister, recommended Methodist Hospital in Philadelphia

because it had a school of nursing for women. The minister also knew about the school of nursing for men at the Pennsylvania Hospital. Both Luther and Dorothy could pursue their education and not be separated. Career choices during the depression were very limited, and scholarships were not readily available. Luther remembers that, "Private duty nurses drew higher salaries than bedside

Photo reprinted by permission of Barbara La Valleur, St. Paul, MN.

nurses and were primarily men." One could make $.50 an hour as a private duty nurse, a respectable wage to earn in those days.

Diploma programs were designed to have students work as nursing assistants for six days, on 12-hour shifts, as payment for their room, board, and tuition. They were paid a $10-$12 a month stipend for personal spending. This is how both Luther and Dorothy earned their way through nursing school, and they were grateful for the opportunity. Nursing school was a way to survive economic hardships because all expenses, plus a meager spending allowance, were taken care of by the hospital. Looking back on his journey into nursing, Luther describes it as something he "stumbled into" as a result of the economic times.

Because Luther excelled in academics throughout his life, getting accepted into a hospital-based nursing program was never a concern. The problem came after he graduated from the Pennsylvania Hospital School of Nursing—founded by Benjamin Franklin and Benjamin Rush, MD, this was the oldest hospital in the United States—whereupon he was prohibited from entering the majority of baccalaureate nursing programs around the country, solely on the basis of his gender.

BREAKING INTO A WOMAN'S WORLD: REVERSE DISCRIMINATION

Upon applying for a night supervisory position at a hospital, Luther was told to not expect promotion to day shift positions because, as he was told, "The facility would not allow patients to know they had a male nurse on staff." This was the 1940s, and it was only the beginning of what he refers to as the "reverse discrimination that lasted most of my career."

It was shortly after Luther and Dorothy graduated from their respective nursing programs that they were married. However, to support his new wife, he took a position as a postal clerk instead of working as a nurse. In the 1940s, he could make nearly twice the salary while working for the postal service than he could make by working as a nurse. During those years, every penny of income counted greatly.

Even though Luther was not practicing as a nurse, he applied to Duquesne University in Pennsylvania in order to continue his nursing education. He made an appointment with the provost of the university and was greeted eagerly. The provost remarked that the nursing college was the only college on campus that did not have both genders, and he was looking forward to having Luther break the gender ice for them.

Together, Luther and the provost went to visit the dean of the nursing college. Luther remembers that the dean unceremoniously announced that no man would ever get a degree in nursing from her program! Both Luther and the provost were stunned with the comment, so the provost referred Luther to other universities that he hoped would be more open to admitting a man into a baccalaureate nursing program. Luther applied to the University of Pennsylvania and was received by the school of nursing with much the same response. A faculty group met with him and stated that if he presented his academic records to the admissions office he would be admitted immediately, but he could not enroll in the nursing program. He remembers being told, again, that no man would ever be admitted.

Luther could not understand what his gender had to do with his competence, but he was met time and time again with similar discriminatory remarks. He was even told that he was over qualified for nursing. He was even asked why he would want to waste his credentials on nursing.

He could not understand the logic or reasoning behind the rejections, but once more he made application. This time it was to Temple University School of Nursing. The dean of Temple's School of Health Professions was not a nurse, and, upon reviewing Luther's stellar academic record, he instructed his secretary to admit Luther immediately. This all happened very quickly, and, after all of the rejections, Luther could not believe that he was finally a baccalaureate student. As a baccalaureate student, he attended nursing school by day and worked all evening at the postal service. Says Luther, "The two easiest sacrifices I could make during those years were sleep and recreation." And so he made those sacrifices.

Luther realized early on that he was viewed with suspicion for entering into a woman's world. In 1937 when he started school, less than 1% of all nursing students in the country were male; today that percentage has increased to only 9%.

During his second year of nursing school, he was denied the educational opportunity to take part in an obstetrical (OB) rotation with his female nursing student colleagues. He appealed the decision, and pointed out that firemen and policemen were permitted access to OB training, and, further, that all the obstetricians affiliated with the hospital were men. The reply? "That is different" was all the rationale he received.

He was still expected to have the theoretical OB knowledge needed to pass the state board exams without the parallel clinical experience. This is one of the few cases in which Luther held his tongue from further fruitless

An opinionated, fun-loving man, Luther Christman frequently wears his feelings on his sleeve. The shirt reads: "Hand over the sunflower seeds and no one will get hurt."

dialog and retreated, for the alternative was dismissal from the program. He was learning how to pick his battles.

THE FIGHTING NURSE?

When World War II began, Luther Christman was eligible for the military draft in spite of having a spouse and a child. He wanted to join the U.S. Army Nurse Corps, but he was denied. He advocated for the commissioning of men into the Nurse Corps in an effort to strengthen this branch of U.S. military service. He worked through many forms of U.S. governmental representation, up to and including leaders within the Pentagon, but to no avail. He was soundly rejected as a nurse in the military.

He volunteered to accept a commission in the U.S. Armed Forces as a nurse, but, again, he was denied and greeted with derogatory comments about men in nursing. He was, however, able to serve his country by working in the U.S. Maritime Service as a pharmacist's mate from 1943-1945, but he remained disturbed by his rejection by the U.S. military services.

He was disturbed not only on behalf of male nurses, but also, and more importantly, he considered this to be an injustice to the service men that were wounded in war. With a nursing shortage in the military, the wounded men were not being provided with the best possible access to care when qualified nurses, including him, were being turned away.

Luckily, this rejection was in written form. Luther sent copies of this document to senators, congressional representatives, and high-ranking military officers because he felt they should be aware that qualified nurses were being denied the opportunity to serve their country at a time when the military was understaffed by approximately 2,000 nurses. He wanted them to know that drafting men into these positions was a viable solution.

General Dwight D. Eisenhower, who was Supreme Commander of Allied Expeditionary Forces in Europe during World War II and later went on to become the 34th president of the United States, and Colonel Mayo, who was stationed in the Pacific area, responded to Luther in support of his idea for including male nurses in the Nurse Corps. Both Colonel Mayo and Eisenhower were indignant that male nurses were barred from receiving commissions, but, worse still, was the fact that they could not serve in any capacity in the U.S. Army health fields. Colonel Mayo wrote in his letter to Luther that male nurses had been drafted but that the military forbade having male nurses serve in nursing roles. Colonel Mayo was outraged at the waste of competent personnel when the shortage of nurses in the armed forces was so intense.

The U.S. surgeon general was called into several committees, and a bill addressing the nursing shortage was introduced into congress. Luther discovered that a bid to draft female nurses was on the congressional agenda. This would be the first time in U.S. history that women were to be included in a military draft.

Luther did not intentionally turn to the media in releasing his opinion, but chose to garner congressional support first. However, his message about male nurses being unable to serve in the military was becoming such

Photo reprinted by permission of Barbara La Valleur, St. Paul, MN.

A relaxed Luther Christman.

a high-profile controversial issue that the media was quick to pick up the story. It was not long before *The Saturday Evening Post* wrote an editorial questioning the military mandate against male nurses. The *Christian Science Monitor* featured a similar story that was reprinted in *The New York Times* and the *St. Petersburg Times*.

As things progressed, Luther was provided with assurances from congressional representatives that the pending law would overturn the military mandate against male nurses. Have you heard the saying, "I won the battle but lost the war"? Well, Luther found himself in a classic case of winning the battle but losing the war as more than two thousand male nurses were eventually drafted into military service after this legislation passed, but none were allowed to work as nurses in the army. It was not until the 1960s and the Vietnam War that men were allowed into the nursing corps.

A WORKING VISIONARY

A month after World War II ended, Luther was released from his duties at the maritime base in St. Petersburg, Florida, and he returned to his postal service job in Philadelphia. This choice allowed Luther the opportunity to complete his baccalaureate education in nursing while still earning an income to support his family. He graduated in 1947 and accepted a job at Cooper Hospital in Camden, New Jersey. He was hired to teach part time in the Cooper Hospital School of Nursing; the remainder of his workday was spent working on the operational side of the nursing service within the hospital. Luther worked at Cooper Hospital from 1947-1952 and made numerous operational changes in a successful attempt to assist the nursing shortage. He brought in corpsmen to help staff the operating room of the hospital when nurses were not available, and he used hospital auxiliary workers as ward clerks in order to lighten nurses' workloads. With this change, nurses could place patient care as their primary focus. As it was, Luther believed nurses spent too much time answering phones and delivering flowers to patients' rooms. Interestingly enough, Luther remembers the nurses having difficulty giving up the ward clerk duties. Many nurses believed that by answering phones and distributing mail, they were better able to learn about their patients. Luther was able to successfully help the nurses through this transition.

Word about the successful changes Luther had made at Cooper Hospital got out, and he began receiving job offers. By 1953, Luther was contacted by the governor of South Dakota to reorganize the state's mental health program. Luther accepted this position at Yankton State Hospital in Yankton, South Dakota. While at Yankton, Luther received a call from someone in the Pentagon. The government had four, certified, conscientious objectors (individuals who for reasons of conscience object to conforming to the requirement of military service), but the government could not find them employment as no employers would accept them. Luther recalls thinking that, "If Uncle Sam needs help, I will give it."

The objectors that Luther agreed to hire had to work for the same wage as a private in the military—$30 per month plus room and board. These four individuals were to be nursing attendants, and they arrived to work the same day that Luther had also employed three Native American workers.

Yankton State Hospital in South Dakota had Native Americans as patients, but the attitude towards employment of Indians was extremely harsh at that time. Luther wanted this negative cultural attitude to change, so he hired the three Native American employees as groundskeepers. On the first day that these seven new employees reported to work, news spread rapidly throughout the town. The members of the Veterans of Foreign Wars and the American Legion were angry and demanded to meet with Luther. They feared that jobs were being given to Native Americans instead of to veterans, and they were outraged.

He went out to the city square for what he thought would be a meeting with the local townspeople. He could feel the anger build in the mostly-male crowd, and he realized the severity of the situation he had blithely walked into. It was more of a nightmare, really. "As soon as I arrived, the circle of people tightened around me, and they started venting their anger at my decisions. Suddenly, they tied my hands behind my back and were about to place a noose on my neck. We moved en masse to the biggest tree in the square, and it was obvious what they intended."

It was at that point that Luther had to think quickly if he was to get himself out of this situation alive. "I raised my voice as loud as I could and asked if I could make a statement. There was a partial lull among the crowd so I could shout... It is obvious that I have erred, and I too am interested in veterans, that is why I wanted more staff. I have limited funding but if seven men will resign immediately from their employment and come to work at the hospital for the same salary these men are earning then I will fire them immediately and employ you in their place."

Dead silence overtook the crowd. These workers were so inexpensive to hire that they would be difficult to replace. No one from the crowd volunteered to accept the low paying jobs. Interestingly, and thankfully, a loud voice yelled out an offer to buy Luther a drink. Together with some from the crowd, he went to a nearby bar and talked for 2-3 hours.

Sometimes a leader is allowed the luxury of time to strategize his or her vision for the profession. On other occasions, being a visionary requires fast thinking. Luther could operate at both speeds.

Ironically, this group of angry men turned out to be some of the strongest local supporters of Luther. Long discussions pursued on what the group could do to assist the hospitalized veterans at Yankton (visiting the patients, buying candy, buying tobacco, assisting the veterans on walks, and so on).

The entire time Luther was in South Dakota, this group of people kept its promise to be part of the solution and did not add to the problem any further. As a leader, this situation provided Luther with the confidence to know he could handle just about any situation in the future—no matter how daunting or threatening. It also taught him that critics can sometimes become great supporters if shown respect in addressing and dealing with their concerns.

Meanwhile, Luther believed that in order to be a competent professional he needed to further his education, so he enrolled in graduate school. By 1962 he completed a master degree in clinical psychology, and he continued on to finish his doctoral degree in anthropology and sociology. He took on a double major at the doctoral level, and many doubted his success at taking on this heavy academic load. Luther would prove his skeptics wrong, as he graduated with academic honors and set the minimum time record at Michigan State University for defending his dissertation—25 minutes; the prior record had been two hours.

As a result of his dissertation, Luther developed his own laws of behavior:

1. Everyone wants the world to be in his or her own image.
2. No one can use knowledge he or she does not have.
3. In every instance, given the free choice between rationality and irrationality, everyone opts for irrationality as their first choice of behavior and are rational only when forced to be rational.
4. Most people, under most circumstances, generally will do what is right, if they know what is right, and if the temptation to err is not too great.

MOVING NURSING FORWARD

One vision for the profession that Luther has maintained is the need for nurses to be educated at the graduate level and at the very minimum the baccalaureate level. He believes nursing is being watered down with the different entry levels, thus making the profession weaker. Drawing analogies to other professions such as teaching, social work, engineering, and medicine, nursing is the only profession that has weakened its educational standards over time.

Luther refers to how the concept of a two-year technical program was turned into a two-year nursing program in order to solve a nursing shortage. He asks the question, "What would medicine be like if physicians had various educational training levels that culminated in an MD. Would a patient intentionally go to see a physician with lesser preparation? I think not."

Luther cannot understand why the nursing profession continues to allow this lower standard to occur, and he refers to his behavioral law #2 that states that no one can use knowledge that he or she does not have. "We cannot expect nurses with less education to function equally in roles held by nurses with higher educational preparation." Further, he believes that, "The various entry levels into practice confuse the public, so that the concept of a nursing professional is never fully understood."

He points to the fact that all teachers, social workers, and engineers have one minimum standard of education that must be achieved before entering that profession. Pharmacists must now hold a doctorate degree, while many medical doctors have combined MDs and PhDs. He worries that if nurses do not recognize the need to standardize the professional entry level, the profession could become extinct, or, at best, permanently arrested in growth. He believes that if the "gap in training between nurses and the other members of the healthcare team is reduced, it is very predictable that the role of nurses can be constricted instead of expanded."

Luther makes no apologies when he says, "The issues of low pay and low status in nursing is a direct result of the fact that the majority of nurses are less educated than any other healthcare professionals... It is the minority that hold bachelor, master, or doctorate degrees, yet nurses are surrounded by professionals who are more highly educated. In essence, nurses are low on the totem pole."

He recommends that nurses not compare themselves to other nurses, but that they look around to other professionals. "Many of the communication problems that exist among physicians and nurses relate to the level of education among nurses." Luther wants what is best for the patients and

Luther at his home. It's not hard to see that he is one of the most passionate advocates for nurses anywhere.

the profession. His philosophy is that, "Knowledge is power and professional practice means a lifetime of commitment to learning."

As harsh as these words may sound, Luther is one of the strongest advocates for maintaining the dignity of nurses. He says that what he believes needs to be heard, and it is safe to say that it agitates many within the profession.

THE EDUCATOR

While Luther worked as a professor at the University of Michigan School of Nursing, he became a consultant to the Southern Regional Education Board regarding best practices for racially integrating the colleges. His suggestions were implemented, and Vanderbilt took note and recruited him to be dean of nursing in 1967.

While negotiating his position as dean, he asked to have a dual appointment as director of nursing at Vanderbilt Medical Center. This would put him on an equal playing field with the dean of the medical college. His request was granted, but he knew his work would be cut out for him. Enrollment had dropped from 120 students in the nursing college down to 90, and there were no signs of improvement. His plan was to create a model that paralleled the medical model of education, and, in essence, allow what he saw as clean integration of concepts.

Luther called this the unification model, and his goal was to integrate both nurses and physicians in the educational process. Nursing professors and medical professors would teach together within a classroom composed of both graduate nursing students and medical students. The rationale was that medical students and nursing students would learn together and have respect for each other's knowledge bases. This would be the initial model for the science-based coursework.

In later years, Luther would propose expanding this model into the clinical setting and plant the basic seeds for what today is referred to as the advanced practice nursing model. The other key component of this model is that nursing professors must spend the majority of their time working in the clinical setting as opposed to the classroom. Luther noticed that physicians who taught in the medical school were expected to focus primarily on their clinical competence while teaching was secondary.

He asked "Would you choose to have heart surgery from a surgeon who spent the majority of time in the classroom? Of course not. You would not feel safe." Furthermore, he adds, "Would you want a surgeon operating on you who learned from a teacher who was not current in practice skills? Yet, it is allowed in nursing."

As a longtime advocate for nurses, and, as someone with a desire to see the profession of nursing advance, Luther tried to implement the unification model. He conceived the notion of a clinical master degree program in psychiatric nursing and applied for a federal grant. Together with Dr. Ewald W. Busse, a psychiatrist from Duke University, Luther worked with a multidisciplinary team including clinical psychologists, nurses, and sociologists in an attempt to implement an integrated clinical model. The initial concept was to take the integrated model used in the classroom settings and apply it first to the psychiatric clinical setting, then, if it was successful, duplicate the model in other clinical nursing specialties. The model would replicate how medical students were educated. Duke University medical staff was excited about the idea of extending this model to include nursing, and they offered to pay for the initial funding from the medical school budget.

Luther, thinking back on this time, says that, "The dean of Duke University's nursing program indicated that she would have to consult the National League for Nursing (NLN) before moving forward." The outcome was that the NLN would not approve an advance clinical nursing role, and, Christman states, "The NLN responded with a threat to remove accreditation of the entire nursing program at Duke if the program was implemented, so the dean refused to move on the proposal.

Luther then attempted to consult with the American Nurses Association (ANA) on the issue. "When ANA provided no response, the physicians working on the concept said they would drop the notion of working with nurses on advancing their educational preparation." Hence, the Physician Assistant program was developed. "The thinking was that nurses did not seem interested in clinical competence and were too difficult to work with and make any progress." As Luther remembers, men were the only ones initially recruited into the role of Physician Assistants until affirmative action policies forced the profession to admit women.

Luther reflects at how different the nursing profession might have been if the cooperation had been extended to all clinical areas, especially with the avid cooperation of physicians.

BUILDING A UNIVERSITY

As much as Luther enjoyed his work at Vanderbilt University, he left to seek new challenges. One of his biggest career risks was leaving Vanderbilt University to participate in starting up a new university. While still dean at Vanderbilt, he consulted at Presbyterian St. Luke's Medical Center in order to assist in the preliminary stages of designing a medical university. After two years of consulting, Luther, along with James Campbell, MD, who was in a top management role at the Rush Medical Center and who was responsible for bringing Luther in as a consultant to the large medical center, made the argument that it was time to launch the process of starting a university.

Luther left Vanderbilt to become one of the original founders of Rush University and Rush University School of Nursing. Within one year, the school received full accreditation and received $5 million for the school of nursing. Luther and James Campbell set a 20-year goal of raising $85 million, and the goal was surpassed in 1992 when they reached a total of $91 million in endowments.

In the early days of the university, Luther was appointed dean of all health programs at Rush University, except medicine. It was at Rush that Luther became best known for developing the Rush Unification Model of patient care that "embraces my vision of nurses as knowledge workers and full partners in patient delivery." He also called this the nurse-physician (physician-nurse versions are interchangeable) practice. It was his goal that "the same nurse would care for the same patient every day, giving the patient continuity of care so often lacking in hospitals. I wanted to move

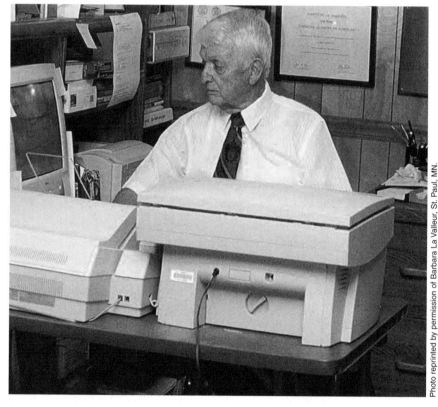

Photo reprinted by permission of Barbara La Valleur, St. Paul, MN.

Luther at his desk. Even retired, he maintains a full schedule.

away from a system that turned nurses into managers of mediocre care and move toward a system that could provide quality care."

As early as the late 1960s, Luther noticed the transition of nurses moving away from bedside care into administrative duties because they believed they were more valued and obviously better compensated. "The best nurses were being pulled away and drained from direct patient care."

Luther believes strongly that the development of the team nursing concept is the antithesis of the Rush Unification model in that it is managerial instead of clinical and "shatters nursing care by creating disorganization." He further believes team nursing is a far more costly model for institutions and pulls nurses further away from what brought them into the profession. "If registered nurses were fairly compensated for their clinical competence, then this drain on bedside nursing would not exist."

By this time in his career in the 1970s-1980s, Luther had become known both nationally and internationally for his ideas and visions for the profession. He had many offers to become dean at such prestigious schools as Yale University and the University of British Columbia. He was so fulfilled with his work at Rush University that he did not want to leave. At times he reflects on this decision as a mistake, because, as he says, "If I had gone to Yale University, my earlier ideas would have been more widely accepted because it would not have been just the school of nursing, but also the medical school behind the ideas for integrated education."

NURSE ACTIVIST

During the nursing shortage of the 1960s, Luther offered solutions to the shortage that were favorable to some, but offensive to others. Affirmative action was one of those solutions presented by Luther. He was an avid supporter of affirmative action programs. He asks, "Why should affirmative action apply only to the male professions?"

A classic example was during the years 1967-1972 he was dean of the School of Nursing at Vanderbilt University. All the deans and top administrators were called into a closed meeting with members of the affirmative action group. At this meeting, they were told that the funding for research at Vanderbilt would be pulled if the university did not get the gender quotas up to 50%—equal representation of men and women. All of the schools were included in this mandate except for the nursing school. Luther was astounded that this kind of discrimination would be allowed and supported. As he says, "It is important that we represent the faces of our patients, and not all of our patients are white females... There is a mysterious lack of affirmative action in nursing, where men comprise less than 9% of the total number of nurses in the workforce."

Luther would spend much of his career fighting for the equality of minorities within the nursing profession. His focus was not limited to gender. He fought for all minorities. In fact, while at Vanderbilt University, Luther hired the first of several African-American faculty members.

Still, gender is a concern for him. Don't be fooled. Luther points out that the medical profession has had to include female representation, which is steadily increasing, in their programs while male representation in nursing is fairly stagnant. He further cites affirmative action as one key to the nursing shortage, saying, "Studies have shown that on average, 96% of men work full time from the time of graduation until retirement, compared to 32% for females. If the profession was 35% male, there would not be a shortage."

During these years, he was nominated to run for president of the American Nurses Association. "I was dean of the School of Nursing at Vanderbilt University, past president of the Michigan Nurses Association, and the favorite to win the ANA election." He was a candidate who was a scholar, a researcher, and a clinical practitioner.

Before the ANA convention, there was considerable campaigning and momentum for his election. On the first day of convention, a group of reporters asked to meet with him. The reporters had been talking with the nurses who were entering the delegate hall about their upcoming vote, and it was reported to Luther that he was overwhelmingly in the lead to win. There was excitement among even the reporters. They hoped to see their headlines read "First Male to Win Presidency of ANA."

That particular headline was never written, as a behind-the-scenes campaign had been launched against Luther that included rumors regarding his sexuality, his stand on diploma nurses, and an accusation that he was considered an "exploitation" on the part of Vanderbilt University because of his dual position as dean and director of nursing. (It was thought by some that if Luther was elected he would use his position as ANA president to exploit the status of the Vanderbilt School of Nursing.) In the end, no matter how hard his supporters tried to right the message, this one-time favored candidate received only 30% of the vote.

In Luther's own words, "The majority of discrimination against me was blatant and not done behind closed doors" as is often the case for women and minorities.

Throughout his professional career, discriminatory comments were often made against Luther in the presence of other nurses, and rarely can he remember a woman suggesting that he was being slighted or that the comments were inappropriate. While at a conference meeting for deans of the Southern Regional Education Board, all the hard work and progress he had made while at Vanderbilt was verbally undermined by a female dean who publicly proclaimed that the good things going on at Vanderbilt were not a credit to Luther's ability (she said that he did not have any ability), but, rather, the successes were due to the fact that he was a male, and, thus, he received everything he requested for no other reason than his gender. (Interestingly, in Luther's five years as dean of the School of Nursing at Vanderbilt, enrollment tripled and a faculty model was developed that received national recognition and saved the university millions of dollars. These accomplishments were recognized and revered by outside professionals far more than by his nursing colleagues.)

Luther persevered, and never considered leaving the nursing profession. Over time, he just became more resilient and a little less shocked at the things that people said.

All of these slights and acts of discrimination that he experienced in nursing led him to found an association called the American Assembly for Men in Nursing (AAMN) in 1980. At the time, there was one association in the country for men in nursing, and it was in Michigan. Over the years, the AAMN started to dwindle in membership, and Luther used resources from Rush University to support years of meetings for the AAMN. The association, which welcomes women to join as members, advocates on behalf of men in nursing, supports them in growing professionally, and encourages men to enter nursing.

THE RETIRED NURSE

Luther Christman has spent the majority of his life advocating for the nursing profession, nursing education, and quality patient care. His opinions on healthcare and nursing issues remain strong today, yet his spirit is as gentle as ever.

Luther continues to receive awards and honors for his long years of service to the profession, on both a national and international basis. For

Luther Christman with Sigma Theta Tau International president Dan Pesut and past-president Eleanor Sullivan at an award ceremony.

example, as a result of the impression Luther left on healthcare professionals in Japan, there is a Luther Christman Center in Tokyo that artistically displays his publications, papers, and portraits.

Retired since 1987, he remains busy writing articles on the profession, speaking to groups across the country, and he maintains his professor emeritus status at Vanderbilt University and dean emeritus status at Rush University.

Luther supplements his knowledge base in science and healthcare research by reading the latest journal publications; however, the majority of his recent years had been spent in the role of caretaker for his wife, Dorothy, until she passed away in July of 2003. After 70 years of being together, the two had rarely been separated.

Luther Christman has numerous legacies he has left to nursing, but his most powerful ones have been his strong, passionate campaign for increasing the standards of the profession and for opening the door of the profession to minorities. As a result of his platform, he has left the profession a better place for others.

What more could one individual ask from a lifetime career?

CHAPTER **5**

supported nursing

what docs got, nurse got

Vernice D. Ferguson

Vernice Ferguson, RN, MA, FAAN, FRCN, was a mover and shaker of major proportions in the profession of nursing, and she remains a strong voice for nursing. She has accomplished many "firsts" as an African American, as a woman, and as a nurse. Her contributions to the Veterans Affairs Health Administration and to the profession of nursing are extensive and should never be forgotten.

Vernice learned valuable lessons early in her life that would serve her well on the journey to becoming one of the most prominent leaders in nursing. Being raised in the United States in the middle part of the 20th century often predisposed African-American children to the idea that there were two worlds: One White world and one Black world. However, Vernice never allowed herself to view the world so simplistically. Instead, she created her own dreams. She was a fighter who felt that race would never get in her way, and, further, "If one gets a good education and becomes excellent in what he or she does, it will be recognized and speak for itself."

Vernice did just that. She went on to become a faculty member at Johns Hopkins University, an institution that years earlier would not have accepted her as a student because of her race. She was determined to never take a back seat in anything she pursued. Instead, she always looked for where the seat of power resided. It is there she would take her place. She lived her career knowing that a leader can never fear change but must embrace the new opportunities as a way of being able to channel creativity.

THE EARLY YEARS

To fully appreciate Vernice's nature, it helps to view her career in relation to the era in which she grew up. Career choices for women in general were limited, but even more so for African-American women. For Black women who grew up in America before the civil rights movement, mentors in nursing were nearly nonexistent.

Ironically, Vernice was one of the early pioneers in baccalaureate education. Those around her family were teachers, preachers, or lawyers. Her mentoring influences came directly from family members and close friends. Family friends stayed at her house in Baltimore, Maryland, because "a Black individual could not go to a hotel to spend the night … I think every Black person who held a PhD during those years stopped by our house at one time or another."

Dinners were set at a big table, and even at a young age Vernice would be called upon to participate in the vibrant conversation of these powerful people. She remembers wanting to be a nurse because her mother always wanted to be a nurse, but her mother did not allow it. As a way of living out her mother's frustration and "because of my love for her, I decided to become a nurse."

Against her father's wishes, she would first become a candy striper at the local hospital, and that, in turn, cemented her dream of entering the profession. It was not that her father was against her going to college—all Ferguson children had college in their future—it was that he wanted her to become a doctor.

Vernice's father was a minister and was in hospitals enough to see how hard nurses were made to work. He was not sure he wanted that life for his daughter. She knew, though, that she could not be anything other than a hospital nurse.

At a young age, she already had the makings of a renegade. She wanted to break the mold and blaze her own trail through life.

Ferguson's choices for a college were limited by the segregation issues of the time. Civil rights and equal rights have come a long way since the '40s, but years ago, Blacks had fewer choices of where they went to school because not all the doors were open. In addition, over 70% of the nursing programs were hospital diploma schools, but Vernice wanted a college degree.

She applied to New York University (NYU) and the University of Minnesota (UM), both of which accepted her. She chose NYU to be near

Vernice Ferguson speaking at Villanova's commencement in 1988.

her family. When she graduated from NYU in 1950, she was awarded the Lavinia Dock prize for high scholastic standing, as well as honors in clinical practice.

To understand what the world was like when Vernice graduated, know that when she was handed the Lavinia Dock award, she extended her hand to the director of nursing to shake, but the director, with all of the Ferguson family looking on, did not have the grace to shake it. "There were indignities that one suffered everyday as a person of color." This affront was one of many during that era. On occasions when racism would raise its head, she would use humor to deal with it, which she found to be more powerful than dealing with it confrontationally.

Upon graduation, it was not difficult for Ferguson to find work. She had one criterion and that was she wanted to work the day shift. "Knowing the hospitals run around the clock, my one condition was that I wanted a day job."

With a new husband, whom she had met and married the year she graduated from NYU, she was determined to have some degree of normalcy, and a big part of that was to have regular work hours. She accepted her first position, at Montefiore Hospital in New York, for one reason only—because they promised no rotating hours. She did not want to work days, then nights, the evening shift, and then back to days.

The hospital had a six-bed research unit funded by the National Institutes for Health (NIH), and, because of her education, she was appointed head nurse in the neoplastic metabolic unit. To be right out of school and in charge of a neoplastic metabolic unit was one of the happiest "accidents," as Vernice puts it, in her career.

This experience led her into research, and with it she had the opportunity to co-author numerous papers with her colleagues. Her main research focus during 1950-1952 was physiologic research in calcium metabolism. In 1955, her first solo article was published in the *American Journal of Nursing* (AJN). The first rendition of the manuscript was sent back with the rejection reasoning stating "it was too sophisticated and nurses were not doing those kinds of things." In order to get the article published by AJN, she had to bring it down a level, which greatly offended her.

"It did not please me to dumb it down, but they were not ready for it because they had not seen nurses in that role before … it was an important message to get in the literature, so I went along with it." Vernice did not have this experience when she published with her colleagues in other disciplines in journals such as the *Journal of Clinical Nutrition* or the *Journal of Clinical Investigation*.

Vernice was happy about being able to write on behalf of the nursing profession, as it gave her an outlet for a secondary love of hers—journalism. It was her way of being able to combine the love of language with the love for nursing, a combination that helped to carry her far in nursing.

AN ADMINISTRATOR AT WORK

Vernice launched her long nursing administration career with the Veterans Affairs (VA) health system. Ironically, she closed her career there as well.

Before retiring from the VA in 1992, she would hold the highest nursing administration position, assistant chief medical director for nursing programs. She would be responsible for the largest nursing service in the world with more than 60,000 nursing personnel.

This journey started for Vernice in 1966 when she was offered the opportunity to become a chief nurse trainee in the system. Chief nurse trainees were hand picked and funded for a full year as an understudy to a major chief nurse. Vernice was sent to Denver, and her chief nurse was a former Army nurse who was considered to be one of the brightest.

She did not stay in Denver as understudy for the full year. Within nine months, she received a call to accept an assignment as chief nurse in Madison, Wisconsin. It was considered a highly prestigious assignment, as most nurses in their first assignment were in small facilities, with advancement taking many years rather than the months that it took Ferguson. In Vernice's opinion, "I hit the golden ring on my first assignment and loved it."

From here, Ferguson's career moved quickly as she was sought out time after time to take on more and more responsibility. These career

jumps took her from Madison, Wisconsin, to Chicago, Illinois, to Washington, D.C., to Baltimore and Bethesda, Maryland.

One thing that was always important to Vernice was maintaining her clinical expertise. She never wanted to be considered just an administrator. "I considered that very important throughout my career so I could keep growing and changing."

In 1980, when she was in the position of assistant chief medical director for nursing programs, the VA began caring for a world of aging veterans. When this aging population trend began, nearly 10-15 years ahead of the rest of the country, she knew she lacked the necessary knowledge in gerontology to lead through this demographic shift. "I knew, being from an acute medical-surgical background, that I could not preside over what I didn't know." In response, she chose to take a sabbatical. She had two reasons supporting her decision: to get the knowledge she needed and to remind VA nurses that, just as physicians take sabbaticals, nurses can too.

She took six months and became a scholar-in-residence at the Catholic University of America to focus on long-term care and elder care at the time when there were 11 teaching nursing homes funded by the Robert Wood Johnson Foundation. "I criss-crossed the country and toured the private sector and the public sector, and I made rounds with junior medical students at Georgetown University."

A major contribution that Vernice brought to the VA system was a new way of viewing the nursing profession. During the 1980s, nursing was viewed as a tradition-bound service. Vernice viewed this as an opportunity to lead in a new and vibrant way—to bring people along to a different way of thinking.

To bring this new way of thinking forward, she brought the first staff nurse to the VA central office for a one-year assignment. Past leadership models included assisting with policy changes, but never had staff nurses been asked as a fresh voice and perspective in helping to set policy within the VA system. This was invaluable in bringing the staff nurse's perspective to the table for deliberation. Unfortunately, with budget cuts, this program lasted only one year but is an early example of shared governance. Vernice had a similar mentoring program during earlier years while working at the NIH Clinical Center.

She views her mentoring programs as one of the major accomplishments she made to the profession. She was creating learning opportunities available for all nurses for whom she was responsible in terms of their growth as professionals and in changing and shaping their future. "To have

Vernice Ferguson at the 1989 dedication ceremonies for the new Sigma Theta Tau International building. Vernice was instrumental in raising the funds for this much-needed new building.

nurses be actualized through my office, my resources, and through me, so they could continue to grow and be whatever they wanted to be in nursing is just one of the ways of giving back."

In addition to her executive administrative role with the VA, Vernice concurrently served in the role of president for the Honor Society of Nursing, Sigma Theta Tau International, from 1985-1987. Initially, Vernice served as president-elect. Two years later, she became president. As this was later in her career, she felt confident in her abilities to manage both her work schedule and her schedule of duties as president. During her term as president, her voice for the profession was used to encourage and mentor young nurses.

It is Vernice's philosophy that "the educators, researchers, and administrators will find their way along, but the young need the extra guidance and extended hand of our profession's more senior and experienced colleagues." Vernice could see the importance of bringing more youth into the profession 20 years ago and used this topic as her platform when speaking as president.

While at Sigma Theta Tau International, Vernice raised a considerable amount of money for a much-needed new headquarters building. She rigorously campaigned for support for the building in Indianapolis, Indiana, which was completed and dedicated in 1989.

Following her years of service to Sigma Theta Tau International, Vernice went on to become the second president of the International Society of Nurses in Cancer Care. It was this role that exposed her to the international world of nursing. "The experiences one gains as a result of working with the global communities of nursing are experiences I feel all nurses owe to themselves."

EQUALITY REIGNS SUPREME

Vernice expresses the importance of the phrases "never take a back seat" and "never take no for an answer" as key motivators in her life. She never believed nurses should take the back seat to physicians or take anything less than what is offered to physicians. "What is good enough for the doctor is good enough for me and the nursing staff."

Case in point, when Vernice was chosen in 1980 to lead the VA nursing program nationally, she attended a national meeting called the Association of the Military Surgeons of the United States (AMSUS). Upon visiting the VA booth, she noticed a fellowship program in gerontology being advertised for the physicians but which was not available for the nursing staff. She believed that if it was good enough for the "docs," it was good enough for the nurses. It took her three years to acquire that same fellow-

Throughout her career, Vernice always managed to be at the table ensuring that nurses had a voice that represented their needs and concerns.

ship offering for her nursing staff, but she succeeded. Her philosophy? "Whatever the boys have, I am going to get the same thing for the girls."

She learned early on that no one discipline can solve all the problems of healthcare. Each discipline has unique gifts that it brings to the table. It was always Vernice's quest to be at the table. The one question she always asked, whether in her role as nurse leader of the VA medical center or chief nurse at the NIH, was "Where does the power lie?"

Her response was always, "Be there ... So, by hook or by crook, I was always in the inner circle ... and you position yourself to be in the inner circle so that you can facilitate nursing in its fullness to have its day in the sun."

Another example of how strongly Vernice feels about equality for all is when she was recruited to work for the NIH Clinical Center in 1973. After several months of the interviewing process, she received a call notifying her that she had been the unanimous choice. The question was asked if she would choose them.

Vernice was mature enough as a leader by then to realize that she now held the power. The search committee wanted to know her salary demands, but she had other priorities to settle first. "Gentlemen," she said, "we are not going to talk about my salary, we are going to talk about the salary for the nurses ... I cannot accept a nurse at the GS6 level" (GS stands for General Schedule followed by the numeric ranking within Civil Servant positions—rankings went from GS1-GS15). In response, they informed her that if they raised the salaries of all nurses, then the dieticians and pharmacists would want more. "Gentlemen, that is your problem, not mine. We are talking now about nursing." She proceeded to negotiate a minimum salary floor for nurses.

The conversation then came back around to her salary demands, so when asked the question for the second time, she turned to the CEO and asked him what his government grade was, and, with his response in hand, she told the committee that she would accept "what he has."

She was told no, of course, and they explained that it was not possible, that no one in the government system jumps several grades at one time, as it is a Whitten Amendment written to prevent favoritism. Vernice informed them she was no longer interested in their position, and she returned to her job at the Veterans' Affairs Health Administration. Interestingly, she received a call a short time later offering her the job at her salary demands. She, again, had stuck to her philosophy that if it was good enough for the boys, it was good enough for the girls. "They would have done it on the spot for a physician … I knew I was their unanimous choice, so I would use this to advance the nursing agenda which the nurses deserved."

Years later, when she left the NIH, she was told that a waiver for the salary she had demanded had been sent down on her behalf to the secretary of the Department of Health and Human Services, which was signed by the secretary days after she was brought on board. Obviously, they wanted her and were willing to make it work, and she knew it and was able to get something for herself, a nurse.

Vernice would not accept the idea that she would not be paid equally to a male executive and that if the NIH wanted her badly enough, they would find a way to make it work. She stood by what she believed in, but she also was wise enough to realize she held the position of power during the negotiating process.

ACTUALIZING NURSING

Vernice's goal throughout her career focused on moving nursing out of the shadow of organized medicine. It was what she describes as one of her greatest career risks, as many times this involved adding more stress to her own days. She considered it her job to move nursing into a more contemporary position. In addition to all her obvious contributions to the profession, one of her major contributions was to explain the nature of nursing to other disciplines and to articulate how the nurses' roles were independent yet collaborative.

Vernice did not approve of organized medicine looking on nurses as being dependent upon a physician's realm. She observed hospital administrators trying to make physicians happy but not doing the same for nurses. It was obvious to her many years ago that in order to bring nursing to its fullness, the profession's unique gifts, body of knowledge, arts, and science would all have to be embraced. Vernice was acutely aware of the value of empowering "the staff nurses down in the trenches," so as professionals they would feel they had the authority to properly do their job.

She wants all voices at every level to be heard and given merit; "orders should not just flow from the top down, without considering those who have the hands-on, day-to-day experiences of working with the patients and their families." This was a lesson that she learned early—from her mother and father—to make every presence and opinion known.

An example of how hard Vernice would push the envelope in actualizing nurses was a time when she fought hard for nurses but won only a pyrrhic victory. She was chief nurse at the VA Hospital in Madison, Wis-

consin, and she eliminated the various levels of reporting in order to empower the head nurses. The head nurses, as a team with Vernice, decided to make a procedural change regarding the standard equipment given to each patient (a metal urinal, a metal bedpan, and a metal emesis basin). The nurses had noticed that much of the equipment was not used by every patient, and they believed that each patient should be assessed for his needs and given the equipment accordingly. This would save extra work by the nursing assistant who had to sterilize the distributed equipment, whether used or unused, on a nightly basis.

Word got back to the chief of medicine, who, upon asking a nurse why the change was made, was told that Vernice had told them to—not that a team of nurses had made the decision together. Hopping mad at this act of impudence, the chief of medicine confronted Vernice, who in turn told him in no uncertain terms that it was a nursing decision and not a medical decision and that he could take issue with her decision only when or if the patients were not taken care of as was appropriate to their treatment and conditions.

Unsatisfied, he accused her of trying to run the hospital. She learned a tough leadership lesson. She had thought that the decision that had been made was a nursing team decision, but, upon questioning by a physician, the nurses took no ownership in the new process. This meant that something was flawed in the way that she had handled the communication in the decision-making process. Next time she would ensure that the nurses felt like equal partners at her side for any journey through change.

Vernice did not stay long at the Madison VA because she was being considered for the chief nurse position at Chicago's West Side VA Hospital (1967-1970). "Mobility," she states, "is a key to continued promotions and success."

Vernice did receive the promotion and was off to her new position in Chicago. Unfortunately, it would not be long before another offer would come in *summoning* her to become a general medical and surgical nursing specialist for program planning and policy development in Washington, D.C. She tried to resist the offer, as she did not like having to leave her new colleagues, but in the end she accepted the position and moved to the East Coast.

Within months it would happen again. Vernice was notified she was now being considered for the position as chief of the nursing department of the prestigious Clinical Center of NIH in Bethesda, Maryland, the same position for which she had negotiated a minimum salary level for her nurses and for which she had negotiated her salary to the level commensurate with the head administrator.

As history has a way of repeating itself, it would not be long before a leadership opportunity would arise and Vernice could now approach things differently, as a result of her earlier lesson. While working at NIH, a new patient computerized system for recording all care, including research protocols, was being installed.

After the computerized system was put into place, the physician scientist of one institute decided to take his group out of the program as user-generated ideas were not being implemented and the program was too complex and too time-consuming to be of use to the group. Shortly thereafter, Vernice's boss, in order to save the computer project, announced that the nurses would serve as agents to the physicians and input their data into the computer.

Vernice, however, knew that it was *not* going to be the way things were. The nurses would not be the physician's data-entry agents. She, in turn, called a meeting with her leadership team and the key leader of the information cadre. Together they discussed what position they would take on the issue of who would be responsible for entering the information into the computer.

"I went around the room to all 13 nurses who were responsible." As she went around the room, each person was asked to identify what they valued the most about the computer program and what they valued the least. They had the same concerns as the physicians: that it was too time-consuming and too complex. In addition, they believed the company was slow to respond to their requests for further refinement of the software.

When Vernice asked the group members for their position on this issue, they rallied for discontinuing the use of the computers just as the physicians had. She left the meeting at 11 pm that evening and called her boss to let him know that the nurses would be joining the physicians in discontinuing the use of the computers, and that, as of Monday morning, the nurses would not be entering data into the computers. There was a long silence on the other end of the phone. Finally, her boss replied he wanted to see her in his office first thing on Monday morning.

At the time, she was also holding the position as president of the American Academy of Nursing (AAN), and she had an important meeting to attend that following week. Knowing that she had just opened a hornet's nest, she asked someone else to cover her obligations at AAN while she worked through issues at NIH, as she felt strongly that when leaders create dissonance in their organization it is their responsibility to preside over it.

To achieve a successful outcome for the nurses, Vernice enlisted the assistance of one of her chief nurses who went on to every unit to tell the nurses the details of the plan and why they were doing it, and then asked the unit nurses if they had everything in place to do their work come Monday morning. She asked the nurse leader of the computer cadre to call the chief of pharmacy that night, and he said he could maintain his department for two weeks in the manual way.

Finally, she had a call placed to the physician of the institute that had first discontinued the use of the computers, and the physician's response was along the lines of "tell Miss Ferguson that we applaud and support the nurses ... this is the first time we have ever known them to take a position on anything."

On Monday morning, as the issues were aired, the top leadership of the Clinical Center formed a committee of nurses and physicians and other parties with a vested interest in successful resolution of the major problems associated with the computer.

Success followed. She had learned from the earlier incident of not carrying the process far enough when there were problems on the horizon. "I learned how to lead better by my earlier mistake of thinking I had the followers with me, and discovered that when the heat was on, they could not be counted on to be supportive. One has to stand for something and sometimes we are lucky in leadership and other times one can lose the job."

The final resolution in this situation was that the computer system was brought down in order to correct the major outstanding problems, and when it was reinstalled throughout the VA system it was recognized as "one of the strongest systems for managing data in the country," Vernice remembers.

THE RETIRED NURSE

Although Vernice technically retired from the profession of nursing, one would never consider her retired, as the pace she leads would put most young nurses to shame. Ferguson continues to travel around the country speaking out as an expert on behalf of nurses and the profession. It was such a part of who she was during her working years that it is now a part of her retirement.

Vernice takes her own advice by continuing to stay active in the profession. In 2003, she was appointed as one of 16 distinguished Americans to advise the secretary of the Department of Veterans Affairs on the future direction in healthcare in the VA through year 2020.

She has also been appointed to the Programs Committee of the American College of Physicians, American Society and Internal Medicine Foundation. This appointment means she will be dealing with improving communications among healthcare providers and those whom they serve. Vernice is privileged to be the nurse who was invited to serve on the committee representing nursing.

"This opportunity will allow me to share that nurses have gifts that all of healthcare professionals need to hear about. When you get to the table to put that voice forth in a way that is respected and wanted, it helps to move the healthcare objective forward."

Vernice during her tenure as president of The Honor Society of Nursing, Sigma Theta Tau International, from 1993-1995.

When Ferguson started out in nursing, she never let any imposed limitations slow her down or keep her from getting to the top. "I never thought of being anywhere other than the top ... I always thought that today takes care of itself, but leaders should be looking at tomorrow."

Ferguson kept her eye on "tomorrow" throughout her career as a visionary seeking to actualize nursing. Her secret to success has always been excellence and enthusiasm. "You have to be enthusiastic and passionate about what you do ... and, of course, excellent at what you do and what you believe, so it gets translated to other people." Those are the gauges that Ferguson uses to mark success.

CHAPTER 6

Nat'l Institute Research of Nursing @ N IH

Ada Sue Hinshaw

Ada Sue Hinshaw, RN, PhD, FAAN, never doubted she would attend college. Weekly walks to the bank with her mother to deposit the coveted $10 into her college account served as a constant reminder of her goal. She also knew she wanted to follow in her mother's footsteps and become a nurse. What she did not know was that her nursing career would be pivotal to the development of the scientific foundation of the profession, the creation of a new institute at the National Institutes of Health (NIH), and national leadership roles that would facilitate nurses' participation in healthcare public policy.

Ada Sue's accomplishments are a result of her research efforts and leadership style. Ironically, she muses, her early success actually resulted from "obliterating the words 'nursing research'" because these two words created panic in the eyes of nurses and blank stares on the faces of those outside the discipline.

Ada Sue Hinshaw is a pioneer nurse researcher who had the opportunity to participate in the building of an infrastructure for a center that would legitimize nursing research as a scientific contribution—the National Institute of Nursing Research. Her journey required she develop new methods of communication, participate in high profile politics unguided by history or rules, and produce results that built confidence.

Justifiably, she has been recognized with many of nursing's most prestigious awards and positions, including Nurse Scientist of the Year, Distinguished Health Leader of the Year, President of the American Academy of Nurses, and two terms on the Institute of Medicine Governing Council.

Colleagues have referred to Ada Sue as "Grace under Fire," and her remarkable career displays the courage and leadership that confirms that title.

THE EARLY YEARS

Ada Sue Hinshaw was the product of a very strong family that valued education, a focused work ethic, and respect for others. Born May 20, 1939 in Arkansas City, Kansas to Oscar Allan and Georgia Tucker Cox, Ada Sue was the older of two daughters. The majority of her childhood was spent in Cherryvale, Kansas—a small rural community of fewer than 5,000 people.

Ada Sue recalls being younger than seven years old when she decided that she would be a nurse. Her mother was a nurse for a local physician, and Ada Sue would visit the office each afternoon. These visits convinced her that she too wanted to be a nurse.

In 1961, she graduated from her mother's alma mater, the University of Kansas, earning a bachelor of science in nursing degree (BSN). Ada Sue was "capped" with her mother's cap—a dream come true for her. Ada Sue's mother not only influenced her career choice but was also a significant role model for her leadership style. Ada Sue describes her mother as a "very strong woman, very soft in manner and style, but very strong." The consistent lesson from her mother was if you want to get things done then you must get a plan and get the right people to help you.

This maternal influence imprinted itself on Ada Sue's self-described leadership style of "shifting things by a shared vision." She says "you don't want to oppose the vision of others," instead, "you should utilize the group vision to obtain motivation through collaboration."

The Cox family survived the Great Depression and World War II by being adaptable and making tough decisions with quiet resolve. In 1942 her mother willingly put aside her nursing career, and the family moved to Oregon so her parents could earn triple their current wages as ship builders.

Ada Sue's father was a brilliant mathematician who was never educated beyond the ninth grade. He was born and raised in the Ozarks by a family that had few financial resources; however, he was gifted with an abundance of raw intelligence. He went on to become a successful small business owner, making the most of the opportunities he had. He was a risk taker who worked hard. He also believed education was the conduit to opportunity and wanted his daughters to have a college education.

Ada Sue far exceeded her father's academic vision, ultimately earning a doctoral degree and receiving some of the highest honors and recognition in nursing, healthcare, and national leadership. When asked about the obvious pride her parents must have felt about her accomplishments, she quickly responds with a turn of the table, saying "I am proud of them. They are very special people."

Growing up, Ada Sue was always social and involved in numerous leadership roles. From a young age, she performed in piano recitals and remembers competing in state recitals before large crowds. Ada Sue does not remember being nervous when performing and learned to love public speaking. In high school, she was a cheerleader, drum major, and president of her senior class. Academics came easily to her, and she knew that she wanted to move straight through college to graduate studies.

EDUCATION AND MENTORS

After Ada Sue graduated from Cherryvale High School in 1957, she enrolled in the School of Nursing at the University of Kansas. To earn extra income, she worked part-time on the evening shift on an Ear Nose and Throat (ENT) ward. It was not uncommon for hospitals to staff their wards with student nurses, and Ada Sue remembers being a junior in college when she was put in charge of the ENT unit. She recalls being "half out of my mind" with terror and very grateful for the supervisors whose experience often saved the day.

In 1961, Jean Hill, the dean of the University of Kansas School of Nursing mentored Ada Sue by suggesting she immediately begin graduate studies once she graduated with her baccalaureate degree. Following Hill's advice, Ada Sue enrolled in the MSN program at Yale University. She chose Yale for its superior midwifery program. Before being enrolled at Yale University, Ada Sue, to use her words, "had never even heard the word research."

In her first year, Ada Sue was able to observe the remarkable work of Yale professors James Dickoff, Patricia James, Robert Leonard, and Rhetaugh Dumas, all renowned researchers, so her interest in research was piqued. She describes it was an honor to be involved with people who were so very bright and excited about what they were doing. Midwifery soon took a back seat and nursing research became her career focus.

In the summer of 1962, Ada Sue returned to Kansas and married Lewis Everett Hinshaw, III. The newlyweds returned to New Haven, Connecticut so Ada Sue could finish her degree, and Lewis enrolled at Hartford Seminary to become a Southern Baptist minister. In late 1965, the Hinshaws moved to the west coast so Lewis could pursue doctoral studies at the Graduate Theological Seminary affiliated with the University of California at Berkeley. Ada Sue worked on an Obstetrics and Gynecology unit at Alta Bates Hospital. This experience proved timely as she was living the obstetrics experience herself. She gave birth to their first child, Cynthia Lynn, on January 2, 1966.

By the fall of 1966, Ada Sue was a faculty member at the University of California at San Francisco (UCSF) School of Nursing. UCSF put her back into the research milieu, and she found herself working with Marlene Kramer who was one of the most outstanding mentors in her career.

Marlene Kramer was the Associate Dean of Undergraduate Studies at UCSF and had built a remarkable research career around a "discovery learning" curriculum and the bicultural socialization of nurses. Discovery learning was an innovative method of teaching, and Ada Sue had the opportunity to assist Marlene in her studies.

Ada Sue believes it was a rare opportunity to be able to work with someone of Marlene's vision and intelligence. The UCSF experience expanded Ada Sue's research skill set and enthusiasm.

Ada Sue recognized a doctoral degree was the logical next step and essential if she was going to stay in academia. She had determined she needed additional knowledge in research methods, statistics, and instrumentation. She was mulling over her doctoral options when she met Gladys Sorenson who was the dean of the School of Nursing at the University of Arizona.

Gladys Sorenson was assigned to critique Ada Sue's presentation at the Western Nursing Research Society Conference (WNRS) in 1970, and she wasted no time in letting Ada Sue know that the University of Arizona was one of only nine universities designated to offer nurse scientist doctoral training grants.

In 1971, the Hinshaw Family was on the move again, this time to Tucson, Arizona, so Ada Sue could pursue a doctorate in sociology. In addition to the training grant support, Ada Sue was drawn to the discipline of sociology because she had an opportunity to work with Jack Gibbs who was an expert in model construction and Bob Hamblin who was renowned for social behavioral measurement.

A doctorate in sociology meant Ada Sue would first need to earn a master degree in sociology, which she completed in 1973. She was halfway through her doctoral program when she gave birth to her son, Scot Allen Lewis Hinshaw on May 10, 1974. Scot was 18 months old when she was faced with becoming a single parent as she and Lewis had decided to get a divorce.

Ada Sue's doctoral dissertation, chaired by Bob Hamblin, built on Marlene Kramer's work in looking at the complexity of professional nurse decision-making. She also studied job stress, job satisfaction, and nurse turnover, which later contributed to her interest in Magnet Nursing Services research. Her doctoral work honed her skills in measurement and methods.

Upon completion of her doctorate in 1975, Ada Sue accepted a dual position as an associate professor in the School of Nursing at the University of Arizona and clinical researcher for the University of Arizona Medical Center. Ada Sue's joining the School of Nursing faculty facilitated Dean Sorenson's vision of building a strong research program. Under Sorenson's direction and phenomenal vision, Ada Sue and Jan Atwood, whom Ada Sue had met during her doctoral studies, participated in implementing the new doctoral program and in developing an academic research program.

Ada Sue Hinshaw delivering a presentation.

Ada Sue faced two distinct challenges in creating an acclaimed research program: human and financial resources. First, there were only six doctorally prepared nurses to further the research initiative, and faculty recruitment was bleak given the scarce availability of doctorally prepared nurses nationally.

The dean of the University of Arizona School of Nursing concluded they would have to "grow" their own scholars who could carry the program forward. The doctoral team of Ada Sue Hinshaw, Jan Atwood, Gladys Sorenson, Janelle Krueger (who left shortly after Ada Sue arrived), Jesse Peregrin, Alice Longman, and Agnes Aamodt did just that.

Second, there was little money to support nursing research. At that time, universities did not fund nursing research, and there was only approximately $3 million dollars available from federal funding to support the entire nation's nurse researchers. Ada Sue realized it was going to be difficult to create meaningful science without significant funding.

Collectively, the doctoral research team submitted grant proposals, and slowly the funds began to trickle in. As the School of Nursing doctoral program at the University of Arizona matured, Sorenson's original vision of a strong research program was realized. The school rose in the rankings among schools of nursing, thanks in large measure to this small group of dedicated scientists who laid the foundation.

Ada Sue simultaneously had the challenge of building a research practice environment at the University of Arizona Medical Center. Jan Atwood joined Ada Sue within a year, and the program began to blossom. Ada Sue and Jan's hospital appointments provided a unique opportunity to marry the worlds of clinical practice and nursing research in order to facilitate an evidence-based environment from a nursing perspective.

One of the lessons Ada Sue learned while filling the hospital clinical research role was the importance of language. The ability to successfully combine the clinical perspective and the research process was directly related to presentation of information in a non-threatening way. Ada Sue possessed the gift of making the complex look simple.

Ada Sue built her research career by saying to staff nurses "I know you have really important clinical questions and those questions deserve information." The researchers would then collaborate with the clinicians to design research methods to address those questions. After three years of conducting nursing research without ever using research terms, Ada Sue and Jan's clinical research group had generated enough interest and enthusiasm that they could introduce words such as *theoretical framework, modeling, design, methods, statistics,* and *research implications* without

Sue Hinshaw, sitting next to Nancy Bergstrom, practices active listening.

people running from the room. This transformation occurred because the nurses and clinicians "could see the power of what was being done."

Ada Sue delighted in "seeing strong clinicians become clinical scholars through gaining and sharing information in a very rigorous manner." This was a remarkable symbiotic relationship—clinicians and researchers—that produced results that changed nursing practice. Ada Sue recognized that she must get the right people together to create the evidence-based environment.

Ada Sue recounts that she modeled many of her later national policy initiatives from the knowledge she acquired from this clinical research role. The clinical research role emphasized the importance of learning to perform strong significant clinical research that could then be practiced, and Ada Sue carried this lesson throughout her research and leadership careers.

She also developed a strong sense of the definition of nursing research. The traditional definition of nursing research was *research conducted by nurses*. Ada Sue's definition for nursing research was *research questions asked from a perspective of nurses that would guide nursing practice; it might also guide the practice of other disciplines as well*. Ada Sue's non-traditional definition became integrated into public policy as she moved through her career.

Always a builder, Ada Sue really enjoys the challenge of initiating new projects. She believes she was able to build a formidable career because she completed her doctorate at age thirty five, thereby affording her three decades to build a science research career. She acknowledges that "it is impossible to get to the policy tables effectively unless you have a strong research career" and a research reputation takes time and networking.

ROUND ONE: THE POLITICS OF NURSES, WOMEN, SCIENCE, AND HEALTHCARE

In 1981, Ada Sue was elected to the American Nurses Association (ANA) Cabinet on Nursing Research. The timing could not have been better for her because the ANA was poised to critically evaluate how to move nursing research into the 21st century. It was a remarkable opportunity to shape the future.

Ada Sue and the other cabinet members put together the 1986 ANA policy paper for directing the future of nursing research. She remembers spending numerous hours sitting on hotel room floors painstakingly writing this policy paper with cabinet members Nancy Wood, who was chair of the policy statement subcommittee, and Ora Strickland and Joanne Stevenson, both subcommittee members. The paper helped to define nursing research and outlined the necessary resources needed to allow nursing research to blossom. Unknowingly, the paper also became the blueprint for the future of nursing research at the NIH.

The profession of nursing was struggling to take nursing research to the next level. The Institute of Medicine (IOM) had just conducted a study entitled *Nursing and Nursing Education: Public Policy and Private Actions* (1983). The study findings indicated it was important to establish an entity for nursing research in the mainstream of scientific investigation. Nurse leaders were thrilled with the IOM finding.

Then, in the summer of 1983, a singular opportunity was presented to the ANA. Congressman Edward Madigan, a Republican from Illinois, contacted the ANA to see if they could collaborate on a healthcare initiative that would support nursing. Madigan's chief of staff, Ellen Reiker, an RN, had urged Madigan to take this initiative.

From the congressman's perspective, there were several political advantages to working with the nurses. First, nurses have always had high public acceptance and they were known to get to the voting polls. Second, women's issues had become important in the political calculus of reelection. Third, healthcare and scientific support to improve patient outcomes had become highly publicized. For Congressman Madigan, working with nurses was a promising combination—nurses, women, healthcare, and science—all elements important in the world of politics and the public. As a result, Congressman Madigan contacted the upper echelon of the ANA and asked, in effect, what he could do for nursing.

The ANA responded by contacting Nola Pender, chair of the Cabinet on Nursing Research, about a proposed National Institute of Nursing (NIN). Pender wasted no time in calling her cabinet members to unify support of the concept. They had been offered a rare opportunity and needed to make it count.

After extensive discussion, it was concluded that they should pursue an Institute of Nursing at the NIH. Though previous efforts to consider such an institute had failed, the political climate now seemed perfect. Seizing the opportunity, the ANA and Congressman Madigan worked closely to formulate a plan to set the wheels in motion. Ada Sue recalls working diligently with Congressman Madigan's staff and other ANA cabinet members to craft the legislation. They were charting new territory for nurses.

In the fall of 1983, Congressman Madigan introduced the legislation to the House reauthorization committee, of which he was a member, to amend the NIH reauthorization in order to allow for proliferation of the NIH to include the National Institute of Nursing (NIN) and the National Institute of Arthritis and Musculoskeletal and Skin Diseases (NIAMS). The proposed legislation had one major strategic flaw—no one had informed the NIH. The NIH responded simply with a public proclamation stating they didn't believe proliferation of the institutes was in the best interest of the NIH.

The reality was the NIH had three distinct concerns regarding the proposed NIN. First, no one really knew what nursing research was, much less whether the end product could uphold the reputation of NIH. Second, nursing research did not come with a treasure chest. Most proposed institutes typically had funding in the neighborhood of $50-$100 million dollars when they came to the table; however, the proposed NIN had only around $3.5-$5.0 million dollars to offer. Third, the American Medical Association (AMA) was not in favor of the development of an Institute of Nursing, and they are a strong voice in healthcare and health politics.

Ada Sue credits the NIH with responding with great wisdom by allowing the process to progress without overtly taking a stance against either proposed Institute (NIN or NIAMS); however, politics surrounding this bill were in full force and nursing had a tiger by the tail.

Although nurses, women, healthcare, and science were attractive from a political standpoint, the proposed legislation was not without obstacles inside and outside the profession. Perhaps the biggest challenge was the dissension surrounding the proposed NIN within nursing itself. The ANA officers and Cabinet of Nursing Research members, including Ada Sue, canvassed the country, speaking at key conferences and meeting with nurse leaders about the development of the NIN.

Nurse leaders were clearly divided. There were those who expressed concern that the profession was not prepared for the high profile NIH world. The lack of experienced nurse scientists had them concerned about being able to deliver a product that could promote the profession. Nothing would be more devastating than failing at this level.

Geraldine Felton, RN, PhD, a national nurse leader and educator, authored an article in *Nursing Outlook* (Jan/Feb 1984) highlighting the concerns of national nurse leaders in taking this bold step to join the NIH. There was also the question of who would lead the NIN. Without tested leadership, this was a journey in uncharted territory.

The other camp believed nursing research would never be capable of developing the necessary research foundation if it did not have the resources and interdisciplinary support to catapult nursing research to the next level. The growth of nursing research had been handcuffed by inadequate funding. In 1960, the US Health Resources and Services Administration (HRSA) had founded the Division of Nursing to provide federal support to clinically educate nurses and nurse researchers. From this beginning grew numerous pre-doctoral and postdoctoral fellowship programs, but grant funds remained lean. At this time, a large nursing research grant was approximately $200,000, which was inadequate to support projects of scientific importance.

The benefits of becoming an NIH institute were three-fold in the eyes of some of the nursing community (Hinshaw & Merritt, 1988).

1. The NIH would provide increased and consistent financial resources for research growth and development.

2. The focus of nursing research on health promotion and disease prevention in addition to clinical processes provided a natural complement to the biomedical research that the NIH was already conducting.
3. Nursing research needed to be developed within the context of other disciplines because nursing commonly draws from so many disciplines.

The fit for the proposed NIN seemed natural and necessary to many nurse leaders. The perspectives of both camps were legitimate. According to Ada Sue, "the situation was a Catch 22," and it was difficult to know if the proposed NIN was setting nursing research up to succeed or fail.

Ultimately, nursing rallied to the cause of forming the NIN, believing the risk was worth the benefit. Nursing leadership was committed to success. If nursing received the opportunity to join the NIH it would bring important knowledge to healthcare discovery—end of discussion.

Obstacles beyond the nursing profession included the Republican Party which concurred with the NIH that "this was not the time to proliferate the institutes." The Republican sentiment was "why do we need nursing research at the NIH when nursing research seems to be established at HRSA?"

According to Ada Sue, nursing leadership believed that staying at HRSA was perceived as inadequate for the development of nursing research and research training. HRSA is responsible for the education and training of clinicians. Only the Division of Nursing at HRSA had research and research training programs. This positioning caused nursing research to be isolated from the mainstream of scientific research located at the NIH. The NIH is the research and research training arm of the government, and it integrates all research disciplines within the scientific community. The proposed NIN was to develop the research component. This concept was difficult for politicians to digest. In fact, gathering a general understanding of the concept of nursing research proved to be a challenge.

The Republicans knew it would be politically unwise to publicly challenge the proposed NIN, but the undercurrent was there, and it extended all the way to the President's office. Should the NINR bill pass the House and the Senate, it was unknown if President Reagan would sign the bill into law.

In the fall of 1984, after an entire year of campaigning by nurses, promotion by legislators, bill revisions in conference committees, and polite suggestions by the NIH, the NIN bill had passed the House and the Senate, and was sitting on President Reagan's desk. Reagan vetoed the bill.

President Reagan wanted to see the results of an Institute of Medicine (IOM) study of the proliferation of the institutes before he would sign any future bills. Because Congress was not back in session for a possible override of the veto, the proposed NIN legislation had come to an end—for the moment.

Much had been learned in the previous year. Both the professional associations and Ada Sue had learned that communication was imperative. Neglecting to inform the NIH about the bill created unnecessary ill will. This is a lesson she will never forget.

Nationally, nurses had begun to rally to the cause with a new-found political savvy. Congressman Madigan remained very committed, and promised to reintroduce the bill. Several federal organizations, including the NIH, suggested, post veto, that nursing research should be studied prior to future consideration.

Between 1983 and 1985, there were several major studies to evaluate the nursing research dilemma, but two were central to the outcome of the NIN. First, was the previously mentioned IOM study (1983) that identified that nursing needed to be located in the mainstream of science at the NIH. Second, was a 1984 NIH Task Force on Nursing Research study chaired by Frank Williams, the Director of the National Institute on Aging (NIA), who had always been a friend of nursing. The latter study was to evaluate the amount of nursing research in current NIH institutes. Ada Sue believed the study was an attempt to suggest that there was sufficient ongoing nursing research and that there was not really a need to create an institute.

The saving grace of this study was the NIH definition of nursing research which primarily mandated that nurses must be conducting the research. This definition really made a difference because it narrowed the field of those conducting nursing research by eliminating non-nurse investigators studying nursing practice. This study found that nursing research activities were not well funded at the NIH.

The NIH in evaluating the proliferation issue used criteria developed by the IOM for new institutes, and across the board, except for the issue of "adequate funding," the proposed NIN met the requirements (Hinshaw & Merrit, 1988). The data were in. Nursing should be in mainstream science and had great potential for growth and met the NIH criteria. Nursing leadership was delighted with the results.

ROUND TWO: COMPROMISE AND SAVVY POLITICS

In 1985, Ada Sue Hinshaw was elected Chair of the Cabinet on Nursing Research. As round two for the proposed NIN began, Ada Sue and the cabinet members made sure that the preparation was meticulous and strategic.

There was overwhelming bipartisan support for this bill on the second attempt; however, Ada Sue emphasized this legislation was not about nursing research. The legislators were investing in nurses, women, healthcare, and science.

Congressman Madigan reintroduced the new legislation in the House in the fall of 1985. The House had two strong champions for the bill— Representatives Edward Madigan on the House Energy and Commerce Committee, subcommittee on Health and the Environment and Carl Pursell (Republican from Michigan) on the House Appropriations Committee, subcommittee on Labor, Health, and Human Services Education. There were three strong champions in the senate—Senators Daniel Inouyue (Democrat from Hawaii), Edward Kennedy (Democrat from Massachusetts), and Mark Hatfield (Republican from Oregon).

This time, the NIH was well aware of the legislation and the evidence generated in supporting the bill. Once again, the NIH publicly was neutral on the process.

Nursing had developed a four-pronged strategy to move the proposed NIN legislation to a successful outcome.

1. Nursing incorporated the Tri-Council which included the ANA, the American Association of Colleges of Nursing, the National League of Nursing, and the American Organization of Nurse Executives to send the message to Congress that the nursing leadership in the U.S. supported the proposed NIN.

2. The ANA did a remarkable job in uniting the professional organizations, with a total of **75** plus nursing organizations carrying the message in support of the proposed NIN to their legislators.

3. The ANA Cabinet on Nursing Research, headed up by Ada Sue, continued to educate nurse leaders on the new evidence supporting the legislation. (Ada Sue was also Chair of the ANA Cabinet on Nursing Research Legislative Network. This network could reach the national legislators in 45 states within 30 minutes by activating the phone triage system.)

4. Nursing formed coalitions with other powerful organizations across the nation to move the initiative. These groups included professional arthritis associations and clinical consumer arthritis groups.

The nurses were mobilized and organized for round two. The nursing voice was strong, consistent, and left little doubt in the legislators' minds that the nurses went to the voting polls.

Fresh in everyone's mind, including the legislators, was the previous Presidential veto. This time the legislative backers of the bill worked diligently at the White House to avoid another veto. ANA and other organizational leaders, including Ada Sue and nurse researchers, were meeting with Congressmen and the NIH staff whenever possible—nothing was left to chance.

In October 1985, as the NIN bill was nearing the Congressional floor for a vote, Ada Sue, as the Chair of the Cabinet on Nursing Research, received what she refers to as the "Cookies and Compromise" call from Eunice Cole, the ANA President.

Ada Sue remembers that she was standing in the kitchen of her little graduate student house baking Halloween cookies with the children when Eunice phoned. Wiping off the layers of cookie dough and quieting the children, Ada Sue began to critically discuss how they were going to move the bill past President Reagan. Eunice believed that to avoid a second veto they would have to be prepared to compromise something.

After extensive conversation, they agreed the ultimate "something" could be the name. The legislative language had been painstakingly drafted to be identical to every other institute at the NIH, so if the NIH wanted to call it the National Center for Nursing Research (NCNR), that was fine as long as the institute prerogative and legislative language remained untouched. Coming into the NIH as a center rather than an institute meant that there were significantly fewer programs to put in place and therefore the investment by the NIH would be significantly reduced. The name was to be the bargaining chip.

In November 1985, the NCNR bill—Public Law 99-158, the Health Research Extension Act of 1985—passed the House and the Senate vote and once again came to rest on President Reagan's desk. There was little doubt by those who had worked on this bill that there would be anything but a positive outcome. The compromise had been made, and the support had been garnered. President Reagan did sign the bill, but once again his signature was affixed to the veto line. Reagan called the legislation "micromanagement of the NIH."

Congress was furious. The Congressional response was swift and decisive with the House voting on November, 12, 1985 to override the Presidential veto by 380-32 and the Senate voting on November 20, 1985 to override the veto by 84-7, thereby authorizing the NCNR at the NIH.

On April 16, 1986, the Secretary of the US Department of Health and Human Services (DHHS), Otis R. Bowen, announced the establishment of the NCNR at the NIH. Two days later, Doris Merritt, a pediatrician who was in charge of central coordination of research training at the NIH, was appointed as the interim director of the NCNR. Doris Merritt had asked to be appointed to the interim director position "because she believed nursing research was going to be a significant contributor," and she wanted to help build the infrastructure.

Doris Merritt had been with the NIH for many years and knew the NIH backwards and forwards, which was a great asset for the incoming NCNR director. Once the NCNR became a member of the NIH family, the center was accorded the respect of all the entities.

The immediate priority was recruiting a permanent director for NCNR. National nursing leadership rallied to promote the NCNR directorship in hopes that there would be many good candidates to choose from. The NCNR search committee contacted Ada Sue about the directorship in June of 1986. She candidly shared that she would be happy to interview but that she was not interested in changing geographic location.

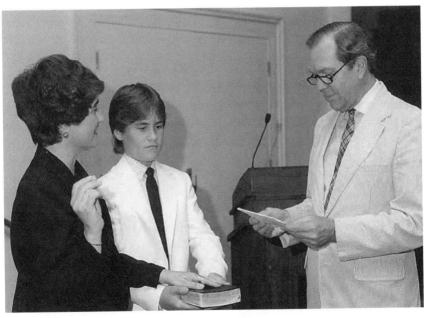

Ada Sue Hinshaw with her son, Scot, who held the Bible as Ada Sue was sworn in as director of the National Center for Nursing Research.

Ada Sue Hinshaw pointing to signed and framed NINR legislation.

Her family was firmly rooted in Arizona. Her daughter was a junior at the University of Arizona, and her son was in the sixth grade. Although her children have always been her biggest professional cheerleaders, Ada Sue did not want to ask them to move to Washington, DC. Moreover, she was eager to tap the new found NCNR funds for the nursing research she had been developing. Her passion was nursing science and academe. Politics had never really been her interest. She was resolute that the interview was purely an exercise in professional support.

In the fall of 1986, the NIH began to interview candidates from across the country for the NCNR directorship. The interviewees had one opportunity to meet with the NIH selection committee, NCNR leadership, and the NIH Director.

Ada Sue recalls that her interviews with Doris Merritt (Interim Director of the NCNR) and Ruth Kirschstein (Director of the National Institute of General Medical Sciences) went very well. There was instant chemistry and an immediate natural fit.

On the other hand, her interview with Jim Wyngaarden, Director for NIH, had been awkward, and Ada Sue felt that he was unimpressed with her. She departed honored to have participated in the process, but sure that Wyngaarden would never support her candidacy. Her professional commitment to support the NCNR had been fulfilled, and her angst over a change in career trajectory evaporated. Ada Sue was satisfied with her contribution to the creation of the NCNR and was eager to return to Arizona to pursue nursing science.

In the December of 1986, Ada Sue received a call from the chairman of the selection committee offering her the NCNR directorship. She was stunned and nearly speechless. She remembers blurting out, "Oh, well, I don't know if I am really interested in this job."

They simultaneously began to laugh and agreed that she needed some time to think about it. Shortly thereafter, Wyngaarden called, proclaiming his enthusiasm to work collaboratively with Ada Sue in creating opportunities for the NCNR at the NIH—all the awkwardness of their first meeting appeared to have evaporated. Ada Sue also had the benefit of digesting the offer and sharing the idea with her family. Shocking even herself, she decided to accept the position. Though this opportunity had not been in her professional plan, it was a detour that could be an experience of a lifetime with far reaching consequences for the profession of nursing.

THE FIRST FOUR YEARS OF THE NCNR

Ada Sue arrived at the NIH on June 24, 1987. Her first order of business was to learn how to navigate the enormity of the NIH. She credits Frank Williams, the director of the NIA, in addition to Doris Merritt, with teaching her how to be a director at the NIH.

Frank mentored her through the creation of the center and taught her how to build it with patience and political savvy. He taught her how to handle the transition from hopes and promises to research results. Frank Williams and Doris Merritt, the acting interim director of the NCNR, taught her how to manage the operations. Ada Sue felt she was surrounded by friends and colleagues. Nevertheless, the learning curve was steep.

The first four years at the NCNR were dedicated to finding funds to support the growth and development of nursing research. By the time Ada Sue became the director, the NCNR budget had grown to $16 million. In 1986, Congressman Carl Pursell, a Republican from Michigan, worked diligently to garner $5 million for establishing the NCNR infrastructure, which helped significantly in addition to HRSA's growing nursing research contribution of nearly $11 million. Doris Merritt, however, never made any distinction between research money and operational money. She simply said NCNR had $16 million to build on. Things were looking up but funding remained limited.

During the first three years of the NCNR, Ada Sue would appear before Congress and testify about the hopes and promises of the rigorous science to come and then ask for more funding. There were numerous grants awarded to academic settings and ongoing research, but there was nothing to talk about yet. Congress wanted to hear from her so she used the time wisely to educate them about what they were investing in—nursing research. Who better than Ada Sue to educate Congress on what nursing research really was? She took advantage of the captive audience and sent a value-added message

For a nurse raised in the Midwest, surviving Washington politics meant learning how to communicate more effectively than she had at any other time in her life. She felt that her language had to be more precise, crisp, and clinically relevant than anyone else's. Precision of language also meant precision of the message.

Prior to her Congressional testimony, Ada Sue would present to Jim Wyngaarden and his staff. These practice sessions helped her gauge the power of her message and anticipate potential questions.

The NIH carefully groomed Ada Sue to handle anything that Washington could send her way. One veteran NIH employee described her as a director "who was admired by all for her intelligence, leadership, and good nature. In fact, no one could believe that she was *that* nice, but indeed she was! Washington politics was never able to change her."

Year four arrived in 1992, and it was time to give testimony to Congress about the results of the "hopes and promises," and it was impressive. Ada Sue believed that credit for much of the NCNR research success belonged to the Division of Nursing at HRSA. Without hesitation, she says "HRSA had trained great nurse researchers and had laid a phenomenal foundation for rigorous science; otherwise it could have been a total loss."

Ada Sue presented the practice round to the Wyngaarden group, reporting Dorothy Brooten's study on nurse practitioners and patient outcomes, and other sterling examples of completed nursing research. Moreover, other NCNR programming had been advanced including the new Center of Excellence grants and an increased number of institutional training awards. Within a few years, the infrastructure for the NCNR had doubled in size with an increased number of staff in the extramural and research training programs. Considering the last four years and the current evidence, Wyngaarden left the meeting telling his colleagues that it was impressive work. He was heard saying "this may not be all bad ... this might be pretty good." The scientific evidence of nursing research was in, and nursing had generated a product that made the NIH proud.

BECOMING AN INSTITUTE

From her first days at the NCNR, Ada Sue strategically began to build the essential institute programs so that the center could be transitioned to an institute. If the NCNR charter had the same language as all other institutes and the necessary programs were in place, then it would be politically difficult to refuse the request to become an institute. Jan Heinrich, the Deputy Director and Extramural Program Director of the NCNR, was very instrumental in the strategic planning to this end. The team had two things to accomplish—put all the required institute programs into place and deliver quality research.

The biggest challenge proved to be building the intramural research program. In 1989, Ada Sue hired Carolyn Murdaugh as the NCNR Director of Intramural Programs, who was able to get the final program under construction. In the fall of 1992, the TriCouncil initiated legislation to redesignate the NCNR to the National Institute of Nursing Research (NINR). To show its support, the NIH also initiated the process to redesignate the center to an institute through the Executive Branch of the U.S. government.

In this effort, Ada Sue approached Bernadine Healy, who was the current director of the NIH, saying "I don't know where you stand on this, but the professional organizations want to prepare legislation to re-designate the center to an institute."

Ada Sue went on to outline the progress of the NCNR and the legislative language, which was already consistent with all the other institutes. She took a deep breath and waited. Bernadine Healy replied that she didn't see why it couldn't be done and that she would think about it.

The defining moment for the proposed change serendipitously took place at a cocktail party. Shortly after this initial discussion, Ada Sue and Bernadine happened to be at a reception with Lewis Sullivan, the then DHHS Secretary, and Jim Mason, the DHHS Assistant Secretary of Health. Standing in the receiving line, Bernadine turned to Lewis Sullivan and Jim Mason and questioned if there was any reason the NIH could not move forward with transitioning the NCNR to the NINR. The response was simple: It's your call. And that was it. The political support for transition from center to institute at the executive branch-level took place in a matter of minutes. Ada Sue credits this triumph to having carefully executed a plan to build the center, and, perhaps more importantly, to networking.

When Ada Sue moved to the NIH, she wisely decided to live on campus so that she could develop relationships with those who moved in the NIH circles. Her neighbor was Jim Mason. Jim had a son who played basketball with Ada Sue's son. Ada Sue gardened side by side with Jim on the weekends. Jim knew the work that the center was producing, and, more importantly, he knew that Ada Sue would not suggest an institute if the "i's" were not dotted nor the "t's" crossed because he knew her.

The initial two-year fight for a center had been reduced to a matter of a few moments for the transition to an institute because of networking, relationships, timing, and the delivery of a quality end product—all the result of Ada Sue's effective leadership.

As a culmination of legislative action by the professional nursing organizations, President Clinton, who took office in 1992, signed the NIH Revitalization Act of 1993 (Public Law 103-43) which elevated the center to an NIH institute on June 10, 1993. Four days later Donna Shalala, the new DHHS Secretary, signed the Federal Register notice and the National Institute of Nursing Research was formally established.

Ada Sue had gone to the NIH with the commitment to "build a scientific structure that would support nursing research and develop credibility for nursing research" and this had certainly been accomplished. Nursing now existed in the mainstream scientific community, and it was a respectable player. By 1993, the NINR budget had grown to nearly $50 million and a decade later the budget is a hearty $131 million. Nursing leadership had taken a risk and had succeeded at the NIH.

LEADERSHIP LESSONS LEARNED

Ada Sue never planned to leave academe—it was her first love—but she committed to join the NIH and the administrative world with the goal of building the infrastructure for nursing research and ultimately facilitating the successful transition of the NINR to an NIH institute. When this was accomplished, she knew it was time to take her skills back to the world of education. Ada Sue was seeking a school of nursing that was committed to research, and the match was made with the University of Michigan. Despite the ice and snow, Ada Sue found this to be a warm environment to create the research excellence that could now be supported by the NINR, which she had helped to create.

Ada Sue's NINR journey provided a wealth of leadership lessons. One of the very first lessons was, in her words, "learning to be comfortable with playing the game and not always winning." She adds, "sometimes you stumble because there are no rules."

The petite Steel Magnolia, as Ada Sue is known by many, is nearly hidden by the podium at speaking engagements.

Though Ada Sue did not win round one, there was much learned from the process. Perhaps most importantly, nursing leadership learned how much it wanted and needed the NINR for professional advancement. Nursing leadership had to establish the rules, and this included better communication, more organization, and more strategy in its efforts.

Ada Sue took personal risks in accepting the high-profile NIH position with significant potential for failure. She knew nursing science, and she surrounded herself with good people who knew not only science but also politics and NIH operations.

Ada Sue's definition of "good people" are those colleagues who will complement not replicate strengths and who were willing to tell you "no." She believes leaders must listen carefully. The dissenting voice is the gift of a different perspective that could make all the difference.

Ada Sue has received some of the highest honors and awards in healthcare, but the Nurse Scientist of the Year award in 1985 was, in her words, "probably the most special because it was awarded by my peers." She also adds, with a laugh, "that it was also the most memorable award as well because it has generated laughter in the Hinshaw family for many years."

She had purchased a special dress for this occasion, a strapless black velvet gown with fur trim at the waistline. As stunning as she looked, what she heard as she stepped behind the podium was her daughter's giggles. As it turns out, with her 5'3" frame, all that the crowd could see was bare shoulders and arms. "Here I was, receiving this most prestigious award, and it appeared as if I was not wearing any clothes!"

On this occasion, the lesson learned was that the principles of detail that apply to research design also apply to fashion. Today, Hinshaw always factors podium confounders into fashion outcomes.

In addition to the NINR, Ada Sue has held leadership roles such as the Institute of Medicine (IOM) Governing Council (two terms), President of the American Academy of Nurses (2000), and Dean of the University of Michigan.

She has been selected for these roles because she is a scholar who is a gifted communicator. Colleagues describe Ada Sue's leadership as the "total package" because she has the ability to bring the players to the table and address formidable issues. She is a consensus builder who has developed the fine art of merging the leadership mission from multiple disciplines so they can work collaboratively.

Ada Sue was honored in 1993 with the Distinguished Health Leader of the Year Award. She is the only nurse to have ever received this award among a list of physicians, government representatives, and many other outstanding healthcare leaders.

When asked about this recognition, Ada Sue smiles and comments "this award meant a great deal because I was lucky enough to represent the nursing profession—who I believe was really the recipient of this award." When it comes time to take credit for the accomplishments, Ada Sue is quick to identify it was the team and never the individual.

She has commonly found herself in situations that were high pressure, chaotic, and uncontrolled. She has always responded by taking a deep breath and steadying herself, recognizing that she was representing the entire profession not just herself. Ada Sue didn't mind taking risks, but she was always thinking of the consequences so that she could immediately begin the damage control.

Living in the Washington, DC area, she learned to rely heavily on her leadership motto of "never taking things personally, even if they are meant to be personal." She always kept focused on developing the center and institute so that nurse scientists could develop the science. Congress may have initially invested in nurses, women, science and healthcare, but what they received was nursing research led by one of nursing's finest scholars, ambassadors, communicators, educators, and visionaries—Ada Sue Hinshaw.

Hinshaw & Merritt, (1988). Perspectives in Nursing 1987-1989. National League of Nursing. 94-95.

CHAPTER **7**

Faye Glenn Abdellah

Faye G. Abdellah, RN, EdD, ScD, FAAN, is considered to be a national pioneer of nursing research concerning long-term care policy, mental retardation, developmental disabilities, home health services, aging, hospice, and AIDS. Imagine any one individual who has held such positions and titles as the first nurse to hold rank as rear admiral 08 (an 08 ranking is equivalent to two stars in the uniformed services) for the United States Public Health Service (USPHS) and deputy surgeon general of the United States. Further imagine that individual holding 12 honorary doctorate degrees and 90 professional honors—all in the same lifetime! Just the thought of such a leader as this can be daunting and intimidating to say the least, but Faye is neither. She is gracious and generous in sharing her vast experiences from an exciting journey through nursing. Faye G. Abdellah started as a rebel and over time learned how to better disguise her rebellious leadership methods under the title of "politically correct," all in a successful effort to move nursing forward.

The fact that Faye was so accomplished is a credit to her focus and determination to succeed. Her mother was of Scottish heritage and very supportive of her daughter's educational desires, yet her father was of Algerian decent and had opposing views about a woman's place in society. Faye knew from an early age that if she were to advance herself it would be through education. It was also quite clear to her that she would be educating herself without her father's support, and it would be at her own expense. She was very determined to step out from the veil of the male-dominated worldview in which she had been raised and make her distinct mark on life. As the eventual mother of nursing research, Faye G. Abdellah did just that.

THE EARLY YEARS

How many nurses can remember the exact time and date when they made the decision to enter the profession? Faye can do just that. It was May 6, 1937, shortly after 7 p.m., in Lakehurst, New Jersey, when she witnessed the tragic crash of the Hindenburg. The Hindenburg airship, the largest aircraft ever to fly, exploded 200 feet in the air during a landing operation. Due to the hydrogen explosion, the majority of passengers aboard were either killed or badly burned. It was an international tragedy that would change lives everywhere, including Faye's.

She was a young teen at the time of the incident, but she knew she never wanted to feel helpless in an emergency again. Burn victims from that crash were in need of immediate aid, and all she could do was to look on at the horrible situation. This incident left an impressionable mark on Faye, and it would guide her career choice. Sadly, the full-circle of tragedy came back to her at the end of her long career in the form of the September 11, 2001, terrorist attack on the Pentagon building in Washington, D.C. During the attack, Faye, the founding dean of the Uniformed Services University of the Health Sciences, Graduate School of Nursing (USUHS/GSN) in Bethesda, Maryland, ensured that her students and faculty administered care at the Pentagon scene and aided the victims and their families through this national crisis. (The USUHS/GSN falls under the direction of the U.S. Department of Defense.)

That young girl who had wanted to help others in a time of crisis had done just that. Faye's vision of training nurses specifically to respond in times of disaster had led her to create a mission-oriented program that is recognized as cutting edge and has already graduated more than 250 uniquely qualified and certified advanced practice nurses (both family nurse practitioners and nurse anesthetists) for the uniformed services. The response of the USUHS/GSN nurses that day told her she was on the right track with their educational preparation and military training in mock disaster exercises. It was also a confirmation of Faye's lifelong contributions to nursing.

AN EDUCATION

Faye was a rebel from the start in her efforts to promote nursing. After acceptance into the nursing program at Fitkin Memorial Hospital School of Nursing (now Ann Mary School of Nursing) in Neptune, New Jersey, she decided to pursue a double major. Faye was strong in the sciences and recognized the importance of science in the practice of nursing. After receiving a diploma from the nursing school in 1942, she attended Rutgers University (1942-1944) in order to study chemistry. Faye had a strong desire to further her education with a baccalaureate degree in nursing. She applied to and was accepted into Teachers College at Columbia University in New York City, and she continued straight through to earn Bachelor of Science, Master of Arts, and Doctor of Education degrees while working as a health nurse at a private school. While at Columbia University, Faye supplemented her income by teaching in a prominent nursing program. Her first position in nursing leadership was as a faculty member at Yale University from 1945-1949. These years at Yale clearly illustrate what lengths she would go to have her voice heard.

Although she was only in her 20s, Faye had very strong, well-developed opinions. It was 1948, and in one particular incident at Yale, she was strongly opposed to an outdated 1937 textbook that graduate students were required to use for a class. The dean would not consider changing the book and was firm about having all students use it.

Faye was not satisfied with the response she received, so she took matters into her own hands. She asked two of her colleagues to help gather the infamous books in the courtyard at Yale. There, she alone set the books on fire! It was quite an effective technique for getting the dean's attention, but it also shortened her career at Yale. The next morning, she was informed that her yearly contract would not be renewed and that she would be responsible for paying the total cost of the destroyed books. Her salary was very low in those days, so it took her a year to pay the book debt. Much to her distaste, she had a steady diet of peanut butter sandwiches during that year. The burning of the books was only one of many rebellious outbursts resulting in relatively severe punishment in the early days of her career.

Losing her teaching contract at Yale University was unfortunate, but perhaps a blessing in disguise. For it was not long after her repayment of the incurred debt of books that Faye met Brigadier General Lucile Petry Leone. Lucile recruited nurses to serve in the uniformed services during World

War II and formed what became known as the Cadet Nurse Corps. Faye heard her speak one day and was very impressed with her vision for nurses in the services. As Faye already held a graduate degree by this time, she decided to enlist in 1949. In one of her military assignments with the USPHS, she was assigned to cover 13 U.S. states in order to study both patient and nursing needs. She was asked to coordinate these efforts with the Western Interstate Commission for Higher Education (WICHE). She was a nursing researcher from the start of her military career.

Some great leaders learn quickly from their earlier lessons, while others have a fierce sense of determination to effect change without regard for the consequences. This was true of Faye for she readily admits she might have been a slow learner when it came to acting as the diplomat in order to accomplish her goals. It would not be long after entering the uniformed services that she would bring about another incident in her career, and this one would make the book-burning day pale in comparison.

The military has a well-known reputation for giving orders and expecting results, no questions asked, but Faye took it upon herself to test this theory of leadership and found herself under house arrest for six months. In 1957, Faye had a vision that would have challenged the United States Public Health Service nursing committee. She proposed reorganizing the nursing research center, then within the Division of Nursing, and placing it within the National Institutes of Health (NIH). This reorganization, in essence, would have allowed nursing to be recognized as a science, in addition to providing a place to house nursing research.

The politics of the situation were tense. She was up against strong opposition from her immediate supervisor. Her goal was to create an institute within the NIH that was focused on nursing research. This, she felt, would help bring well-deserved scientific recognition to the profession of nursing. The reactions to her proposed reorganization played out as a turf battle, with those in possession of power fighting hard to keep it. Faye fought hard for her cause only to suffer a terrible defeat in the end. This defeat included six months of house arrest, which further meant no access to a telephone or secretary—quite a challenge for a researcher in 1957. Faye, amazingly, was not hindered by this setback. She continued to publish numerous articles and work on some of her most important research during this time.

It was nearly 30 years later, in 1986, that the NIH finally established the National Center for Nursing Research (NCNR), bringing Faye's vision to life. (In 1993 the NCNR was elevated from a center to an institute.) It

The calm demeanor belies the ever rebellious spirit of Faye G. Abdellah.

is because of her early visionary work as an advocate for furthering the science of nursing research that many fondly refer to her as the mother of nursing research.

THE MOTHER OF NURSING RESEARCH

Abdellah took many risks during her career. Many, including Faye herself, consider it a wonder that she received two stars from the USPHS, as time and again she bucked the system, causing displeasure from many in power, and followed her own ideas and used her own approaches. She recalls being figuratively "beheaded" at least three times in her career for continuously challenging the system and for, as the saying goes, going against the flow.

She went on to accomplish some of her most important work in the area of nursing research while in situations of adversity. Some of her early writings contributed to the idea that nurses should use a problem-solving approach to nursing practice that is based upon science rather than on the mere following of physicians' orders.

During her six months of house arrest, she turned what could be a "lemon" of a situation into "lemonade" by completing some seminal research that later had a tremendous impact on the profession of nursing. Faye's research during this period was focused on remedying the issues facing nursing in the late 1950s. Ironically, many of the nursing issues that were the focus of her research remain the focus of today's nursing studies: The workforce environment, patient safety, and patient and nurse satisfaction. She also faced issues related to a nursing shortage.

Prior to Faye's vision of bringing science into nursing research, nursing studies had been conducted rather rudimentarily and were considered very

Faye speaking at a Sigma Theta Tau International event.

basic research. Data had been collected through fundamental statewide nursing surveys with no science applied to the methodology of gathering data or analyzing it. Faye worked hard to change the way research was being conducted and created a new problem-solving method called the Typology of 21 Nursing Problems, which was later published in 1960 (*Patient-Centered Approaches to Nursing*, New York: Macmillan).

Faye's problem-solving model established a framework for resolving identified patient problems so the patient could reach a state of complete health or cope with the condition(s). The Typology of 21 Nursing Problems was developed as the unique body of scientific knowledge of nursing that later served as a model for many nursing theories. Today Faye's model is still used, but the focus has shifted from a problem-solving model to an outcome-based model. This shift reflects the change in both nursing care and science over the past 50 years. This conceptual shift was the first seed of what today is called evidence-based practice.

Another of her many accomplishments was the development of the first federally tested coronary care unit, a facility that was established as a result of what she learned during her research on patient care. This facility allowed healthcare workers to save thousands of lives.

A VOICE IN NURSING

Throughout her career, Faye never stopped speaking out on behalf of nurses and patient care, often in non-traditional ways. For example, during the 1970s she served as director for the Office of Long-Term Care located in the U.S. Department of Health and Human Services (DHHS) where she was responsible for overseeing 17,000 Medicare-funded nursing homes across the United States. In this role, it was not unusual for her to make unannounced inspections at nursing homes across the country.

One particularly unforgettable inspection at a nursing home in San Diego, California, caused her to make and receive some trouble. She recalls that the staff at many of the substandard long-term care facilities she visited would try to keep her on the first floor in order to hide code and statutory violations and other evidence of substandard care. This visit proved no different. "As a nurse, I knew if there was trouble to be found it would be in areas other than the first floor." During the visit to the San Diego long-term care facility, she became so upset at what she saw that she knew something had to change. The next day during her opening address at the conference of the American Health Care Association, she launched

an attack intended to light a fire of change in the membership by saying, to quote Faye, "the animals in the San Diego Zoo had better care than the patients in the homes you licensed." Shortly thereafter, she was escorted out of the conference and the building.

The next morning, she received a call from Casper Weinberger, then secretary of the U.S. Department of Health and Human Services, who was her "top boss." She was slightly concerned that after her public declaration of the prior day, she might have earned herself a pink slip. Instead, she received praise for bringing attention to the matter. Faye recalls Weinberger saying, "Faye, whatever you are doing, keep it up." As was her pattern, she had once again acted without concern for any personal consequences but with a burning desire to effect change.

At this point, 20 years into her nursing career, Faye began to change her tactics. She was starting to realize that more ground could be gained by camouflaging her rebellion and going undercover, so to speak. She was maturing as a leader and getting smarter in her tactics. No more book burnings where she would earn much attention but few of the results she desired. She was developing into a savvy strategist.

LEADING THE CAUSES

As mentioned, Faye G. Abdellah is considered to be the national pioneer of nursing research with over 153 published works to her credit. The numerous papers and books she has written over the years are cataloged and can be found in the National Library of Medicine in Bethesda, Maryland. These writings reflect the breadth of her professional interests in nursing science and cover topics related to patient care, nursing practice, nursing research, and the care of the elderly.

Many of the hurdles in the nursing profession that Faye came across during the 1950s were a result of poor documentation. Although it was the cause of much frustration for her at the time, she understood that it was difficult for anyone to prove a case for a nursing action when the documentation and research had not been established. Over time, she realized staff nurses had the creative ideas for improvements in nursing and, frequently, in healthcare in general, but they lacked the research skills to validate their ideas. This realization allowed her the insight to find the basic tools needed to carry out an evidence-based nursing practice.

Realizing that the staff nurses were the eyes of the researcher was a valuable lesson that she was able to use throughout her career. But she also knew that in order to make change, she had to document, document, document or no one would listen to her case. She felt strongly that to be equal to others in the medical field, nursing research needed a scientific base so that a similar language could be spoken across the healthcare fields. "Nursing was slow to realize the importance of developing a nursing science and, hence, was slow to catch on to evidence-based documentation," said Faye.

The lack of documentation in nursing was a constant frustration for her, one that wouldn't be remedied quickly. It would take another 20 years for nursing to clearly value the importance of documentation; something she felt held the profession back from being recognized as a science.

At the time, few staff nurses were researchers, but, as she had found, many had wonderful ideas—Nobel Prize-winning ideas in fact. Faye recalls that it was a staff nurse who first observed that 100% oxygen given to premature infants could cause blindness. That particular staff nurse did not know what to do with the information because she did not know how to collect and document the data. Consequently, someone else using the staff nurse's observation did the research and won the Nobel Prize.

Rather than uncovering the way the Nobel Prize winner had obtained the information that led to the Nobel award, Faye decided she could do more for nursing by working with staff nurses to encourage documentation of ideas and data collection. This action was not meant to necessarily make researchers out of staff nurses, but to encourage innovation and teamwork between staff nurses and nurse researchers. Eventually, Faye hopes, these early efforts will bear fruit and earn a Nobel Prize for a nurse.

MISSION FOCUSED

Regardless of her rebellious instincts, Faye was now more politically correct, and the recurring theme of her leadership paralleled the military's philosophy in which the primary focus is on the mission. "Whether it is [serving] in France, Korea, or Vietnam, or other things that prepare one for being a nurse, being mission-oriented means not letting anything deter from that," said Faye.

After 50 years of service in the USPHS and the uniformed services, it is obvious Faye enjoyed the military lifestyle. Being a female could make things more challenging at times, but she found equality within the military that she did not find in the civilian world.

Without a doubt, being a high-ranking woman in the military can cause resentment among male counterparts and subordinates. And, as Faye once said, "There is still a ceiling and when you hit that ceiling there is a lot of resentment."

Even after she earned the title of U.S. deputy surgeon general in the 1980s, she continued to hit the gender ceiling. Being a female deputy surgeon general (1981-1989) raised some eyebrows among her male counterparts, and "they did not hesitate to ask me what I did to earn the position."

Faye realized she had a choice and that she could take the positive or the negative approach to dealing with sexist individuals. She chose the positive and used humor as her support, as she had to work with some of these same individuals on a team.

Being deputy surgeon general provided numerous opportunities to work on team skills. Within the military setting, there is, as Faye says, "less throat cutting between physicians and nurses than in the private sector, because the mission is primary and one has to be part of a team." The interdisciplinary relationship needed within the healthcare environment is achievable in the military but can be very difficult to come by in the civilian sector.

One male colleague who embraced what Faye had to say was former Surgeon General Dr. C. Everett Koop. Dr. Koop and Faye worked closely

Rear Admiral (retired) Faye G. Abdellah accepting the Archon Award for her colleague Dr. C. Everett Koop.

together as a team for nine and a half years, with her in a position that was never before held by a woman or a nurse. Dr. Koop and Faye were actively involved in the formation of national health policies related to AIDS, drug addiction, violence, smoking, and alcoholism. It was through their concerted efforts that smoking was banned on both domestic and, later, international flights.

In 1988 and 1989, Dr. Koop presented Faye with the Surgeon General's Medallion and Medal in recognition of her contributions as chief nurse officer and deputy surgeon general for the USPHS and her exemplary service to the surgeon general.

ABDELLAH AS MENTEE AND MENTOR

The most valuable advice Faye believes she could offer new nurses with leadership ambitions is to find a mentor. "I am a firm believer in mentors and the strength that relationship can offer another individual."

For Faye, mentoring does not have to come from another nurse but could come from anyone. She believes leadership is leadership, and to choose a mentor outside of nursing can broaden an individual's perspective. An example Faye uses to illustrate the power of this kind of mentorship is Sister Rosemary Donnelly, former dean of the Catholic University of America School of Nursing. While serving as an intern in a senator's office, Sister Donnelly drafted successful hospice legislation that had a positive impact on the healthcare arena. Sister Donnelly's ability to achieve this goal was, in part, the result of working closely as a mentee with the senator.

Faye is very proud of being able to mentor young nurses and guide them through their careers. Her earliest mentor was the late Lucile Petry Leone who established the Cadet Nurse Corps during World War II and was the first chief nursing officer for the USPHS. Some of the earliest advice given to Faye by Lucile, which helped to shape or change some of her decisions, was the advice to continue on into graduate school. "I had a dream of developing a nursing science, and my mentor was very encouraging in my decision to continue on with my doctoral degree."

With such a full career, Faye also gives credit to the many colleagues who influenced and mentored her along her journey. Virginia Henderson was one such role model, as it was Henderson's 14 principles that had the most impact on the development of her typology model.

Faye was always passionate about the need for a specialized school to train nurses at the graduate level, specifically for the military. In 1993, as part of a collaborative vision shared with Senator Donald K. Inouye (a democrat from Hawaii), Faye founded the Graduate School of Nursing, the first military school for nurses, at the Uniformed Services University of the Health Sciences.

This graduate school prepares nurses to respond to the special requirements of weapons of mass destruction and the demands of the military. The year 2001 emphasized the importance of preparing the very finest advanced practice nurses (APNs) for the uniformed services. Several APNs were called to duty immediately and served on-site at the disaster when the Pentagon building was struck. These nurses not only took care of the victims but also ensured that the families received access to counseling and lodging in Washington, D.C.

Abdellah spent much of her nursing career in the arena of public health and felt strongly that graduate nursing students of the GSN should

have knowledge of public health in addition to their Master of Science in Nursing degree. She felt it was a necessity because of the various public health needs and settings to which these students would be deployed.

LESSONS LEARNED

For nursing in general, Faye believes that there are other countries that are ahead of the United States when it comes to nursing education. For instance in Japan there are no two-year nursing programs and no diploma programs. Students go directly from high school to a baccalaureate program and then go on for their master degrees.

Raising the entry-level requirements of professional nursing to the baccalaureate level in the United States is the place to start. Like many other professional nurses in the United States, she believes the two-year programs cannot, in the time allowed, prepare students for the demands of a rapidly changing healthcare environment, particularly if evidence-based nursing practice is to become a reality.

"I admire countries like Japan, Australia, and Norway because they set up their nursing system differently from ours [the United States], as a result of learning from our approaches. We need to realize that we are the only U.S. health profession that does not mandate the baccalaureate degree as the entry-level preparation."

Most other countries like Japan and Australia never started down the path of the two- or three-year programs. However, Faye is quick to acknowledge that other countries have to face different issues than the United States does. For example, in the former Soviet Union, nurses do not teach in their own discipline—physicians do—resulting in all physician-directed nursing programs.

Nursing education is not the only area where Faye recognizes mistakes can be difficult to rectify. Her personal mistakes as a nurse leader offer many lessons. She learned from her failures that it is very difficult to change the behavior of others. She resolved that one has to find what she calls a *hook* in order to drive behavior to change. For example, while working collaboratively with the World Health Organization during the 1980s, she was assigned to Kenya to encourage Kenyans to come to clinics for a smallpox injection. Nothing she was saying or doing had any effect in getting the locals into her clinic. Three weeks of failed attempts made her realize that she needed another strategy. Pushing aside traditional teaching, she came up with an idea.

A colleague of hers who was with her in Kenya happened to be taller than seven feet, and she thought that perhaps this could be her hook. She went back to the areas where she had previously failed to convince the locals to consent to the injections and said, "If you want to see the tallest White man in all the world, come to the clinic." She never mentioned the smallpox injection during this announcement. The nationals came in droves to see this tall White man, and they then accepted the injections.

Faye found this strategy to be successful in teaching healthcare classes to teenagers in the United States. She was never effective in stopping teen smoking habits until she found her hook. After numerous unsuccessful attempts at educating teens (particularly girls) against smoking, she found the ammunition she needed to make the difference. An article in the *New England Journal of Medicine* documented that smoking in young girls caused premature wrinkles. She went back to high schools and shared this perspective and was greeted with comments like, "Why didn't you tell us that in the first place?"

Again, the lesson learned was finding the hook in getting behavior to change. Whether it was viewing the tallest White man in the world or being concerned about wrinkles, she was able to find the one thing that would be meaningful to an individual or group—the one thing that, in turn, could provide for behavior change.

Faye was instrumental in changing behaviors on a larger international level as well. She implemented exchange programs for the United States and France and the United States and the former Soviet Union. She worked with the nurses in these exchange programs in an effort to further nursing education in developing countries.

Her leadership assistance and intervention in Yugoslavia resulted in the enactment of a law requiring the establishment of training programs for hospital managers.

THE RETIRED LEADER

Throughout her life, Abdellah demonstrated remarkable courage and determination for pursuing her vision. From the young girl who resisted her father's imposed patriarchical belief of women to the leader who publicly scolded the licensing agency responsible for maintaining the standards of nursing homes across the country, her courage to step up and take the risk was always evident. The courageous risks she took in her leadership roles were all in an effort to move nursing forward or to improve patient care around the world. Her influence even crossed into nursing's educational system, as it was her Typology of 21 Nursing Problems that had the most dramatic impact on programs in nursing and the development of nursing theories.

As a result of her courage in pursuing change, Faye can be sure that her mark was left on the profession. Overcoming the fear of taking a risk and failing is one of life's most valuable lessons, and Faye's career accentuates this point. She was so focused on the desire to effect change that fear of the consequences became secondary. The consequences for some of her actions never caused her to quit or take her eyes off her mission. Where most would have given up, Faye came back stronger, which is a tribute to her perseverance and courage.

Faye G. Abdellah spent most of her professional career in the U.S. Public Health Service. She retired as U.S. deputy surgeon general in 1989 and founded the Graduate School of Nursing at the USUHS in 1993. Even though Faye is retired, she is the busiest retired nurse one can imagine. Her life includes teaching graduate nursing students, conference speaking engagements, writing, and acting as an activist; she has not yet slowed down.

"My heart is in nursing, and I think young people coming along now need to carry the torch." This living legend certainly has earned the right to pass the torch.

Abdellah, G., (1960) *Patient-Centered Approaches to Nursing,* New York: Macmillan.

CHAPTER 8

Sue Karen Donaldson

In the late 1950s, while attending Cooley High School in Detroit, Michigan, Sue Karen Donaldson, RN, PhD, FAAN, dreamed of Broadway's lights and a career in music and drama. She had no idea that her college entrance exam scores and the influence of a biology teacher would dramatically change her plans. She would ultimately trade the drama of the theatre for the drama of defining the discipline of nursing, which would facilitate the growth of the PhD programs in nursing.

Sue's path as a nurse leader was largely serendipitous, spontaneous, and most importantly, compelling, and it has been defined by risk-taking behaviors that began at a very young age. She is driven by what needs to be accomplished but not what will be demanded of her. She also admits that in many circumstances her naiveté provided an unrestrained environment for free thinking because "what was there to lose?"

Sue entered nursing by way of the biological sciences. She became a scientist who was a nurse first. Her academic fate groomed her to become a master of debate and logic, which she applied to advancing the discipline of nursing. Sue is driven by precision of language and is gifted in her ability to articulate complex concepts in high-pressure interdisciplinary forums.

This profile in leadership reflects how Sue discovered the power of collaboration with Dorothy Crowley. Sue and Dorothy pushed, pulled, and prodded one another to the next level of intellectual thought. Their intellectual volley put them on a scholarly treasure hunt for answers that would bridge the chasm of what is the discipline of nursing.

EARLY INFLUENCES

Sue Donaldson was born in Detroit in September of 1943 to Esther and Howard Bolitho. She was the middle of three daughters who were separated by approximately 3.5 years each. Her father was an accountant, and her mother was a homemaker who provided what Sue describes as a "perfect childhood." It was a lower-middle class existence filled with love and support. Her parents never pushed performance, but they were quick to identify opportunities and positive outcomes.

Sue was a good student who could be defined as focused and persistent. Toward the end of her grade school years, her school invited student participation in a closed-circuit program at WDTR radio station in Detroit. The tapings took place at a station in inner-city Detroit, and participation required parental permission and transportation. Sue knew her parents would say no. Her mother did not drive, and financially, taking a taxi cab was out of the question. This, however, was an opportunity she did not want to miss.

Theater was one of Sue Donaldson's first loves. Here she is, sitting at the table, in her high school play Arsenic and Old Lace in 1961.

Undaunted, Sue obtained a schedule of public transportation, forged her mother's signature, and once a month made her solo trips through the most dangerous sections of Detroit. It was not uncommon to have time to spare between bus transfers, and she spent that time devouring the wonders of Detroit's museums and libraries. It was this experience that developed Sue's lifelong love for art and literary culture.

Sue's clandestine radio career, at the tender age of 12, went on for many months before an unfortunate call from the school alerted her parents to her trips into the city. Her parents were mortified. Her mother became hysterical, reminding her of the danger associated with inner-city Detroit. Her father didn't know if he should punish her or congratulate her.

This unfettered courage and nerves of steel attitude set the stage for her future leadership roles.

NURSING EDUCATION: THE PATH

In 1959, Sue's SAT scores demonstrated a strong ability in math and science. Helen Blades, Sue's high school biology teacher, encouraged her to pursue a doctoral degree in biology, but she also encouraged Sue to go into healthcare in order to assure relevance of the science to clinical practice. Helen had earned a master's degree in physiology, and she was influential in lighting Sue's scientific fire through classroom discussion and extra scientific readings. Her dreams of a career in music and drama were supplanted by visions of dentistry, medicine, or nursing with a goal of having an impact on the state of healthcare. However, Sue soon learned that women were still very much unwanted within the profession of dentistry. She was told women did not have the arm strength to perform the job. There was more subtlety to the rejections of the world of medicine. Interest was feigned, but only a variety of excuses were offered, with the same exclusionary result: Women were not invited in. It was this gender bias that opened the door to nursing. Additionally, Sue's older sister, Elizabeth, was a bedside nurse who loved her work. This passion for nursing left an indelible impression on Sue. It was Sue's sister who convinced her that nursing would be a perfect stepping stone to her career as a scientist.

Sue visited the School of Nursing at Wayne State University and spoke to several nursing faculty in the admissions department. She confessed that she did not have a "Florence Nightingale complex" and never planned to be a bedside nurse. She fully expected the faculty at Wayne State to advise her not to apply.

Unbeknownst to Sue, the leaders at Wayne State had been engaged in discussions to explore how they could facilitate nurses moving to the nurse-scientist role; therefore, the faculty was seeking nontraditional nursing students like Sue. She was accepted and began her studies at Wayne State about the time the federally funded Nurse Scientist Program was being initiated. Faye Abdellah, assistant U.S. surgeon general at the time, had been instrumental in developing this program and as luck would have it, Faye Abdellah was an invited speaker to the School of Nursing at Wayne State.

It was on this occasion that Sue had an opportunity to meet one-on-one with Faye. Sue was awestruck as she spoke with the highest ranking nurse in the nation, regally dressed in her full Navy uniform, to plan Sue's academic future as a nurse scientist. It was an experience that left a lasting impression. Faye advised Sue to consider the University of Washington program and to waste no time getting to doctoral studies. Serendipitously, Sue was surrounded by the right leaders and influences at the right time and in the right place.

Wayne State University proved to be the perfect training ground for Sue. She describes it as a very special place where the faculty were committed to the leadership theme. The faculty recognized the special interests of the students and were quick to mentor their development. In undergraduate studies, Irene Beland, who was an author of prominence and "very biologic," shepherded Sue directly from the baccalaureate degree to master studies. This direct entry into graduate studies was not the norm, but she was heeding Faye Abdellah's advice.

Virginia Cleland, who was an undergraduate chemistry major, chaired Sue's thesis study and understood her scientific drive. Virginia helped Sue assemble the proper human and financial resources for Sue to begin her research career. It can be said that the leadership influences of Faye Abdellah, Irene Beland, Virginia Cleland, and other Wayne State University nursing faculty ultimately helped to expand the old vision of nurses as merely bedside nurses into a vision of a modern nurse-scientist.

While completing graduate study, Sue married O. Frederick Donaldson, III. They had been high school sweethearts, and both had visions of doctoral education. Fred was a geographer and a master linguist. When they told their families they would be moving to Seattle to attend the University of Washington, the Bolithos and the Donaldsons were dumbfounded. It was the only time Sue can remember seeing her father cry.

Their family heritage had been firmly rooted in Michigan, and moving west was only for those willing to climb into a covered wagon.

Fred had received his notification of acceptance to the University of Washington, and Sue believed she had a reasonable commitment for being awarded a nurse scientist traineeship. Upon their arrival in 1967, Sue discovered she "had been forgotten," and the program had been filled without her. She was devastated. Sue learned a valuable leadership lesson: Assume nothing and get everything in writing.

They had spent all their money and energy to pursue their doctoral dreams, and she had been left on the doorstep. The next year was spent creating opportunities. Ultimately, she was admitted to the Department of Physiology and Biophysics at the School of Medicine at the University of Washington and shortly thereafter did receive a nurse scientist traineeship spot.

It had been a trying year. Getting home for family visits also required ingenuity and out-of-the-box thinking because they were so financially strapped. Sue and Fred were only able to afford a one-way airplane ticket home to Detroit, and then they would artfully negotiate with the Cadillac dealership to drive an executive car to the West Coast for customer delivery. This provided them with a means of free transportation and a small stipend. Sue indicates the first year in Seattle contained the lesson that persistence and creativity produced results.

Sue and Fred divorced midway into her official doctoral trek; however, they remained close friends, and she kept the Donaldson name. Within a few years post-divorce, Sue met and, in 1972, married W. Glenn Kerrick, who was also a doctoral student in the Department of Physiology and Biophysics at the University of Washington. Sue and Glenn shared a common interest in science, and they both wanted children. Glenn was ahead of Sue in the doctoral program and encouraged her to stay on track as she continued in her research and nurse scientist program.

It was the nurse scientist traineeship that introduced her to Dorothy Crowley, who was the senior faculty coordinator from the School of Nursing at the University of Washington. In addition to her baccalaureate in nursing from St. Louis University (1950), Dorothy had two graduate degrees from Catholic University of America—an MA in nursing education (1953) and a PhD in sociology (1961). Dorothy served as Sue's mentor in the nurse scientist program. The two became close friends largely due to their mutual interest in science.

THE NURSE-SCIENTIST

Sue soon realized that she had a foot in two worlds—the world of physiology and biophysics with the PhD program and the world of nursing within the graduate program. She found the influence of each discipline contributed greatly to her thinking and career development.

The physiology and biophysics program supported her desire to become a scientist, but it was a world of academic isolation. Sue was told by "well-meaning" faculty not to speak of nursing or clinical matters, as they had no relevance to the scientist role. It was a male-dominated environment with a culture founded on logic and the art of confrontational debate. The female-dominated nurse scientist program was comprised of a group of students from various disciplines such as anthropology, psychology, and sociology who openly shared individual perspectives of science and healthcare. It was an environment completely devoted to clinical matters and compromise of disciplinary differences. This dual existence, in two very different worlds, provided Sue with an academic grounding that

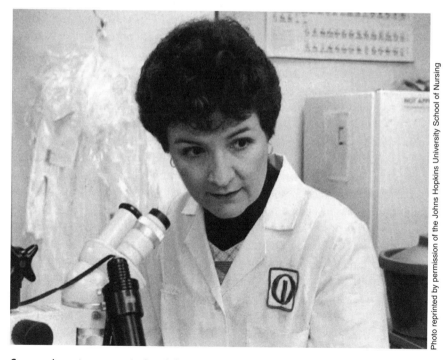

Photo reprinted by permission of the Johns Hopkins University School of Nursing

Sue at the microscope in her laboratory at Rush University in Chicago in 1979.

allowed her to speak of the language of numerous disciplines from a perspective of knowing.

Contrary to her original notion, Sue had become more than just the scientist she had set out to be. She was now a nurse who was becoming a scientist with an insatiable curiosity and a love for debate. Sue's debate skills were honed by the best in the all-male physiology department who engrained in her that everything was based on debate.

She indicates that she had an epiphany of sorts as she was indoctrinated to asking and seeking answers to tough questions. Logic was the basis of all decision making, and defending one's position was natural and expected. She learned a leadership lesson: Always be prepared and protect yourself with a thick skin.

This indoctrination sometimes created problems for Sue. She recalls pointing out to a nursing colleague at a faculty meeting that her idea was illogical, which Sue expected would initiate a healthy debate; however, she was shocked when the woman began to cry. According to the world of physiology and biophysics, there was no crying in science. Thankfully, with help from Dorothy Crowley, Sue re-socialized herself to a softer approach, or she may have ruined her career without ever knowing how or why.

Dorothy, a little more politically savvy than Sue, was nonetheless a terrific debate partner who also had thick skin. It was not long before Sue and Dorothy found themselves debating the definition of nursing as a discipline, a debate that would bring about *great change for nursing*.

THE DISCIPLINE OF NURSING: THE ONGOING DEBATE

In 1970, Sue was firm in her conclusion that nursing did not have a discipline. "That was my conclusion because I couldn't state it, nor could anyone else I knew." Nursing programs across the nation were repeatedly having their proposals for PhD programs rejected because the central issue—how to uniquely define the discipline of nursing within a research-based knowledge structure—could not be resolved.

Nursing was viewed primarily as an educational program to prepare professionals for practice and as an academic division that imported knowledge from numerous other disciplines to serve as the basis for education. This view of nursing as a profession but not as a science explains why there were only a handful of approved PhD nursing programs and numerous university rejections through the 1970s. The situation perplexed and challenged Sue and Dorothy.

Between the years 1970-1973, the question "What is the discipline of nursing?" became a daily debate for Sue and Dorothy. In a corner of the university's cafeteria, Sue and Dorothy would share readings and theories on the subject. They would leave the cafeteria and begin the treasure hunt for answers to the questions raised during the running debate.

Included in the cafeteria banter was the question of whether or not the nurse scientist program would add clarity to the question. They concluded that the whole concept of the nurse scientist program was not going to define the discipline because, as Sue said, "Even if you put them [the nurse scientist students] in one location, they were not going to speak a common language that would build the science of nursing." These scholars were simply going to bring the perspectives of their various scientific disciplines to the table.

These philosophical cafeteria discussions grew in frequency to include stealing moments in hallways and on coffee breaks. There were no relevant theories or conceptualizations that escaped their critique. The cast of observers expanded to include colleagues from the nursing and the physiology and biophysics departments. Sue and Dorothy took their discussions back to their colleagues for further debate and would return to the cafeteria to debate the expanded set of ideas.

These colleagues, recalls Sue, "Who really didn't want to hear about nursing as a profession or practice, were very respectful that nursing was trying to define its science and its disciplinary boundaries." Nurses, on the other hand, had a vested interest in the outcome of the debate, and their interest was piqued by the ideas. The dialogue was still ongoing when Sue graduated in 1973. Dorothy had become more than a debate partner—she had become a treasured friend. Dorothy was kind, patient, and protective of Sue. She was frequently reminding Sue to "listen and not ruffle the feathers of senior faculty."

Dorothy was a constant reminder of reality. Sue recalls with humor today that Dorothy was "quite concerned" that Sue had scheduled her dissertation defense date only two weeks prior to her pregnancy due date. Dorothy pointed out to Sue that even though she was the most organized, controlled, and well-planned person she knew, it would be the baby, not Sue, who would pick the delivery date, and perhaps she should take this into consideration regarding her defense.

Sue rebuffed this suggestion. According to Sue, the gestation of humans was nine months, and logic and biology convinced her that the pregnancy would not interfere with her dissertation plans. Life had always gone as planned, and she didn't see that a baby would change that. Kenneth Foster Kerrick, Sue's only child, arrived February 22, 1973, shortly before Sue's scheduled dissertation defense date. Dorothy was correct; the child had selected his arrival date.

Dorothy arrived at Sue's home after Kenneth's birth armed with food and friendship. She had been worried about how Sue would adapt to motherhood. Sue had often unrealistically wondered how a baby so small could impact her life as dramatically as everyone suggested. When Dorothy walked through the door, she saw Sue as she had never seen her before—out of control. The house was a wreck, Sue was running in circles, and the baby was crying. Yet, Sue could not have been more thrilled with her 6 pound 11 ounce dose of reality. Dorothy had a visible sense of relief as she remarked, "Thank God, everything will be OK because the baby is in charge!"

Ultimately, Sue successfully defended her dissertation at the beginning of May that year. Although life post-Kenneth had shifted priorities to motherhood, there was always time to continue the nursing discipline debate with Dorothy because "there had to be a solution." Sue joined the faculty of the University of Washington in July 1973, and these discussions continued in the halls of the School of Nursing.

THE DISCIPLINE OF NURSING: THE DONALDSON & CROWLEY FRAMEWORK

Sue reflects back on these seven or eight years of discussions with Dorothy as very stimulating intellectual exercises that were unconstrained by deadlines, agendas, or the need to apply value to the process. They were exchanges that did not have rules and were unrelated to a career trajectory. The discussions were fueled by freethinking without destination that seemed to progress slowly to new levels. "We weren't doing anything real. We never thought of presenting or publishing our thoughts," says Sue.

The end product was defining nursing as a unique discipline and placing it within the context of other disciplines within higher education and research. There had been hundreds of publications where the authors discussed the need for nursing research and nursing science, but no one ever articulated the realm of nursing vis-à-vis the realms of the other sciences.

In the summer of 1973, Sue received a dual appointment as assistant professor in the Department of Physiological Nursing, School of Nursing, and assistant professor in the Department of Physiology and Biophysics, School of Medicine, at the University of Washington. Her blended degrees

In 1977, Sue received the Young Investigator Award from Deborah Heart and Lung Center while at the University of Washington. Pictured with her are (left) President Reuben L. Cohen and (right) Dr. Harry Goldberg.

were a great asset to the School of Nursing, often affording her a seat at the table of committees, as a voting member, that were generally reserved for more senior and tenured faculty, such as the Nursing PhD Planning Committee.

The faculty in the School of Nursing at the University of Washington had been working on a PhD in nursing program and had been turned down on their first attempt. Once again, Sue was at the right place, at the right time, and with the right blend of academic preparation for the next series of events that would lastingly impact the academic world of nursing.

In 1975, with the breakup of her marriage, Sue settled into her new role as a single parent and full-time faculty member. She obtained grants from the National Institutes of Health, and she set up her laboratory while the debates with Dorothy continued.

In late 1976, Sue was sent by the dean of the School of Nursing at the University of Washington to Denver as a biologic consultant to the planning committee for the renowned Western Interstate Council for Higher Education for Nursing (WICHEN) 10th annual conference. The conference title *Optimizing Environments for Health: Nursing's Unique Perspective* fit nicely into Sue and Dorothy's ongoing debate regarding the discipline of nursing.

The six-member committee's goal was to sort and categorize the numerous abstracts into sessions for the upcoming conference in May 1977. The group spent an entire day in a hotel suite shuffling abstracts without ever finding a system that fit. No one knew Sue and, in fact, had difficulty remembering her name.

Sue understood she was nearly invisible due to her junior status. It was, indeed, a "speak when spoken to" environment. Her role was simply to lend her biologic knowledge when needed. It certainly wasn't within anyone's mind to ask her for a disciplinary framework.

At the end of the day, after numerous failed attempts, they were no closer to meeting their goal. Sue, who had waited patiently all day, began sorting her stack of abstracts. She had, in effect, operationalized the Donaldson and Crowley debate. She had grouped the abstracts by disciplines and realms within the disciplines. No one really noticed her efforts until she announced she thought perhaps she had discovered a format that fit. For the first time all day, the abstracts seemed to have been organized. The committee looked at her both stunned and suspicious.

After they digested Sue's proposed format, the litany of questions began. They wanted to know how she knew how to build the disciplinary framework, from what paper had she pulled the information for the framework, and who had she been working with in putting the framework together. They began to talk as if she wasn't in the room openly commenting that "she was an unknown in the world of nursing" and "how did she do this?"

Sue immediately began to back peddle. It was clear she had ruffled some feathers. The only thing that seemed to stop the barrage of questions and offered a modicum of credibility was the revelation that Dorothy Crowley was her collaborator. Dorothy was well-known and respected by everyone in the room.

An influential committee member decided to take control of the situation, and she walked over to the hotel phone and called Dorothy. After a brief discussion that validated Sue's description and explanation, the committee member handed the phone to Sue. Dorothy, with great agitation, informed Sue that they had now become the conference keynote speakers in order to explain their framework, which was *not ready* to be explained.

Dorothy further reminded Sue that not a single thought had been committed to paper or synthesized in a manner that was presentable outside the cafeteria, much less to a group of esteemed nurse scholars. The tension was palpable, and Sue knew she had inadvertently created a difficult situation. Dorothy closed the conversation by saying, that "There is no way out of this" and suggested that they start writing.

Sue and Dorothy had only a few months to create a product that would allow their reputations to remain reasonably unscathed. During this time, Dorothy was the associate dean working full time to mastermind the entire PhD program in the School of Nursing at the University of Washington and was pressed to devote time to other projects; however, being meticulous and thoughtful, she made the time to help Sue produce a quality product.

Dorothy, who was usually very protective in keeping Sue out of controversial situations, made it quite clear that Sue would be going to the podium, stating, "You got us into this, and you are going to be the one to deliver the message." Dorothy predicted the room would be filled with some nursing leaders who had been working on a similar effort and that the two of them would be "shredded." Sue, who had nerves of steel when it came to public speaking, didn't mind the podium assignment, but she agreed that they needed to get up there, get to the point, and then get out. Sue and Dorothy were co-authors of the paper, but they took care to write in language that was natural to Sue in order to minimize miscues, as she was the face behind the speech.

There was a third contributor who was unknown to the public. She was Anne Klingensmith. Sue remembers that Anne was a wonderful administrative assistant to Dorothy who was "far too intelligent to be working for us." Anne became the self-appointed project monitor and navigator whose intuition contributed significantly to the end product. As Anne typed the paper, she would edit for content and clarity. Throughout the nearly 20 iterations of the paper, Anne would point out nonsensical issues, as well as the appropriate fit or placement of information. Sue and Dorothy often incorporated her suggestions and knew if they could satisfy Anne they had a chance of pulling it off.

By the end of April, Sue and Dorothy had still not finished the paper, and they were due to board the plane for the conference in a matter of days. They knew the presentation had to be close to perfect, because the critics would assuredly be numerous and vocal.

Recognizing the angst that was driving the iterations, Anne took charge and entered the room, announcing that the last draft had come together and that she was going to give Sue and Dorothy 30 minutes with it. When she returned, Sue and Dorothy reported they had more work to do but would have it for her in the morning. Anne walked across the room, retrieved the final draft, and announced, "It's done."

That last draft of the paper contained the following three categories of existing inquiry, which became the essence of the framework and definition of the discipline of nursing:

1. **Concern with principles and laws that govern the life processes, well-being, and optimum functioning of human beings—sick or well.** For example, a concern with the discovery of laws that govern health, knowledge of reparative processes, and prevention was manifest in the late 19th or early 20th century in Nightingale's writings and certainly in Rogers' concern with laws and principles governing life processes in the past two decades.

2. **Concern with the patterning of human behavior in interaction with the environment in critical life situations.** As evidence of this theme, Rogers' writings reflect a concern with life rhythms and their relationship to environmental rhythms. Similarly, Johnson's writings in the 1960s focused attention on systems of behavior, pattern-maintenance, and pattern-disruption. The conceptual frames for most nursing curricula today include coping processes, adaptation, and supportive and non-supportive environments.

3. **Concern with processes by which positive changes in health status are affected.** Peplau focused on nursing as an interpersonal process, an educative and maturing force; whereas Kreuter as well as Leininger and others addressed the particular type of process system seen as a unique nursing contribution. (Donaldson, 1978, p.113-120)*

THE RISK OF HER CAREER

The conference organizers had no idea what Sue and Dorothy would present in their keynote lecture. Given the title of the conference, *Optimizing*

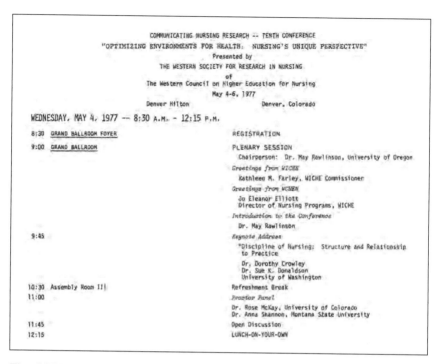

The 1977 program for the WICHEN conference at which Sue presented the paper "Discipline of Nursing: Structure and Relationship."

Environments for Health: Nursing's Unique Perspective, no one expected a description of a framework defining nursing as a discipline. Eyebrows were raised when the title of the paper, "The Discipline of Nursing: Structure and Relationship to Practice," was made public.

When Sue and Dorothy arrived at the conference in Denver, they were asked more than once about the "unusual title." Heads turned when it became clear that Dorothy, the recognized senior scholar, was not the lead author and would not be taking the podium.

The question of "Who is Sue Donaldson?" was asked more than once. Curiosity was piqued.

Dorothy was more than a little nervous. She also felt that the best possible outcome was that they give the paper and get out of town.

The WICHEN conference began on Wednesday May 4, 1977, and May Rawlinson, chairperson of the conference, introduced Sue to a room that was filled to capacity with the elite of nursing. Sue took the podium and Dorothy managed the overhead projector. In a brief 30-35 minutes, Sue delivered the paper essentially word for word as it was ultimately published in *Communicating Nursing Research* and then reprinted in *Nursing Outlook*.

It was difficult for Sue to gauge the reaction of the crowd as she spoke. Ten minutes had been slated for questions and answers, with concern that this would be too brief a time to be able to field the expected debate and critique that Sue and Dorothy were convinced would follow. But they were completely unprepared for what came next—silence. The saying "you could have heard a pin drop" rang very true at that moment for both Sue and Dorothy.

And then the conference organizers began exchanging glances, trying to determine how to gracefully move beyond the moment. Just as May Rawlinson moved to the microphone to end the silence, Dr. Marjorie Batey stood up to speak from the back of the room. Marjorie was the associate dean at the School of Nursing at the University of Washington and the editor for WICHEN publications for many years. She offered the only comment. She explained that the silence represented total shock, and that it would take time to digest what may have been the most profound paper ever written on the topic.

The conference moved on without further discussion of the keynote address. Feeling an enormous sense of relief, Sue and Dorothy faded to the background for the remainder of the conference. Dorothy, evidently relieved that their worst fears weren't realized, thought that the address went fine, while Sue, not as optimistic, remarked that she did not think that the address had been well received. From Sue's perspective, the silence had been deafening and validated the fear that the elite of nursing were displeased.

Sue and Dorothy left Denver agreeing on one thing—the paper would be published in the WICHEN journal and it would likely be viewed merely as one of those "radical" papers. And they expected that to be the end of the story.

THE RIPPLE EFFECT

The first day back at work, Sue wore jeans and hole-filled tennis shoes, planning to rewire and move equipment in her physiology lab. It was with great relief that she would relax for the first time in months. As she neared her office door, there was a note taped at eye level from her secretary indicating that the dean needed to see her as soon as possible.

Dorothy had already seen her own summons and had been trying to contact Sue. Together, they quickly concluded that since each had received the same message, then the hurry-up meeting must have something to do with the conference, which they had mistakenly concluded to be history.

Dorothy, who was concerned that the visit to the dean would require artful explanation, was more than a little concerned about presenting a credible image given Sue's "mad scientist" attire that day. For a change, it was the wrong place at the wrong time—and, worse still, in the wrong clothes—for Sue. There was no graceful way out, it seemed.

At their meeting, Dean Rheba de Tornyay got quickly to the point. She needed a copy of the WICHEN paper. Rheba had received a communication from Rozella Schlotfeldt, who was the dean for the School of Nursing at Case Western Reserve University, that the Donaldson and Crowley paper had so clarified the definition of the discipline that she was going to recommend they adopt this thinking into their graduate curriculum. It didn't look like they were in trouble after all.

Dean de Tornyay was very proud of what Sue and Dorothy had produced but needed further information to answer the inevitable questions. Sue and Dorothy were surprised at this attention, as, they explained, there had been virtual silence and a complete lack of reaction to their presentation.

Schlotfeldt's communication may have been the first hint of acceptance, but it certainly was not the last. The momentum for schools to incorporate the Donaldson and Crowley framework into programs began to build itself over the next 6-12 months.

According to Sue, it was difficult to assess who was more amazed by the unfolding events after the WICHEN conference. The pair had no idea that their freethinking sessions of eight years had any applicable value. They were dumbfounded by the reaction.

The three themes in the Donaldson and Crowley paper began to appear in numerous discussions and publications including an American Nurses Association statement defining and framing nursing. Sue is quick to say that they did not invent the three encompassing categories that defined the disciplinary structure but that they were the first to frame the discipline in this manner.

According to Sue, the three categories were effective because they defined what nursing should be focused on and included the unique contribution of nursing to society and people. Additionally, Sue and Dorothy believed the categories suggested boundaries for systematic inquiry and theory development.

THE PAYOFF FOR THE NURSING PROFESSION

The Donaldson and Crowley paper became, for many institutions, the means to justify a PhD in nursing. The paper defined the boundaries of the discipline of nursing in a manner that made sense to the profession and to the world of academe. Prior to the paper, it was not uncommon for nursing PhD program proposals to be rejected because nursing had not defined itself as a unique discipline. In order to author a PhD in a field, there must be a unique discipline.

The more common doctoral degree was the Doctor of Nursing Science (DNSc), which was recognized as preparation for clinical researchers for translational research based upon existing knowledge. The PhD program,

Sue and Dr. Michael Johns in 1995 in front of the famous dome of Johns Hopkins Hospital.

by contrast, universally means preparing researchers for generating original knowledge of a discipline. Ironically, it had been the University of Washington PhD program that prompted Sue and Dorothy to take the discussion to the next level with the issue of "unique versus borrowed contribution" of other disciplines to the knowledge base and science of nursing.

In the years that followed the WICHEN conference, numerous nursing programs cited the Donaldson and Crowley paper when formulating their PhD programs. Though the paper was not universally accepted, it was commonly considered the best framework available at the time. (The University of Washington, home to Donaldson and Crowley, was unable to use the framework as planning of the PhD program had already been well-developed by the time the paper was presented, and it would have required significant restructuring to incorporate their framework. Thus, the committee elected to go ahead with its original plan, which ultimately was accepted by the university.)

Additionally, Sue and Dorothy were often contacted to consult for universities regarding their framework. They spent time visiting Vanderbilt University, the University of Colorado, and the University of Pennsylvania in discussions with the presidents and various committee members.

Sue recalls that on numerous occasions she spoke with department members within other disciplines about the paper, affirming for her that the discussions transcended the function of nursing within healthcare and transcended even the profession of nursing. Excitingly, these discussions often took new paths whereby nursing was discussed as an intellectual exercise.

The identity of nursing as an academic and research discipline was impacted significantly by the introduction of the Donaldson and Crowley paper. There was finally a framework for nursing that made sense to nurses and to scholars in other disciplines. At more than one conference, Sue indicated scholars from other disciplines came to the microphone and announced that they *finally* got what nurses were trying to say for decades but hadn't been able to effectively communicate.

The Donaldson and Crowley paper was by no means the first or the last words on the subject; however, a significant stir was created that contributed to the clear definition of the unique contribution of nursing as a discipline. The paper was the small push needed to create the momentum for nursing to be embraced as a discipline. Sue and others believe that as a result of the paper and the discussions and debates that followed and the inclusion of the paper's framework into many newly approved nursing PhD programs, nursing was now on even ground with other disciplines.

The outcome of this dynamic period and serendipitous journey was compelling. In the mid-1970s, there were fewer than eight nursing PhD programs nationally. Today this number is *83*. The debate about the legitimacy of nursing as a discipline has ended.

SUMMARY

Dorothy Crowley died in 1980 from lung cancer, and this was a huge loss to nursing and to Sue personally. She lost a friend and a leader who had patiently taught her how to lead. Dorothy had mentored, socialized, and educated Sue to academic leadership. Sue dedicates all her speeches about the discipline of nursing to Dorothy and has carried the content of their debates forward and developed it beyond the scope of the initial paper.

Sue's leadership in nursing can be attributed to this further development of the Donaldson and Crowley paper. Sue may have wanted to be a scientist, but Dorothy reminded her that she was a *nurse scientist.*

The serendipity surrounding the Donaldson and Crowley paper was the product of seven years of freethinking and collaboration without the pressure of deadlines, agendas, or tenure. Sue and Dorothy did not intend to change the world. They simply wanted to apply facts and logic to a question that demanded an answer. The value of this academic freedom of thought must not be underestimated. In science, this kind of exercise has resulted in scientific breakthroughs that have changed society.

In 1964, Townes received the Nobel Peace Prize for LASER (Light Amplification by Stimulated Emission of Radiation) research, which was an exercise in scientific freethinking that had no apparent value. When a journalist asked someone on Townes' research team how LASER technology could be used, he replied that perhaps in 40–50 years an application would be found. We all know that by the 1990s, LASER technology was pervasive in society.

Sue and Dorothy did not think that what they were doing was anything *real* or had any value beyond the cafeteria; however, years into their discussions and debates, the outcome of their discussions and debates—the Donaldson and Crowley paper—facilitated an improved understanding of the discipline of nursing. Although the initial response was unexpected si-

Sue presenting the keynote speech, "A Quarter Century of Breakthroughs in Nursing Research," at the 25th annual meeting of the American Academy of Nursing in Mexico in October, 1998.

lence, over the years this seminal work was critiqued by many and remained salient to its purpose.

Sue believes the development of ideas requires being willing to disseminate the findings and be open to discussion and critique. Critique is a powerful and essential tool to improve the product by putting it out to the brightest minds to evaluate its merit from their unique experience and knowledge base. Sue states if she had the opportunity to write the paper today, there would be very little she would change.

Sue may have begun her career proclaiming she did not have a "Florence Nightingale complex," but there is little doubt that she and Dorothy advanced nursing in a manner that would have pleased Nightingale herself. Sue managed to bring the best of science to nursing and the best of nursing to science.

*Donaldson, S.K.B., & Crowley, D.M. (1978). The discipline of nursing. *Nursing Outlook,* *26 (2),* 113-120. Reprinted from Nursing Outlook, V26, 1978, with permission from Elsevier.

CHAPTER 9

a leader in Professional organizations

Margretta "Gretta" Madden Styles

Gretta Styles' career illustrates the importance of leaders developing an area of expertise. In Gretta's case, she had many areas of expertise encompassing education, professional organization administration, and credentialing. She has lived by the motto, "Build an area of expertise and others will seek you out." Her leadership journey was serendipitous and not mapped out in advance, but the impact to the profession has been very profound. She was one who remained open to new opportunities and challenges, with a lifelong commitment to learning. Gretta was and continues to be a national and international force in nursing. Her leadership as president of the American Nurses Association, the International Council of Nurses, and the American Nurses Credentialing Center tells the story of her level of influence. No other nurse has held all three of these positions—and during times of such importance to nursing.

THE EARLY YEARS

Gretta Styles, RN, EdD, FAAN, was the youngest of eight siblings and attributes much of her success and drive in life to her birth order. To really appreciate Gretta, one must know that a favorite book of hers is *Born to Rebel* by Frank Sulloway, written about youngest children and family dynamics. Gretta did not live the life of the youngest, spoiled child, but on the contrary she worked hard and juggled much to achieve her success.

As the youngest child, "I felt I had to fight harder to be heard and seen."

This survival mechanism taught her two powerful lifelong lessons:

1. How to be self-sufficient, and
2. How to have the tenacity to achieve those things that seem out of one's grasp.

Perhaps these early lessons help shed light on how Gretta later became president of the American Nurses Association (ANA), president of the International Council of Nurses (ICN), and president of the American Nurses Credentialing Center (ANCC).

Throughout her life, religion and family played an integral role. Born in the small town of Mount Union, Pennsylvania, she had the typical aspirations of small town people who have felt stifled during their youth. She wanted to break out of town and experience what the world had to offer.

A sense of adventure followed her throughout life. Gretta was a pilot flying solo over cornfields by age 16, bungee jumping at 50, and parachuting out of a plane on her 55th birthday. From a young age she learned to push limits and took great pleasure in high-risk adventures. Says Gretta, "I enjoy being backed into a corner in situations where I have to fight my way out." Perhaps this is a natural inclination for a future leader.

THE FOUNDATIONS OF A CAREER

Gretta, who was scholastically very strong, graduated from Juniata College in Huntingdon, Pennsylvania, with a Bachelor of Science in both chemistry and biology in 1950 at the age of 20. By this time, her commitment to religion was taking on a stronger role in her life. So much so that following graduation, she lived for a year in an Episcopal convent in Puerto Rico.

It was while living in the convent that, among other duties, she was responsible for teaching in a diploma nursing school. Since she had a BS, she was asked to teach some of the basic science courses in the school of nursing. She found herself fascinated by the study of science and nursing, so she made the decision to go back to school.

Gretta chose the nursing profession over medicine because she wanted to be more intimately involved with patients. Thus, she set out to dedicate her life both to God and to the profession of nursing.

Upon fulfilling her one-year commitment to the convent, Gretta knew she wanted to pursue a religious vocation and take vows to become an Episcopal nun.

She decided to go home to tell her family of her decision. Sharing the news of her decision with her family was one of the most pivotal times in her life, for she adored her mother and needed her approval. Her parents, along with all her brothers and sisters, were devout Methodists. The fact that she would consider leaving the religion in which she was raised was accepted by her parents, but entering the sisterhood was upsetting to her mother. "When I told her of my decision, she cried for about a week and then had a massive coronary. From that point, until she died in 1957, she was severely limited."

As a result of her mother's response and internal conflict, Gretta never officially joined the convent, but personally and in secret she took the vows of poverty, chastity, and obedience. No one was aware of the vows she held herself to, as she decided to fulfill her other dream of becoming a nurse.

In 1951, there were only two programs in the country offering a generic Master in Nursing degree that admitted individuals with baccalaureate degrees in subjects other than nursing, and Gretta had her eyes on the one at Yale University. In three years, the students were prepared as nurses and were eligible to "sit for the RN licensing exam." Gretta applied to and was accepted into Yale University.

While at Yale, then with only males in the undergraduate program and few females at the graduate level, Gretta had many opportunities to date, but she still felt obligated to her vows. Religion and nursing had become so entwined for Gretta, she felt called into missionary work. This would have allowed her the outlet to practice her two life passions.

As she neared graduation from Yale, she interviewed with a representative from the church. When he found out she was a pilot, he recommended she meet a gentleman by the name of Doug Styles, registered at a local Episcopal seminary, who was also interested in flying and missionary work. Never did she imagine she was to meet her future husband.

Doug Styles created an internal dilemma for Gretta as she struggled with her personal vows and the feelings she felt for this wonderful man. She turned to God for the answer. If it was meant to be, then she would ask God to give her a sign, so she could be released from the vows. "Send me a rose," she prayed.

"I was a senior at Yale, and the next day my roommate's boyfriend came to pick her up for a date, and he asked if he could speak to me." Her roommate came to get her and brought her out to the commons area. To her surprise, her roommate's boyfriend handed her a rose. "He said, 'I just felt I wanted you to have this.' " Gretta had not told her roommate or anyone else of her prayer to God; it had been her personal secret. Upon receiving this sign, she felt secure in her decision to date the man who later would become her husband.

JOURNEY INTO THE NURSING PROFESSION

Gretta graduated in 1954 with a master degree in nursing, a rarity at that time, so she was in great demand. Her first position out of graduate school was working as an instructor in a school of nursing in Tampa, Florida. Shortly out of school, she became pregnant with her first child, and it was not long before her husband's career took them to Fort Lauderdale, Florida. Just after moving to Florida, a second child was born.

She remained a stay-at-home mom for only a brief period of time. As much joy as motherhood brought Gretta, something was missing in her life. One day her husband, who was the rector of a local parish, came home and told her he had found her a job.

He could sense that she was depressed and not fulfilled professionally, so he located a position for her as the associate director of nursing at a local community hospital. She was 27 years old, with no administrative experience, and now she was second-in-charge of a brand new hospital in Pompano, Florida. She was determined to make it all work. The tenacity she had shown as a child would be very useful.

Gretta was in this position for two exciting years. The director of nursing, an experienced administrator, gave her every opportunity to participate in the management and development of the new facility. One moment she would be helping out in the emergency room, the next she was dealing with a policy issue with other administrators.

Because Gretta was in the minority of nurses who held master degrees, she was sought out repeatedly for new opportunities. When in 1963 the Kellogg Foundation allocated funds to four states to support the development of associate degree programs for nurses, Florida was one of the receiving states. It was Gretta who received the call to develop this new type of program at Broward Community College in Fort Lauderdale, which she successfully established, with the help and advice of the president of the institution and the experienced director of another Kellogg-supported associate degree program in Bradenton, Florida. In this position, she became familiar with academic leaders in Florida, including Dorothy Smith, the dean of the College of Nursing at the University of Florida, an outstanding visionary and pioneer in bridging university education and clinical practice. Gretta was gaining new types of expertise and examining the greater landscape for nursing.

Before retiring, Gretta would establish another school from scratch at The University of Texas Health Science Center at San Antonio (UTHSC). At both schools, she started from the ground up and had her work cut out for her. "There was not so much as desks, pencils, or chalkboards." She loved the challenge of starting afresh or working with institutions dedicated to pursuing new directions.

Those early lessons of being self-sufficient paid off. Since associate degree nursing programs were just being developed, there were few established models from which to draw or use as a template. She had to figure out on her own much of what would be taught and at what level on her own.

During her three years at Broward Community College, the president of the college presented leadership opportunities to her. She was able to gain experience with public speaking within the community and work with local hospitals and other institutions to strengthen the bonds with the college.

However, she found that she was being drawn to baccalaureate education. She enjoyed her time with the associate degree program, but she knew it was not how she wanted to spend her working life. She wanted to move to a university setting but knew she would need a doctorate for such a position. "My husband and I wanted another child, so we agreed that I would combine a maternity leave with an educational leave."

So she went to the University of Florida in Gainesville to work on her doctorate in higher education. While there, she became pregnant but, before she completed her dissertation, her husband had a coronary at the age of 39. She gave birth to their daughter, their third child, while he was recovering.

Her husband's health altered their situation, and decisions were made accordingly. The family hastily relocated to North Carolina in 1967, where Gretta served for two years as associate professor and director of undergraduate studies in the School of Nursing at Duke University and finished her dissertation during her first year in this position.

Because of her husband's health from this time forward, Gretta was the primary breadwinner, with the family following her and her career around the country. Gretta's expertise at new program development had gained recognition by many in higher education. Within two years of her arrival at Duke, Marilyn Willman, the president of the then-University of Texas Systemwide School of Nursing, recruited her to become founding dean at the school in San Antonio. The family packed up and went to Texas so she could take her place on a health science campus. Doug Styles served in a number of parishes as they moved about the country. At one point he founded a chapel at the airport in San Antonio, Texas, in order to combine his two loves: flying and his ministry.

The set-up at the University of Texas Health Sciences in San Antonio was unique in that there were only four schools: dentistry, pharmacy, medicine, and nursing. There was no campus administrator, so each dean had much autonomy and independence. Gretta was the only female dean among her male colleagues, and, perhaps, this worked to her advantage.

Before long she was appointed chair of the committee of deans, a nominal role, but not without its benefits. When the president of the Texas Board of Regents that governed the entire Texas higher education system would come to UTHSC, Gretta was often the contact person, and this provided many serendipitous occasions for her to promote the school within a huge statewide university complex. She learned to use these opportunities to great advantage. This was a period of feverish growth on an essentially new campus within a developing Hispanic-American metropolitan area; building and programs were flourishing. The new school of nursing thrived within a community that welcomed its arrival and had the faith to phase out a popular hospital diploma program to make way for state-supported university education for nurses. An excellent faculty was recruited; affiliations with hospitals and other healthcare facilities were fostered. Baccalaureate and master's degree programs were established; a diverse student body gathered. An expansive continuing education service, spreading throughout South Texas, was organized.

Plans were developed for a new building for nursing. In this endeavor, Gretta had the experience of working closely with architects and faculty in designing the facility, recognized by many as outstanding functionally and aesthetically. A federal grant was approved but remained unfunded as demand for new schools increased and the waiting list grew longer. Before she left San Antonio in 1973, she discussed the project with the president of the Board of Regents, hoping that the building would be under construction during his tenure. Because the delay was slowing the development of the school, he persuaded his colleagues on the board to move forward without the federal grant. After its completion, Gretta returned to appreciate this accomplishment. On a subsequent visit to San Antonio, she expressed disappointment at the decision of the regents to dissolve the University of Texas system-wide network of nursing schools, now placing each under the authority of campus administration. She had felt this would foster competition, rather than the cooperation that she had enjoyed as a dean within a centralized nursing entity. However, she did recognize that, through a diversity of experiences, she was learning to adapt strategies to settings.

Opportunities and challenges continued to present themselves. After five years at the University of Texas, she was recruited to the deanship at the well-established and highly regarded Wayne State University (WSU) School of Nursing in Detroit, Michigan. In addition to the undergraduate and master programs, WSU was strengthening its research agenda and adding a core of nationally recognized, expert faculty in this area.

The nursing faculty had hoped to launch a doctoral program but had not yet been approved to do so. Gretta had the track record they needed to get the job done, so again she packed up the family and moved to Detroit, Michigan. She set out to do what she was hired for and within five years, Wayne State had a PhD program in nursing.

As history has a way of repeating itself, Gretta was again recruited away by an offer too good to pass up. She had always had her eyes on the School of Nursing at the University of California, San Francisco (UCSF), because she loved its fine reputation, its superb faculty, its clinical strength, and its international student body. Now she was being asked to take the position there as dean.

She took it and remained dean there for 10 years from 1977 to 1987 and was Livingston Chair, a prestigious faculty appointment, for another five years.

While at UCSF, Gretta had great respect for the chancellor and many of the other deans, but she never hesitated to speak her mind and hold her ground on issues. For example, space was the most cherished commodity on campus. She resisted several efforts to have the space assigned to nursing reassigned. She also applied her strategic skills to establish a center for health care policy within the school.

In one instance, she gained a great deal of personal and political respect because she quietly persisted on a particular issue of great concern to her as a "budding activist" committed to equal rights and as an advocate for nursing. The university annually held celebratory ceremonies at an elite, all-male club in San Francisco. After several years of expressing objections, she told the chancellor that the school would not participate in the ceremonies unless the venue was changed.

The chancellor, a fine physician and gentleman, was taken aback and could not understand her conviction on this issue, as the women at the university were being included in this celebratory event. She, however, believed that it was a place where power was brokered only among men. She could not support an environment where women were not sitting at those tables on a daily basis making deals and sharing an equal role.

She never mentioned her conversation with the chancellor to anyone, but word leaked out within the university. The setting for the event did change, and as a result, Gretta received invitations to speak to women's groups across the campus and to provide advice to females within the other health science schools. Being looked up to as a fighter for women's rights was never her intent during the initial conversation with the chancellor, but it was the outcome of her standing up for her principles.

LIFE IN GLOBAL NURSING: REGULATION AND CREDENTIALING

Gretta Styles' step into global nursing was brought about by a combination of international need combined with Gretta's expertise. The International Council of Nurses headquartered in Geneva, Switzerland, is a federation of the national nursing associations of 125 countries and is the global voice for nurses.

In the international arena, Gretta directed the 1983 ICN worldwide project on the regulation of the profession, including of nurses, nursing education, and nursing services.

Publications resulted that addressed professional and governmental regulatory models.

While Gretta was dean at Wayne State University, the American Nurses Association was struggling with the issue among all nursing specialties about who would set standards and oversee certification, which was also tied to the controversy regarding entry into practice. There was a wide representation of stakeholders with their own opinions on these matters, and Gretta was asked by the ANA board to chair a comprehensive, multi-organizational project on the regulation of the profession.

It was a daunting undertaking, as she would have to juggle her position as dean while chairing this committee for ANA. It would later prove to be a fruitful decision for her career trajectory. It demanded expertise in consensus-building, as well as in the field of credentialing, most of which she developed on the job.

After three years of successfully chairing the ANA credentialing study, it was no surprise that the International Council of Nurses viewed her as an expert in regulation. Countries around the world were in need of nursing regulation guidelines because many had no laws, had undefined standards, or virtually had no authority over the profession.

Gretta was asked by ICN board members to be a consultant in the area of regulation, which she did for many years. She moved on to become chairperson of the Professional Services Committee, a member of the board, and president from 1993-97.

Similar to her past positions, Gretta was quickly being recognized for her leadership abilities and was carving out her specialty niche in the profession. She studied what the issues were in the profession of nursing around the world and then spent six months in Geneva, Switzerland, writing a position paper on regulation.

Gretta and an ICN colleague organized and taught workshops for the representatives of national associations on strengthening regulation in their respective countries. Her position paper and educational workshops had a major impact on nursing from a global standpoint, because they enabled laws to be established, strengthened, or greatly revised in countries with weak nursing practices. These changes allowed nurses to move into more central positions and, in essence, established more authority for nurses.

Working with the ICN, Gretta learned to appreciate how other countries used her information and direction to advance the profession of nursing within their own territories.

When assessing how far nursing practice has progressed within a country, Gretta essentially uses two criteria:

1. Look at the educational requirements and the development of higher education, and
2. Assess the leadership positions in the government held by nurses.

Looking at Australia as an example, Gretta notes that "Australia is really the first large country to require the university degree." With the government's support, Australia transitioned from hospital education to technical institute education and then finally to university education, where students are allowed to pursue a Bachelor of Science degree in nursing. Australia made this transition to baccalaureate education as the entry level into nursing in a relatively short period and is now moving to add an advanced practice model. Nurses in many countries hold powerful positions, many times within the government. It is often the case in small countries that nurses are highly influential in shaping and practicing health care.

In terms of how much work remains to be accomplished in nursing, Gretta believes the United States could be a much stronger member in the ICN by providing support for nurses in less advanced countries, as do some of the other national nurses associations. Gretta traveled extensively while working for the ICN and spoke out on behalf of nursing internationally. One of her most memorable speaking engagements was during a ceremony in Athens, Greece.

She was the distinguished keynote speaker featured at the Acropolis addressing local dignitaries and nursing professionals from many countries who were gathered in the ancient amphitheater. She was alone, with a small podium, on the large stage. During her presentation, the wind started picking up strength, and she was sure that her notes were going to blow away at any moment. As an educator who taught public speaking, she found herself talking to the audience, while at the same time problem solving how she was going to handle the precarious situation. Gretta has always been one to passionately express her point through use of hand gestures. This was especially true in this case, as she spoke about nursing victories, using the "V" for victory sign.

As some of her papers were flying away, she needed to think quickly. She decided to use one hand to gesture, while keeping a constant finger on the notes with the other hand. As she would finish speaking from a page, she would lift her finger and let the wind blow it away, increasing the dramatic effect of her presentation. By the end of her speech, she received a standing ovation and, as the guest of honor, was taken to sit next to an elderly lady wearing an outfit much like a Red Cross uniform. The woman had been moved to tears by the presentation and asked Gretta what she could do for the profession.

Photo courtesy of the University of Florida College of Nursing.

Photo courtesy of the University of Florida College of Nursing.

Dr. Margretta Styles speaks at the The Critical Link: Nursing and the Future of Health Care, The Dorothy M. Smith Nursing Leadership Conference sponsored by the University of Florida College of Nursing. Styles, a UF alumna, was a keynote speaker at the conference and spoke on nurseforce and nursepower.

Dr. Styles catches up with her old friend Dr. Betty Hilliard who is one of the earliest faculty members of the University of Florida College of Nursing and is considered by many to be one of the pioneers of Florida nurse-midwifery.

Dr. Styles interacts with guests at the conference including Dr. Dennis O'Leary, president of the Joint Commission on Accreditation of Healthcare Organizations, who was also a speaker at the conference.

After conversing for a few moments, Gretta realized this was one of the wealthiest women in Greece, the matriarch of an old Greek family. Gretta suggested she be patron of the national nurses association.

A year later in 1990, Gretta was invited back again, but this time to be awarded an honorary doctorate from the University of Athens at another memorable ceremony.

PRESIDENT OF THE AMERICAN NURSES ASSOCIATION (1986-1988)

By 1986, Gretta had earned a reputation as a leader both nationally and internationally. Even as she was completing her tenure as dean at UCSF and engaged as an ICN consultant on regulation, she was asked to run for president of the ANA even though she had never served in a board position. The election campaign ended in a large victory for her, but she remained in office only two years. She was one of the few nursing leaders in recent decades who served one term as president of ANA, while the maximum is two terms. "I just did not want to do it again," said Gretta. She was juggling her work with the UC in San Francisco and the ICN in Geneva, Switzerland, and commuted between Kansas City, ANA's former headquarters. She was feeling terribly divided and was certain that she was neglecting her family.

One of the toughest leadership challenges facing Gretta in this role was dealing with the issue of entry into practice. "ANA had its position favoring the baccalaureate degree, but it was not being implemented through licensure." ANA appointed a task force to study the possibility of requiring the baccalaureate for membership or separating its membership along educational lines.

"It was very divisive, and two state nurses associations that had fought hard for the professional entry model threatened to leave ANA if we did not make the baccalaureate distinction. As president, of course, I did not want ANA to be torn apart and spent a lot of time trying to convince them to remain with the federation."

One of Gretta's most memorable leadership moments came during this time while attending a meeting at the New York State Nurses Association (NYSNA). The controversy over educational requirements was raging. "It was at that moment that I reminded nurses that if they disaffiliated from ANA they would lose their contact with the ICN." There was a gasp from the audience, many of whom look forward every four years to attending the ICN Congress, and the ultimate vote kept the NYSNA with the ANA. It is difficult to assess the influence, if any, of her comment.

While president of ANA, one of the last things she inaugurated was the establishment of the Commission on Organizational Assessment and Renewal, which she chaired after leaving the presidency. One proposal from this committee was to admit organizational affiliates, such as specialty associations, into ANA's membership structure, a concept implemented shortly thereafter and gaining momentum today with ANA's recent reorganization.

Another key recommendation from this committee was to create a separate body for its credentialing services (certification of specialists, accreditation of continuing education bodies, and recognition of "magnet" nursing services). A few years later the American Nurses Credentialing Center was formed as a corporate entity within ANA. Gretta went on to become president of ANCC (1996-98), even as she completed her four-year term as ICN president, and took a major role in the further development of the Magnet Recognition Program. She later became director of Credentialing International, ANCC's global outreach, offering services and consultation.

Gretta's history of serving as president for ANA, ICN, and ANCC provides the nursing profession with a valuable resource for understanding organizational structure, regulation, and credentialing. Changes to the organizational structure of both ANA and ICN are currently in progress, which is none too soon from Gretta's viewpoint.

Gretta believes both organizational models are outdated for the times and the membership they serve, and she further believes they could become more encompassing and effective. She has long advocated an AARP-like model of minimum dues augmented by fees for services, tailored to individual members for ANA. And she has favored bringing students into ANA, as do many national nurses associations in other countries, believing that this would foster leadership development and encourage loyalty to our professional association.

"Both ANA and ICN are working to broaden their membership base through similar strategies.... More streamlined, greater flexibility, less homogeneity... ICN serves more than 125 national associations with a permanent staff fewer than 30. Frequently, when the ICN undertakes a project, it brings in a consultant who works with the staff and the board for the life of the project, sometimes for a number of years. There is no need to conform to an existing bureaucracy, so the work gets done and done efficiently and economically by a recognized expert." Gretta suggests that this mechanism has allowed the ICN to remain financially stable and may be a future model for the ANA and other organizations to consider.

THE RETIRED NURSE LEADER

If Gretta were to sum up how she would like to be remembered in nursing, it is as a "professionalist." This is a unique term she coined for herself and others who, as she says, "strive to develop the profession, all aspects of it."

"I am not just a researcher, educator, administrator, or practitioner; I am interested in developing all aspects of nursing to achieve true professional status, with all of the rights, responsibilities, and recognition attached to other well-established professions."

Meanwhile, Gretta has not slowed down her work pace. She has been involved in the writing of ANA's white paper on the nursing shortage and is captivated by the stream of powerlessness running throughout the nursing commentary and literature. She is convinced that educational and work environments must be transformed to change the professional culture. Nurses must be partners, and nothing less, in the health care enterprise and policymaking.

As to the workplace, the magnet hospital studies have pointed the way to putting power into the hands of the nurses, and in essence, this change creates a different culture within an organization, a more empowering culture. Moreover, through her own consumer experiences, Gretta has witnessed the power of advanced practice nurses working more autonomously and authoritatively.

For such a prominent nurse leader, it is difficult to define Gretta Styles' career by any one specialty area, as she had many. The three pronounced specialty paths threaded throughout Gretta's nursing profession were education (primarily educational administration), professional organization work, and credentialing. Much of Gretta's career focused on harmonizing the interests of all nursing organizations, generalized and specialized. Interestingly enough, she has maneuvered through her career without having a formal mentor but has had many supportive colleagues.

By the nature of the shortage of graduate-prepared nurses in the '50s, she was handed responsibility quickly. It was a time in which the circumstances allowed, even encouraged and demanded, rapid leadership acceleration. Gretta learned early on in her career to be open to new opportunities and to take risks. What she lacked in experience during the early years, she more than made up for in courage. The option of failing in new ventures never crossed her mind. Gretta had become well rehearsed in life's early lessons of reaching for those things that appear beyond grasp.

Reflecting over her career, she offers that it is much like the saying "build it and they will come," but with the twist of "make yourself an expert and people will find you." The key, as Gretta sees it, is "getting all the education you can, developing an expertise in particular areas, and then opportunity seeks you out."

As proof, Gretta reveals that she never had to apply for a position or an organization office during her career. The jobs reached out to her. She was known for being able to take projects to the next level and show results. Outcomes are what employers are seeking. Even today, Gretta Styles is highly sought after for her experience and expertise, which allows her to maintain a broad vision and perspective when seeking solutions.

But with all her honorary doctorates and numerous awards, "it is family, one's values and beliefs" that make up a large part of Gretta and is how she wants to be remembered. She also wishes to be remembered for never breaking a promise to family, friends, or colleagues. She has, without doubt, left her own unique mark on the profession and her outstanding contributions should not be forgotten

CHAPTER 10

Nursing education teacher

Rheba de Tornyay

The genesis of Rheba de Tornyay's leadership journey can be linked directly to her efforts to retain her personal integrity while in nursing school. Her hospital nursing program had treated young nurses like "delinquent girls" rather than budding professionals, and she was determined to change this misguided educational system.

Rheba de Tornyay, RN, EdD, FAAN, devoted her career to nursing education and scholarship with the goal that nursing must attract and retain the best and the brightest students. She is renowned for her leadership role as dean of the University of Washington, for her early election to the Institute of Medicine (IOM), and for her role as the founding president of the American Academy of Nursing (1973). She has held national healthcare leadership advisory roles for the Pew Foundation and the Robert Wood Johnson Foundation (RWJF) – of which she was the first woman and first nurse to be elected to the board of trustees.

Rheba Tornyay is also the author of a book, *Strategies for Teaching Nursing,* that has been revered for decades. Her extraordinary people skills have often prompted colleagues to describe her as a dignified stateswoman who built relationships for all of nursing. She, however, describes herself as "not the smartest or the most-prepared person" but rather "lucky, committed, and passionate." Her career, however, underscores that her passion and commitment created her "luck."

Perhaps even more notable than her own accomplishments are the number of contemporary nurse leaders who would identify Rheba de Tornyay as the person who most influenced their nursing leadership growth and development. Her mentorship is widely recognized as promoting not only the individual but the profession. She has been known to remind nurse leaders to evaluate the consequences of their choices and to be mindful of growing others. Nursing has benefited from her high-profile leadership because, as one colleague puts it, "national nursing programs were initiated because Rheba de Tornyay was there to shepherd them. They were Rheba's programs pure and simple, and we all benefited."

EARLY INFLUENCES

Rheba Fradkin de Tornyay's earliest memories are of the Great Depression, which, she says, "marked my generation enormously." Born April 17, 1926, she witnessed individuals and communities struggling to survive at the most basic level—food and shelter. She recalls, "We were taught as children that whatever you do, you do it right."

Complaining about work was unthinkable. Having a job was all that mattered. There was an internal drive to succeed motivated by survival, and education was seen as the ultimate opportunity for future survival. Although her parents received little education, the message was clear that she and her sister would go to college.

The Fradkin family owned a chicken farm in Petaluma in northern California. It was a family business that built a strong work ethic. Everyone helped on the farm. Rheba had a particular affinity for the farm animals, and it was her self-assigned responsibility to care for the sick animals. She wanted to be a veterinarian but was told that this was not a job for a woman. When she started at the University of California at Berkeley in 1944, she had no idea what she wanted to do with her life. Rheba recalls, "After two years of horrible grades and feeling very confused" she stumbled into nursing.

World War II was raging, and all civilian students were required to take a National Service Requirement course. Rheba selected a Red Cross nurse's aide preparation class, and it was here she was introduced to the fine art of caring for people. She calls this "the luckiest break of my life" because no one had ever discussed the possibility of a nursing career with her.

NURSING EDUCATION

The University of California, San Francisco (UCSF) did have a nursing school, but she was never counseled to go to a college nursing program.

Dean Rheba de Tornyay, right, with Margretta Styles, center, and Ildaura Murillo-Rohde, PhD, RN, MeD, CS, DA, FAAN, dean and professor emeritus, State University of New York, Brooklyn, at the University of Washington School of Nursing's First Annual Elizabeth Sterling Soule Endowed Lecture in 1979.

She was delighted to leave behind her miserable grade point average and start over at Mount Zion Hospital School of Nursing in San Francisco. The Mount Zion in-residence nursing program proved to be an influential period in Rheba's life.

During her three years of nursing school she was branded as a troublemaker because she objected to the way students were treated, and so she organized the student body. She complained about the working conditions of student nurses, invasion of privacy (the school would open personal mail, among other things), and student nurses generally being treated like "delinquent young girls." Rheba was soon elected student body president and eventually helped to organize other student body presidents to form the Bay Area Student Nurses Association.

This organization ultimately became the precursor of the California Nursing Students' Association. This was one of her first nursing leadership experiences, but, unfortunately, the Mount Zion nursing faculty did not see it as leadership but rather as mutiny. Rheba lost all privileges and was restricted to her room for the express purpose of "reflecting on her attitude."

In a moment of "reflection," Rheba wrote a letter to the California State Board of Nursing. The letter carefully outlined the list of student nurse complaints. She was sure that this strategy would result in an investigation and eventual change. The State Board of Nursing responded with nothing more than a "thank you for your letter" letter. Rheba was frustrated and demoralized.

Months later she attended a banquet and found that she was seated next to the executive director for the California State Board of Nursing. The executive director turned to Rheba and said that she had asked to meet the author of the letter. As it turned out, the State Board of Nursing had not responded fully to her letter, as they did not want to cause her trouble in school. Seeing this revelation as validation of the complaints, Rheba asked the executive director why the state board hadn't done something about it. In response, she was told that she should be quiet and get herself through nursing school because "nursing needs you." The executive director continued, saying, "If they flunk you, there is nothing we can do, and nursing will lose you." She bluntly advised Rheba to "settle down and get over it." The message? Focus on the greater good rather than the moment.

From that point, Rheba made a commitment to devote her career and energy to reforming the system that challenged her personal integrity. She was going to be a nurse educator; however, she believed it was essential to first acquire some clinical experience.

In 1949, de Tornyay embarked on the two best things she ever did in her career: working in psychiatric nursing and leaving psychiatric nursing. She chose psychiatric nursing because her diploma preparation had little emphasis on the psychosocial aspects of nursing. She became a junior psychiatric nurse at Langley Porter Neuropsychiatric Hospital at the University of California, San Francisco, which she describes as disturbingly similar to the hospital portrayed in the movie *One Flew Over the Cuckoo's Nest*. In the absence of effective pharmacology, psychiatric treatment commonly included prefrontal lobotomies and shock therapy. The experience was emotionally draining, but she learned a great deal. Her stint at Langley Porter had a lasting effect. When asked what contributed most to her success as a dean, she always answers "psychiatric nursing." It was in this area that she learned to work with groups and to listen for more than just the words that were said. She believes both are essential attributes for a successful administrator and teacher.

Rheba with co-author Heather Young.

While finishing a Bachelor of Science in Nursing (BSN) degree at San Francisco State College, Rheba worked at the Maimonides Rehabilitation Center, believing the schedule and workload would accommodate her studies. The administrator was a social worker who had created a work environment that encouraged autonomy and control of practice. Rheba flourished in this environment and discovered another professional passion—long-term care.

She enjoyed every moment of caring for the elderly and became a champion for issues on aging and long-term care. Rheba later served on national committees, advisory boards and co-authored a book titled *Making a Good Move to a Retirement Community* that was co-authored with Heather Young. The School of Nursing at the University of Washington ultimately created the de Tornyay Center for Healthy Aging in honor of her professional contributions in this area.

THE TEACHER

Rheba's next career move was to begin her teaching career at none other than Mount Zion Hospital School of Nursing. Ironically, she had been invited to join the faculty of the school that she had reported to the State Board of Nursing. The lesson? "Never burn a bridge."

To enhance her teaching skills, Rheba returned to graduate school. In 1954, she graduated with a master degree (MA) with a major in education from San Francisco State University. Upon completion of her graduate studies, Rheba took two important steps—she married Rudy de Tornyay on her graduation day and soon thereafter joined the San Francisco State University (SFSU) faculty. It was there that Rheba seized the opportunity to implement needed curriculum changes and create an environment where individual student expression was encouraged rather than punished consistent with a collegiate environment. Rheba was hooked on teaching nurses.

Within a year of joining SFSU, she became convinced that a doctorate was essential for her to be a successful teacher and to attain tenure, and so she began her doctoral studies at Stanford University. The Stanford years were another influential period in her leadership development. During these "eight very long years," her advisor, Fred McDonald, created a scholar. The journey was a test of Rheba's character, stamina, and patience.

Fred McDonald was a tough taskmaster who taught her how to write and "wasn't always pleasant about it." When she finished her dissertation, she vowed to put a plaque on the floor of his office proclaiming "Here stood Rheba de Tornyay—hour, after hour, after hour, after hour."

She withstood the test, however, and earned a favorable reputation for her work in the adaptation of Stanford's microteaching techniques for preparing nurse educators. Fred McDonald recognized Rheba's extraordinary teaching talent, and upon completion of her doctorate, he hand-delivered her to Helen Nahm, dean of the School of Nursing at UCSF. Helen Nahm wanted to revamp the nursing education program, and Rheba was just the person for the job.

In 1967, Rheba joined the UCSF faculty and introduced the microteaching technique she had learned at Stanford. Within four years, 360 UCSF graduate nursing students had engaged in the new educational process. Rheba published these teaching techniques in a book titled

Clinical Nurse Scholars 1989. (Rheba is in the back row, third from right.)

Strategies for Teaching Nursing (1971), which she identifies as her single greatest contribution to nursing.

The book went through three revisions over 30 years in print, providing the framework for how to teach. Rheba had noted that graduate studies were focusing on the clinical rather than the functional areas of teaching. As a result, her book was a guide for effective methods to teach nursing students.

For decades, she had "young and not so young" nurses rushing up and saying that the book had changed their lives. According to a faculty colleague who worked at UCSF at the time, Rheba's courses on teaching soon penetrated the faculty ranks. Many faculty members secretly bought her book and modeled their classes after her techniques. Students are harsh critics, and the faculty could do no less than to learn from Rheba.

While at UCSF, Rheba discovered a lifelong mentor in Helen Nahm. In later years when faced with a significant challenge, Rheba would often find herself asking, "What would Helen do?"

Helen Nahm's leadership advice had been explicit, practical, and logical—think of the consequences. She taught Rheba to think not only of the consequences of a decision but the consequences of not making a decision.

Rheba also learned the art of reflection. This was a strategy she employed early in her leadership development, in which she would ask how the situation had gone and what she could have done differently. Reflection can fuel self-doubt; however, Rheba *never* doubted her goals or what needed to be done. Remaining focused on the goals allowed Rheba to move through difficult situations with confidence and determination.

DEANSHIPS AND NATIONAL LEADERSHIP

Rheba served as the dean of the school of nursing at the University of California, Los Angeles (UCLA) from 1971-1975 and the University of Washington from 1975-1986.

Experience taught her that some of the best deans are those who are the best teachers. The best teachers are masters in group dynamics.

Rheba is concerned that today's dean-search committees are too heavily focused on recruiting top nurse researchers. She believes that deans must nurture and facilitate research; however, research is only one component of program success. She likens the role of a dean to a conductor of an orchestra. The musicians are experts with their own instruments, but it is the conductor who leads them to play from the same page, at the same tempo, and in just the perfect harmony to deliver the end product—music pleasing to the listener.

UNIVERSITY OF CALIFORNIA AT LOS ANGELES

When Rheba accepted the deanship of the School of Nursing at the University of California, Los Angeles, she knew the school had a troubled past and wondered if it would remain open; however, she always loved a challenge. The program was almost in a "failure to thrive" situation, because, philosophically and physically, the UCLA nursing program existed on the periphery. Applied fields were not central to the university's mission, and the nursing school was located in a space that was inadequate, with a budget that was insufficient.

Rheba felt a huge responsibility toward the faculty and students, and that sense of responsibility sustained her drive as the dean. The UCLA deanship was a lesson learned that program success requires central administrative support. Great faculty and students are not enough to build a strong program. There were undoubtedly numerous "What would Helen do?" moments, and Rheba had ample causes for reflection.

It was during the second year of her deanship at UCLA that Rheba's prominence as a national leader in nursing began to blossom. Lucile Petry Leone, director of the Cadet Nurse Corps during World War II, approached her good friend Helen Nahm (dean at UCSF) for a recommendation of a young nurse who worked well with physicians, had an interdisciplinary approach, and got along with people, for membership in the Institute of Medicine (IOM). Rheba fit the description, so Helen suggested her.

INSTITUTE OF MEDICINE

In 1972, Rheba became the third nurse to be elected to the IOM, National Academy of Sciences. This national leadership opportunity was a remarkable accomplishment for both Rheba and nursing. She was keenly aware that the IOM did not need, then or ever, a nurse carrying the battle cry and waving the flag. Rheba explains this by stating, "We all know good people

Rheba and scholars at a University of Washington School of Nursing scholarship reception April, 2001.

who get so caught up in their need to make a point that the real message about nursing never gets heard."

The IOM was a pivotal time for Rheba. She describes that she learned an enormous amount and met some of the brightest minds in healthcare. Among the contacts she developed was John Hogness, who later became the president of the University of Washington. When Rheba's name later surfaced as the potential dean for the School of Nursing at the University of Washington, President Hogness already knew her well.

AMERICAN ACADEMY OF NURSES

In 1973, Rheba was selected for another prominent leadership role—the American Academy of Nurses (AAN). The board of directors of the American Nurses Association (ANA) wanted to create a special organization, the AAN, that would function as a think tank for the profession. The AAN would develop ideas but not necessarily implement them. Rheba was notified by the president of ANA that she had been appointed as a charter fellow to the AAN. The ANA appointed 36 charter fellows whose original mission was to create a working group, not just an honorific group, that was committed to leading the nursing profession.

The charter fellows drafted the bylaws knowing that the AAN would be an elite organization. It was decided the AAN would be the forum to recognize the great thinkers of the profession who could point the way for the nursing profession. The AAN would nurture and honor the very best of those in nursing in terms of knowledge and practice.

The charter fellows were concerned that the AAN not follow a sorority model, hence they carefully spelled out how fellows were to be elected to membership and how the AAN would conduct business. Membership would not be couched on who one knew but who had made significant contributions to the profession and were poised to do so in the future.

A sensitive point was the relationship of the AAN to the ANA and how the AAN could maintain functional autonomy when it did not have financial autonomy. According to Rheba, some of this tension regarding financial autonomy continues today.

The AAN was a remarkable leadership experience. Rheba remembers the enormity of the role being articulated by one of the charter fellows who mused, "Did it ever occur to us that maybe we're a small group of professionals driving a huge workforce?" Rheba was the first elected president for the AAN (1973-1974) and describes her election as the single event of which she was most proud.

UNIVERSITY OF WASHINGTON

In 1975, when Rheba was recruited to the University of Washington, she found the environment was refreshingly unlike UCLA. When she interviewed with the president, John Hogness, she was not shy in telling him that she wanted to build the best school of nursing in the nation. She got the job.

The University of Washington had historically supported and nurtured professional schools such as nursing and other health sciences. This was evident by the high caliber of nursing faculty. Rheba was extremely pleased with the amount of support the school received. The challenge was to take the program to the next level. She did just that.

Under her leadership, the School of Nursing was able to establish a PhD program, and the faculty continued to grow and produce national nurse leaders. Moreover, in 1984, when universities and colleges initiated rankings for nursing programs across the nation, the University of Washington was ranked number one. For the last 20 years, the School of Nursing at the University of Washington has remained at the top of the rankings, which is a testament to leadership at all levels.

Rheba remembers an interesting experience with the program ranking. As dean, she always taught a class of first-year students, and she shared with the class that the School of Nursing at the University of Washington had been ranked number one in the first year of rankings. Her excitement and enthusiasm quickly became dampened by the students' response, which was a bit like the proverbial deer in the headlights. There was a barely audible "We're number one?" Unbelieving of their flat reaction, Rheba replied, "Your confidence in your school overwhelms me, what is the matter with you?" She discovered the ranking completely intimidated them. They shared with her their fear of not being able to measure up and maintain the school's prestige. Rheba never forgot the lesson learned from this experience: Success often imposes burdens at all levels.

Rheba certainly felt the burden of being number one. She was cognizant that this meant preparing the highest quality nurses to care for patients, as well as advancing the scholarship of the discipline. She was concerned by the evolving paradigm shift in the educational value system. She noted that those in the educational system seemed to value faculty who secured RO1 funding (externally funded research grants) for individual research over teaching clinical and contributing to community service. She was concerned that *she* might be creating problems for her own profession because this misaligned value system could impact patient-care outcomes. Viewing teaching as second to research could mean the students might not get what they needed to provide high-quality care.

This concern was realized when she visited a hospitalized friend who asked Rheba if she could help provide oral care, which had been badly neglected. Upon further investigation, Rheba discovered recurrent deficits in basic care. She was so disturbed by the neglect that she walked down the hall to a colleague's office, shut the door, and questioned her role as a leader.

Had nurses forgotten to teach the basics such as oral care? Are the machines more important than the comforts of the patient? Had the educational value system emphasized research over those who taught basic patient care? Leadership comes at a personal price, and successful leaders are always checking the course of their actions.

Rheba suggests leadership at the dean level is a tricky business where one is always trying to find the perfect balance. The role of the dean requires avoiding displays of favoritism, appreciating faculty as individuals, and never forgetting that faculty members are not your peers. She warns that not everyone is going to like all the decisions that are made, but hopefully most will respect the leadership. The mark of an effective dean, she believes, is often defined by silence.

The Three Deans: University of Washington School of Nursing Dean Nancy Woods is flanked by her predecessors Rheba, to the left, and Sue Hegyvary, to the right.

What this means is that, from Rheba's perspective, whenever you find a faculty member who has been spending all his/her time talking about the dean, there is something very wrong because good leadership is often more conspicuous by its absence than its presence.

Rheba believes her tenure as dean at the University of Washington was the capstone of her career. It was an opportunity to work with some remarkable talent, and she believes that she is a better person for the experience. Rheba lives within blocks of the campus on a hill that overlooks the campus and remains very invested in the leadership and outcomes of the University of Washington.

Occasionally, she will serve as a guest lecturer on her favorite topic of aging and remains active in the de Tornyay Center for Healthy Aging. She continues to mentor young faculty seeking tenure, telling them what their department chairs and the dean may not tell them. Rheba is explicit in defining the value of professional choices and has bluntly directed, "I don't care if you want to do it or not, here is what you must do." She is the voice of experience, which contributes invaluable advice that illuminates the professional path for many.

LEADERSHIP—THE VALUE OF PEOPLE SKILLS

Rheba identifies herself as a consensus builder, predictably bristling at authoritarian methods. Early in her career, she overreacted to authoritarian styles, but as she matured she realized the buck had to stop somewhere. She came to understand that trying to please everybody meant she would please nobody.

Rheba developed the "ego strength" to gather the information and make a decision knowing it was not always going to be popular. Colleagues who have worked with her say that she could present highly controversial decisions and everyone would leave feeling they were listened to, respected, and understood.

She possessed the ability to bring disparate groups to consensus. Rheba identifies her greatest leadership asset as the ability to get along with people. She's a conductor who knew how to create the music.

Throughout Rheba's career, nursing has struggled to integrate knowledge. She becomes visibly agitated when she speaks of how disjointed communication can appear in nursing. Rheba comments, "Nursing organizations would produce position papers that nobody understood and that never went anywhere."

She is concerned that doctoral education contributes to this communication breakdown. Rheba remembers working with doctoral students to help them translate their dissertations into practice. Her philosophy, one she held long before it was popular, is that all research should be able to be translated into practice applications. She carried this message to all who would listen that nursing must use a common language that is explicit and simple or the work would remain isolated. She believes nurse researchers have a responsibility to produce knowledge that can be used beyond nursing. She worked within nursing and across disciplines to merge the disciplines to one healthcare discipline with one common goal—patient care.

She believes nursing is further isolated by appearing territorial in the delivery of patient care. Rheba recalls sharing with a physician colleague a frequently held nursing perspective that nurses are the patient's advocate. She was shocked when he angrily fired back the question "What do you think I am, the patient's adversary?"

From that day forward Rheba, cleaned up her language. She never forgot the basics of healthcare are that we all care and we all need to respect that.

She is passionate that nursing needs to be a "partner in the health professions." Rheba has always believed that the health professions are really one discipline, rather than many, working from the same knowledge base for the purpose of providing quality patient care. Rheba labored throughout her career to transcend the silos of the separate professions in healthcare delivery. She firmly believes there is no room for a separatist world view.

When the nurse practitioner movement first emerged, Rheba wanted to explore if it was possible for nurses and physicians to use a common language and collect the same data while taking a patient history. Thus, she decided to take the physical diagnosis course taught to medical students. She discovered there was a definite difference in practice when it came to patient interactions. The medical students were more regimented in performing physical examinations, starting at the head and working down to the toes, preferring not to be interrupted. If the patients asked questions, the questions were deferred until after the examination.

Nurses asked patients to tell them about what brought them to the hospital and filled in the blanks according to the patients' responses. She found the medical students were often somewhat frightened by patient interactions. She learned a great deal by rolling up her sleeves and experiencing the process firsthand.

In 1986, she was appointed director of the Robert Wood Johnson Foundation Clinical Nurse Scholars Program. The program was designed to turn clinical nurse scholars into top researchers and academicians. As the director of the program, she assisted in the selection and grooming of an entire generation of nurse leaders. One of the fellows shares that " Rheba de Tornyay was capable of getting the best from everyone—there was no limit to her ability to promote nurses."

LOVES TO TEACH NURSES

Rheba modestly suggests that many of her accomplishments were an "accident of fate." Timing and luck contributed to some of her leadership opportunities, but the real test is what the leader does when the opportunity presents itself. Opportunities are often lost without hard work. On the other hand, an opportunity seized and developed with a good outcome creates numerous future opportunities. Rheba reflects that when she had the honor of representing nursing, she understood that at times she was representing healthcare and not just nursing.

She worked hard to keep the nursing influence at the table and did not hesitate to remind her colleagues of this privilege and obligation. Colleagues describe Rheba as a "regal and dignified stateswoman" whose talents elevated the vision of the nursing profession, integrated disciplines, and created national leadership roles. Much of Rheba's success can be attributed to her ability to build relationships and her ability to remain focused on the principal outcome of all healthcare providers—the patient.

Rheba worked very hard at making leadership appear effortless. She did such a remarkable job that colleagues commonly suggest that leadership came easy for her, which she likens to "you have been married for 50 years because it is easy for you." Anyone who has ever been married knows longevity doesn't just happen, nor is it easy. Professional or personal leadership success is based on hard work, commitment, and passion. Making it look effortless is the hallmark of a leader.

As she surveys her career, Rheba recognizes that at times she was too impatient and moved change too quickly. This resulted in losing people along the way because she did not take the time to create "buy in" by the essential players. Change is never accomplished alone, and incorporating the talents of the members of the group into an idea requires coordination and strategic planning. For her, the ideal situation occurs when the idea comes back to the leader as an original group idea. Along the way, she has learned that patience supports this transition of ownership.

Rheba was successful at developing her leadership role beyond academia. She had a national reputation that allowed her to participate in the most influential healthcare forums. Often she was the first on these committees—the first nurse, the first woman, or both. And then, when her term would be concluded, she would ensure that her replacement was a nurse. She was able to do this because *she* provided a valued perspective and built relationships. Including the relationship that has helped the most to sustain her leadership for over 50 years—the relationship with her husband, Rudy de Tornyay. He is her best friend, mentor, and supporter, and he has frequently been her most useful critic in teaching tactics and politics.

Rheba has a personal passion beyond nursing. She is an expert cook. Rheba owns every cooking tool ever manufactured, and the person she admires most is Julia Child. Rheba describes Julia as more than just a master cook, she is master teacher who knew how to incorporate the principles with remarkable clarity. Julia is adept at demonstrating the manual skills, delighted in trying new methods, and learned how to adapt to the changing times—all traits valued by Rheba. She so admired Julia's teaching methods that she required her students to watch one of her shows remarking, "If nothing else they got a good recipe out of it." Rheba and Julia are both masters of their trade who stood the test of time and left their professions richer for their contributions.

In many ways, throughout her career, Rheba de Tornyay has been one of the great conductors of the nursing profession. She worked hard to get nursing on the same sheet of music, patiently merged the disparate interpretations of tempo, generated enthusiasm for the performance, and invited the influential outside world of healthcare to listen to the remarkable outcome. Her accomplishments were never about "Rheba" but devoted to advancing the profession and advancing nursing education. Her efforts have created national opportunities, which in turn have created professional credibility. She has paved the way so that those who followed had less to prove to be effective leaders.

Nursing owes Rheba a debt of gratitude for the courageous, dignified, and thoughtful leadership she provided over her five decades in nursing. It is little wonder that she has been honored by the AAN as a Living Legend.

CHAPTER 11

nursing education — Dean

Claire Fagin

"I have found in life one must be visible in fighting for what one is passionate about, and hope the rest will follow." Claire Fagin, RN, PhD, FAAN, was never supposed to be a nurse, as it was clear on all accounts that her parents were grooming her to be a physician. Her aunt was a successful physician, and Claire was the anointed child to follow in her footsteps. Even though she was more than a little pushed to go into medicine by her parents, Claire had her own ideas for her future. Perhaps as a premonition of her future leadership style, she followed her own mind, even under times of great duress, refusing to be swayed off course. In the 1960s, for example, she was one of the nurses who led protests and marches against the Vietnam War.

As the first woman appointed as interim president of an Ivy League university, Claire is without a doubt one of nursing's heavyweight champions. Her determination to elevate the profession to new levels has been a constant theme throughout her career. Whether she was in Washington, D.C., lobbying on behalf of health policy or consumer health issues, or creating innovative ways to educate nurses, Claire has had a fire within her that would not allow her to sit idly by and watch what she viewed as an erosion of the profession. She remains an avid fighter for the profession and for all that is right in nursing.

Claire Fagin in a Vietnam War protest march (above) and then preparing to speak at the protest.

THE EARLY YEARS

Claire grew up in the Bronx in the 1940s, viewing the world as her oyster and never allowing herself a narrow view on what a woman could make of her life. She came from very humble beginnings. Her mother was a Russian and her father was an Austrian. Together, they bought a grocery store, moved the family from the east to the west Bronx, and managed to survive through the depression years. Regardless of their humble economic standing in those years, and despite the fact that World War II had begun, Claire's parents expected big things of her in the educational arena. There would be no excuses as to why their daughter would not have the best education possible, especially as she was going to be "the doctor in the family."

While in her first year at Hunter College, the idea of going into the nursing profession came to her when she was walking home one day. Claire just happened to be passing a recruitment poster for the U.S. Cadet Nurse Corps. She immediately became interested, and she pulled a girlfriend into her scheme. Together they went to the office of the New York City Nursing Council for War Service. It was a day that would change her life forever. One of the most influential people in Claire's life was a woman, Dorothy Wheeler, whom she met that day at the nursing council.

Claire had been contemplating entering a diploma program, but after meeting with Dorothy Wheeler, she refocused her sights on a baccalaureate program. Wheeler had convinced Claire that baccalaureate educational programs were the programs of the future. As she was already in college, Claire believed it made sense to continue on in college as opposed to finding a hospital-based nursing program.

NURSING: THE NEW GRADUATE

The format of Claire's nursing program was unique to the time, due to the ongoing war. "The style of education was very clever," says Claire. It was designed as a four-year program, but the nursing diploma could be awarded after three years, with the remaining year focusing on the liberal arts requirements. Students would take a course a month so that if they were called up by the draft they could complete the college credits they were earning during the month of schoolwork. For instance, a nursing student could take English for a whole month and then chemistry for a whole month. With students being drafted mid-semester, this schedule made good sense. Ironically, Claire, who had wanted to serve her country as a nurse, never actually entered military service.

During college, Claire most enjoyed working in the psychiatric ward and chose this area for her senior cadet period. She also enjoyed pediatrics, and so she designed her career to enjoy the best of both.

While completing her fourth year at Wagner College, Claire worked at Seaview Hospital in Staten Island, N.Y. It was while at Seaview Hospital that Claire worked with children who were hospitalized at one-to-two years of age due to the effects of tuberculosis. She observed the issues the children experienced as a result of separation from their parents, and she became so intrigued by what she witnessed that she knew she had found her niche. Claire was too young at this time to realize the impact her first job would have on her overall career in nursing, as later her research on the topic of childhood separation anxiety launched her into the spotlight of the national healthcare arena.

Shortly after the completion of the Bachelor of Science degree in nursing, Claire went to work at Bellevue Hospital as a ward instructor. Reflective of the times, almost all BSN nurses were placed in positions one step up (but not removed in this case) from first-level staff nursing. Leadership opportunities came quickly relative to educational level and experience, even if that meant fresh out of school. "Having no mentor to guide me after I graduated from college influenced my opinion on mentoring. Because most of my career I had relatively short-term mentorship interactions but no real mentoring that occurred over time, I believe these short-term interactions can be just as powerful."

Not long after graduating with her BSN, the travel bug bit Claire. She had desires to move to California. She had received luggage as a graduation gift and went so far as to pack up all her things in order to move west. Planning to travel with a Wagner classmate who was also working at Seaview, they went to hand in their resignations at Seaview Hospital.

However, the move out west was never to be. Claire and her classmate were greeted with a shocking surprise when the nursing supervisor informed them both that more notice was needed. The supervisor threatened them saying they would be given bad references indicating they were unreliable workers.

Even though Claire had never missed a day at work, including walking miles to the hospital in knee-deep snow after the great snow storm of 1948, she feared that if she left for California she would never work again as a nurse, a thought that strikes her as silly today. But the threat did the job, and she and her friend both remained at Seaview for another four months.

After the Seaview experience, Claire was seen to be an "expert" in pediatrics. So when she returned to Bellevue, Mildred Gottdank, the director of instruction, put her in a unique position of working with teens in the hospital setting. This was a very innovative unit, and in addition to working with youngsters on the ward, she and two colleagues, a psychiatrist and a vocational psychologist, provided home visits as needed. "It was very progressive nursing for those years," said Claire. Much of this follow-up care was done on her own time, without compensation, but she did it because it was how she felt nursing should be practiced. One day while listening to another nurse talk about graduate school, the conversation stimulated Claire to start considering returning to school herself. She realized her knowledge deficits, in that when she would report on a patient it was done based on intuitive thinking and not theory.

Another nurse on the unit with Claire, Gertrude Stokes, held a master degree and had a knowledge base beyond the other nurses. Claire admired her and wanted to be like her. It was clear psychiatric nursing was her chosen specialty, but financially, graduate school seemed cost prohibitive until she spoke with Hildegard Peplau, a renowned psychiatric nurse/author. "I was making a ridiculously small salary in those days ($2,400/year), but Hilda said, 'There are scholarships available from the National Institute for Mental Health (NIMH) that you could apply for. Just take whatever exams are needed and apply for the fellowship.'"

Claire did just that and received a full scholarship into Peplau's psychiatric nursing program at Teachers College in New York in 1950. She took a leave from Bellevue with the intent to return upon graduation.

NATIONAL LEAGUE FOR NURSING

After receiving a Master of Nursing degree in 1951, Claire tried to go back to Bellevue, but they wanted her to move into a supervisory position. Or, as she puts it, "they wanted me to become a clipboard supervisor."

She was uninterested in the position and wanted to continue working directly with patients. Claire was now over-qualified for her previous position and found it would be difficult to go back. She refused the new position as supervisor and, thanks to Hildegard Peplau, went to work for the National League for Nursing Education (later renamed the National League for Nursing [NLN]) on a one-year contract.

It was a big decision, but one that would benefit her career. Claire, who is a self-admitted poor salary negotiator, accepted the position of psychiatric nurse consultant and director of a study on the functions and qualifications of psychiatric nurses for $4,500 a year, two-thirds the stated salary, because she was considered too young to make the funded salary, $6,000 a year.

The study Claire directed was designed by Hildegard Peplau and funded by NIMH. She worked with many other nurse leaders to produce her first publication, a monograph that emerged from this study.

Claire learned perseverance during these years. She was a young psychiatric nursing consultant who was in a position that required her to interview other nurse leaders throughout the country. Many times, as a result of her apparent youth, she was viewed with skepticism and not taken seriously by those nurses who were older and more experienced than she was. She worked at getting their respect; in some cases she was successful and others perhaps not.

During this time while working for the NLN, Claire met Sam Fagin. They married in 1952, and he has been her strongest supporter ever since. At this time in her life, she had already begun to make a name for herself. With a master's degree now, she found the opportunities to be abundant. After working only a few months with the NLN, Claire was offered a new position as assistant chief of psychiatric nursing at the new Clinical Center of the National Institutes of Health (NIH). She was courted by fellow Teachers College student, Gwen Tudor, who had been groomed to be the chief of psychiatric nursing at the center. When her one-year contract ended and the study was completed, Claire moved to the Washington, D.C., area where Sam was working and shortly thereafter went to work at Clinical Center.

The opportunity would allow her to develop the center's psychiatric children's unit and head up the entire educational in-service program. This new position was a very rewarding job for Claire, as she was able to design the program from the ground up. She was able to orchestrate exactly how she thought psychiatric care should be delivered in its ideal sense. Once again, Claire found herself in a progressive environment. The flattened nursing organizational structure and hierarchy, the autonomy provided to the nurses, the participation in research, the extraordinary opportunities for collaboration among members of other disciplines, and the inclusion and education of nonprofessional staff in deliberations were among the characteristics that made this division notable. "We were ahead of our times in many respects," says Claire.

While at the center she had the opportunity to meet many notables from the United States and other countries. One of the visitors was a film-maker/psychotherapist from Tavistock Clinic in England who worked with John Bowlby. His name was James Robertson, and he had developed a film titled *A Two Year Old Goes to the Hospital*. This film led to changes in England's legislated practices regarding parental visiting in its hospitals and was extremely stirring for Claire, stimulating her reading about adult-child separation, which led her in new career directions.

NURSE EDUCATOR

Claire planned to remain in clinical practice after receiving her Master of Nursing degree and had become so well-known for her innovative work in psychiatry that she was now receiving offers for university faculty positions. However, instead of taking any of the faculty positions, she took a new clinical position at Children's Hospital in Washington D.C., where she developed the role of liaison nurse for the very well-known department of psychiatry there.

At Children's Hospital, she worked with nurses and physicians and wrote a grant proposal for NIMH to study the liaison role. Shortly before the grant was funded, however, she and Sam decided to return to New York where he would pursue another graduate degree in mathematics. Although she searched for a clinical position, none were available at that time.

So, contrary to her desire to stay in clinical practice, she took a faculty position at New York University (NYU) in 1956. There she worked with Dorothy Mereness, another renowned psychiatric nurse developing a new graduate program in psychiatric nursing, and with the indomitable Martha Rogers, who was just beginning to articulate her theoretical framework for nursing. Working at NYU, Claire was pressured to get a doctoral degree, so she took one course during her first two years there.

In 1958, Claire and Sam adopted a baby boy whom they named Joshua. For two years she was a devoted full-time mother, and, although she enjoyed the role, she missed the challenges offered in nursing. "It turned out that all my friends who did not work were shopping, and I was never a shopper."

Claire talked with Dorothy Mereness, who encouraged her to challenge her mind by taking the Graduate Record Exam (GRE) in preparation for a doctoral program. She applied to and was accepted at New York University and was provided an NIMH scholarship. In the midst of all this, her son was hospitalized, allowing Claire to look closer at the issue of separation anxiety in children. This event determined the path of her doctoral research and much of her career to follow. "I think many people choose doctoral research related to some kind of inner problem they have, and, for me, it was obviously separation."

Because of her earlier readings about separation and her contacts with James Robertson, Claire and her husband would not leave their son's side during his hospitalization. For Claire, this experience reminded her of when she was a very small child and had experienced the trauma of separation. Claire's mother was ill when she was four months old, which was the reason she lived with her aunt and uncle until she was one-and-a-half years old. While she doesn't have a direct memory of that initial separation, she does recall feeling anxious when she was separated from her aunt and uncle and returned to her mother.

She remembers the torturous feeling of being pulled away from the adults she had become so attached to. Because of both her personal and professional experiences in working with children being separated from their parents, she knew this was the area where she could make a difference. The role parents play in their child's hospital recovery became the focus of her doctoral research study.

Claire's dissertation addressed the relationship between the recovery of hospitalized children and the effect parents had on recovery outcomes. The concept of "rooming in" came about as a result of Claire's work in this area. She finished her research in 1964, and in 1966 it was published as a monograph by F.A. Davis. As a result of her dissertation, she became somewhat of a celebrity as she was interviewed on the *Today* show with Hugh Downs and Barbara Walters. Says Claire, "There is no nursing journal of that era that did not have an article referencing my research on rooming in for toddlers and separation anxiety."

Her research helped to change the attitudes and rules about parental visitation in pediatric facilities. The research ended up being so powerful and well-received that in a follow-up survey Claire conducted 10 years later it was found that the majority of the pediatric units in hospitals in the country had already changed to allow for rooming in.

One of the most powerful lessons Claire learned from the success of her dissertation is that nurses can make changes in healthcare. "Many times nurses don't feel they are in a position to make change, but I want them to understand that nurses can make change happen providing they have both persistence and visibility for their work."

While Claire was still working on her doctorate, the Fagins adopted another son, Charles, and their family life was the top priority for these two parents, one in doctoral studies and the other in a very prestigious engineering position.

Upon completing her doctoral degree, Claire returned to NYU to develop and implement a new program in child and adolescent psychiatric/mental health nursing. This program, funded by NIMH, was extremely successful, and when Dorothy Mereness left NYU to become dean of the University of Pennsylvania's School of Nursing, Claire took over the leadership of both graduate programs at NYU.

Under her leadership, the student body increased in number and diversity, and the programs were extremely innovative in introducing community psychiatry to the students—then a very new development in the field.

These were intense years on the home front, as Claire's career was starting to soar. She was supermom at home and a high-ranking professional during the working hours. When Charles was in nursery school and beginning elementary school, she would take him to school in the morning and get on the subway to go to NYU. Then, in time for her son to leave school, she would jump back on the subway and do a marathon run to be sure she was back home in time for his arrival. "I could feel my heart pounding, and it was a wonder that schedule did not give me a heart attack!"

The money Claire earned in those days all went to pay for a housekeeper to cook and clean and to pay for part of the boys' school fees. Her schedule was work, family, and entertaining at dinner parties at home. She readily admits she wouldn't have been able to do it without the additional help at home.

Even with the heavy load of her family and work schedule, offers to climb the career ladder kept coming. She left NYU in 1969 for a position as chair of the nursing department at Lehman College, which is part of City University in New York. She wanted to develop an undergraduate program focusing on primary care, and she gathered a stellar group of faculty equally committed to making a difference in undergraduate education.

One of her innovative developments while at Lehman was a recruitment and retention model for minorities to enter and remain in nursing. In the late '60s and early '70s, this was a very progressive concept. It demonstrated great foresight and vision for the profession.

By working with a strong team of faculty, Claire developed a highly respected nursing program. She stayed at Lehman for seven years, with much success, but found that at the end of that time she was ready to leave. Claire had achieved much success while at Lehman and wanted the challenge of trying to create a similar success on a larger university campus that included a medical school and hospital. The family decided that she would scope out what was available across the country—with the only requirement being that they be able to go sailing.

At one point, she considered the University of California at San Francisco (UCSF) and even interviewed for the position of dean, but found the chemistry was not there on either side. Meanwhile, the University of Pennsylvania was aggressively recruiting Claire as its primary candidate for dean of its School of Nursing.

UNIVERSITY OF PENNSYLVANIA

Shortly after interviewing at UCSF, Claire received a call from the University of Pennsylvania asking her if she would be interested in applying for the dean's position in the School of Nursing. Initially, she had no interest in pursuing discussions, but the University of Pennsylvania search committee was on a mission, and they told her if she didn't come to them they would just show up on the campus at Lehman to meet her.

The last thing she wanted was for the recruitment team to show up on campus and disturb the faculty, so she conceded to visit Pennsylvania as a consultant to the search committee. Once she arrived on campus and met the search committee, the medical school dean, and the vice president for health affairs, she knew that they would not relent in their pursuit of her. She also knew immediately that it was a perfect fit.

She eventually accepted their offer to become dean of the School of Nursing at the University of Pennsylvania. With Claire at the helm as dean, large strides were made for the School of Nursing. "I am proud of many milestones at Penn, but among my high points were the support of foundations for programs, a research center, a primary-care program, an MBA/MSN program, a doctoral program, campus renovations, governmental grants in almost all areas of nursing, and private funding for faculty positions and scholarships."

An integrated faculty practice model, similar to what had been done at Rush University, Rochester, and Case Western Reserve, also proved to be very powerful. The University of Pennsylvania School of Nursing had achieved top recognition in the country for this program and for the research conducted during Claire's tenure as dean and for the "standing faculty" that had grown four times in size. "I was dean at the school longer than most others. The normal term is 12 years; the first appointment is for seven years, and then one goes up for review with a possible second term of five years. I stayed for 15 years."

Claire felt that her heart would always be with the University of Pennsylvania because of all the energy and passion she had poured into the School of Nursing. She believed any other administrative experience would be anticlimactic to her career. She also believed she had done what she came to do, so she stepped "up" into a full-time faculty role at Penn in the School of Nursing.

Claire assumed the role of Leadership Professor, an endowed chair, where she restarted her research work and focused on nursing home reform. She received a pilot grant from the Robert Wood Johnson Foundation after having started the work with a small university research foundation grant. She was in her mid 60s and a funded researcher, a notion that still makes her chuckle.

She had a one-year leave coming to her and decided to take it in two semesters split over two academic years. So in January of 1992, she became a scholar in residence at the Institute of Medicine to pursue her study of nursing home reform. For a three-month period, she and her husband lived in Washington, D.C., from Monday evening until Friday morning. When the three months were up, she went back to Philadelphia and returned to her full-time professorial position.

In the spring of 1993, Claire took the other half of her leave and went to the University of California at San Francisco as a presidential chair for the winter quarter and finished her research study on nursing home reform.

Following her project on nursing home reform, she and her husband took one of their customary trips to France. Claire kept up with the news in the states and while reading the *International Herald Tribune* in a café in Paris, she came across an article announcing the pending resignation of Sheldon Hackney, president of the University of Pennsylvania. She and Sam were to fly home two days later.

On the day of their arrival home, she was called and asked to schedule an interview with the chairman of the board of trustees to further discuss the position of president. Claire told her that she only wanted to be considered if they were really serious. "They told me before I went in for the interview that I was no long shot."

While she thought she would have to sell herself in that interview, she found instead that the interview was to offer her the job.

Her reputation all those years as dean of nursing and the many alumni visits and speeches she had given around the country laid the foundation for the final offer being given that first visit. Claire left the meeting feeling she knew what the presidency was about and what she was getting into.

University of Pennsylvania commencement, May, 1994. Dr. Claire Fagin and Marvin Lazerson. Behind Dr. Fagin are University of Pennsylvania Trustees chairman Alvin Shoemaker and commencement speaker, former HUD secretary, Henry Cisneros.

PRESIDENTIAL CHALLENGES

One thing she made clear from the start was that she did not want to be considered a candidate for the permanent position of university president. It would be a one-year post, and she was to start immediately.

She and her husband moved into the president's house on campus so they could be immersed in the experience. Immediately upon taking the position, both she and Sam knew that this immersion would be essential.

Claire was the first female chief executive officer of any Ivy League university in United States history. She was excited to get started and anxious about the pressure she felt to hold her own for women leaders. The outcome of her time as president would set the tone, perhaps, for other women who followed in her footsteps.

Claire realized two big statements were being made when she was selected as president of the university. The first statement being made was that she was a woman, and the second that she was a nurse.

Many on campus found it amusing that a person who had been dean of the School of Nursing was now in a role where the dean of the School of Medicine was reporting to her. On the surface, the role reversal could bring serious issues to the table with egos involved, but that was not how it turned out. Because Claire had a prior working relationship with the dean of the School of Medicine, the transition to higher authority with her new role was not an issue.

During her first week on the job as president, she was dealt one of her biggest setbacks as a leader. Two incidents erupted on campus with racial connotations, and both escalated far beyond anything she had ever dealt with before.

One was the "water buffalo" incident, which referred to something that had happened months before but had not surfaced. A group of African-American sorority sisters were celebrating an annual event and chanting below the dorm windows after midnight. A freshman shouted at them and called them water buffalos. He was charged with verbally insulting black females. Once the story surfaced, it hit the media outside the university and eventually attracted both national and international attention, in addition to taking up much of Claire's time. It also quickly introduced Claire to the relevant administrative policies and the faulty student judicial review system.

Over some period of time, and with many heated discussions, the women withdrew their case, but the problem never really went away; instead it just moved on to new territory. To this day, the story lingers and resurfaces in the media on occasion.

Claire's long history of working with minorities at NYU and Lehman did not seem to help her in this situation. While she was able to eventually build trust, it took much more time than she would have imagined.

The second incident, which occurred the day following her acceptance of the position, was the confiscation of the student newspaper, the *Daily Pennsylvanian* (*DP*), by members of the Black Student League. This incident also was widely covered in the press, and resolution of the issue was elusive. The stimulus for the confiscation was the regular appearance of a highly charged column criticizing African-American students. This was a First Amendment issue, and major national columnists and the paper's board never let Penn's administration forget this.

The students involved in this issue were great kids on both sides, and many meetings were held. By spring, there was a very constructive collaboration in the *DP* and *Vision* (a paper published by African-American students) on race on campus. In addition, *Firing Line*, William F. Buckley's debate program, was filmed on campus in December of 1993 with the topic being First Amendment conflicts. All of this led to some reconcilement on the part of the students although the case continued for some time.

Claire was additionally challenged by the fact that the majority of her executive administrative staff was new during the time she assumed the office of president. She would have to deal with her own high learning curve, in addition to working alongside a new VP of finance, a new interim provost, and a new senior VP of development and planning. Fortunately, the new interim provost had been the dean of the Graduate School of Education. This individual was a valued colleague and a great match to work alongside.

Claire's years as a psychiatric nurse could not have paid off any more profitably than in this new position. "My skills as a listener and communicator were critical given the issues and problems I was confronting. There still was many a day I could have sat down and cried, but I just didn't have the time!" The conditions going into the office of president were far more turbulent than Claire had originally expected.

One of the greatest career risks Claire knew about, when she agreed to accept the position of president, was that this experience would be the capstone of her administrative career, whether it ultimately turned out good or not. Upon assuming her new role, she did what she had always done be-

fore as a leader—she wrote a list of those things she needed and wanted to accomplish during her tenure.

With the problems and issues facing the university, it would have been easy to get distracted "fixing things" instead of creating momentum to move forward. Even with the rocky start, under her reign the university reached new heights as Claire gave much time and attention to alumni development, to faculty, and to students. In sum, by the time she left, the university was at higher rank than at any other time in its history and had its best-ever results in fund-raising.

REFLECTING ON LEADERSHIP

With much literature written about various leadership styles and differences between the genders in how each leads, Claire has no doubt that it was her years spent as a nurse that gave her the best foundational training to be successful in any leadership role. "As open communication is a key ingredient in any leader, I was well-prepared. I used every form of media, including the Penn TV system, town meetings, print, and radio in order to communicate with the campus population. I think I was successful in creating a family-type environment at the university, which replaced an atmosphere of distance or even distrust."

There is one lesson Claire would have liked to have mastered, but did not, and feels that it's a puzzle to be solved: how to institutionalize change. "This was not only my problem, but this is leadership's problem in general. When positive changes are implemented for any system or organization, there is no guaranteed way to ensure the changes are permanent after one leaves. In other words, it is easy for any new leader to quickly undo successes that have been achieved within an organization. I find that disheartening."

Another institutional observation that Claire makes regarding women leaders is that women leaders are scrutinized via a different set of standards than are their male counterparts. For instance, after leaving the office of president at Penn, an article was written in the November 1994 edition of the *Philadelphia Inquirer* about several women leaders at the university. One of the women being written about was Claire.

"The article contained niceties about the females that one would not read in an article about a man. Instead of describing solid characteristics of a leader, the article referenced my warmth and the affection that I inspire. The part of the article dealing with my accomplishments at the university greatly downplayed any good I had accomplished. And the examples I could give about the other women written about in that publication did them no justice either."

Situations such as these have made Claire a strong advocate for supporting women and highlights for her that sometimes women "do our gender the biggest injustice by failing to support one another, and we frequently stress the expressive parts of ourselves rather than the knowledge and skill characteristics." She thinks that this is all too often the case within the profession of nursing. Paraphrasing Suzanne Gordon, Claire says, "We focus on goodness and virtue rather than on knowledge."

Claire's interim term as president of the university ended in June of 1994. A woman was appointed president following Claire's interim year, and that fact provides her with great satisfaction about a job well done.

IN HIGH DEMAND AND YET TO RETIRE

Completing a successful reign as president of an Ivy League university is a difficult act to improve upon. Initially, Claire was welcomed back into a faculty role in the School of Nursing, but she knew that it was time for her to retire from the University of Pennsylvania.

Her post-university desire was to work as a consultant for foundations. As there did not seem to be opportunities in Philadelphia, in July 1996, Claire and Sam sublet an apartment in Manhattan, and within one month of living there, Claire was approached by the president of the Milbank Memorial Fund and asked to propose a study of the erosion of care. This led to the publication by Milbank titled *When Care Becomes a Burden* (Milbank Foundation, 2001).

In addition, Mathy Mezey, the director of the Hartford Institute for Geriatric Nursing at NYU, asked Claire to be chair of their board of advisors. Several years later she had the opportunity to work with the executive director and senior staff of the John A. Hartford Foundation, and in 1999 and 2000, helped them develop and implement a new initiative in geriatric nursing: Building Academic Geriatric Nursing Capacity (a program housed at the American Academy of Nursing).

Claire says that most of her nursing career paralleled where she was in her own developmental life, and "now I figured I was geriatric, I might as well be a geriatric nurse."

Claire is one of the key individuals involved in building the workforce in the area of geriatric nursing, which she considers to be the future of the profession. She views her current work as another mark in her career. "This actually is very thrilling for me. To be making another mark at this stage of my life amazes even me!"

After a long, successful career, Claire has yet to slow down.

One of the issues that she has always been most passionate about is changing the entry level of nursing to the baccalaureate level. "I ran into Mildred Montag one day in an elevator and asked her if she was satisfied with the changes she brought to nursing by introducing the associate degree nursing program. Her response was that she never meant it to be this way and found the situation as disheartening as I did."

Says Claire, "This had been my issue for years, upon years, upon years. Even I can't carry the torch anymore. This lack of agreement on credentials and pretending that nursing is a field that can prepare practitioners in two years is what is eroding the profession. Since educators can't seem to deal with this situation, our only hope is if the hospital nursing directors quit hiring any nurse who does not hold a minimum of a baccalaureate degree." (Aiken, et al. 2002, *JAMA*.)

Without a doubt, Claire's passion to move the profession forward is as strong as ever. She has innovative ideas and opinions she is only too willing to share with the younger generation of nurse leaders. Considering her contributions, it is easy to understand how she was made a "Living Legend" by the American Nurses Association, received the Distinguished Scholar Award from the American Nurses Foundation, and was named an Honorary Fellow of the Royal College of Nursing in 2002.

Aiken, L., Clarke, S., Cheung, R., Sloane, D., and Silber, J. (2003). "Educational levels of hospital nurses and surgical patient mortality." *JAMA*. 290,12.

CHAPTER 12

Linda H. Aiken

It is difficult to mention Linda Aiken's name without being reminded of her voluminous publications on healthcare public policy or her research on workforce, work environment, and patient outcomes—all work that has helped shape healthcare as we know it today.

In her remarkable career, Linda has left an indelible stamp on the value of nursing to patient outcomes. Her research on characteristics of magnet organizations has provided compelling evidence that these health-care institutions experience superior outcomes. As a result, the American Nurses Credentialing Center (ANCC) began designating them as Magnet Hospitals in 1994.

Her research quite simply gave new meaning to the word "magnet." Along the way, the world of healthcare discovered a formula for potential success, and the outcome has been a concept that a decade later is sweeping the nation.

Linda believes her work has benefited nursing primarily because it was "not nursing centric but healthcare centric" with nursing woven into the analysis. This approach has allowed her to expand public policy agendas, including that of nursing, to attract a more global audience.

Linda believes she succeeded in the public policy arena because she managed three careers—nursing, sociology, and health services research. In each of these areas her emphasis has been singular—outcomes. She always asked the important question: Are the right things happening?

Many of Linda's colleagues believe the word that best describes Linda is "vision."

She has a big-picture mentality, and she sees the horizon with re-markable clarity.

Her outcomes vision sounds simple—create an evidence-based practice—however, making that vision a reality often means challenging systems, processes, and infrastructures on a national and international scale to produce the evidence.

Linda is a risk taker who thrives on being told something is impossible. She is gifted in making the impossible look ordinary. She has taken the perspective of nursing to some of the most influential healthcare forums in the world because she is a nurse first. "I live and breathe my work through the eyes of the clinical nurse." So says Linda, and her work has proven it time and again.

EARLY INFLUENCES

Linda Harman Aiken, RN, PhD, FAAN, FRCN, was born on July 29, 1943, to Grace and William Harman. The Harman family, with two daughters and two sons, lived in Gainesville, Florida, just a few short blocks from the University of Florida campus.

The university culture is the predominant memory from her childhood. The family attended all the football games, often hosting the pre- and post-game activities at their home. Her mother was a University of Florida Alpha Chi Omega sorority alumni advisor, and university students frequently boarded with the family. In short, the Harman household was steeped in the University of Florida tradition. As a result, Linda was destined to be a Florida Gator. However, the University of Florida had academically rigorous standards, and Linda had to work feverishly to assure her acceptance.

The good news for nursing is that the University of Florida had a newly created College of Nursing by the time Linda was college bound, or she might have selected another career. When it came time for college, Linda and her mother assumed that her career options were limited to teaching and nursing because "that was what women did." Linda's mother, who graduated from the College of William & Mary, was always a tremendous influence in her life, and she strongly imprinted on her children that women must obtain an education. She also drove home the point that women should be financially independent. Linda's mother was a teacher, and her father was a businessman who later became a teacher, but teaching was not Linda's interest.

She recalls that the Cherry Ames series on nursing was a significant influence on her decision to consider nursing. The Cherry Ames books put an excitement and thrill into nursing that attracted Linda, along with many of her friends, to the profession.

THE NEW GENERATION OF NURSES

Linda and her husband, James Aiken, were high school sweethearts who married just before college. They made a commitment to see each other's educational dreams come true, and both achieved their doctoral degrees. The couple welcomed their first child, June Elizabeth Aiken, on January 6, 1961, one week before Linda began her freshman year at the University of Florida College of Nursing.

Linda Aiken and Dorothy Smith on the occasion of Dr. Smith's induction as a Living Legend by the American Academy of Nursing in 1996, about one year before her death.

One of Linda's first classes was taught by the dean of the nursing college, Dorothy Smith. On day one, Dorothy told her students that the University of Florida College of Nursing was creating a "new generation of nurses." The University of Florida had just opened a new health sciences center. This center was highly interdisciplinary and supported academic parity across disciplines. The University of Florida College of Nursing used the unification model of instruction that supported faculty in dual academic and clinical practice roles.

It is still difficult for Linda to believe, but Dorothy, the dean of nursing, took an interest in her as an 18-year-old university freshman. Dorothy later became a treasured mentor who helped shape Linda's career. She believes that Dorothy Smith is the most extraordinary nurse she ever met, and it was through Dorothy that Linda learned about vision and leadership.

This new generation of nurses was expected to ask the critical questions and lead the change in healthcare. Dorothy, who was also the chief of nursing practice at the University of Florida Shands Teaching Hospital, imprinted on her students from early on that evidence-based practice was essential, and that publishing was a professional responsibility. This was before the words evidence-based practice were ever spoken. Students were encouraged to create the scientific foundation for nursing if they couldn't find it in the literature. The expectations were explicit, and the bar was high.

According to Linda, this highly interdisciplinary and inquisitive learning environment created a cohort of "troublemakers" who went on to be national leaders. Her cohorts included Margretta Styles, Sue Hegyvary, Susan Sparks, and Patricia Chammings, to name a few.

Linda said that when she first read Marlene Kramer's book titled *Reality Shock,* she felt it was the story of the University of Florida cohorts. The troublemakers' reality shocks were that the rest of the nursing world was not practicing what had been taught to them at the University of Florida College of Nursing.

The world of clinical practice was light years behind Dorothy Smith's vision. Linda had been educated to see the big picture while the rest of the nurses were focusing on the moment, which created the sense of frustration, urgency, and impatience that drove her career. Linda became motivated to convert the rest of the world to the tenets of her University of Florida education—evidence-based practice, meticulous inquiry, and vision.

Linda believes her education at the University of Florida was a gift of a lifetime. Not only was she mentored by Dorothy Smith, but the dean of the medical school, George Harrell, and the provost of the health cen-

Photo courtesy of the University of Florida College of Nursing.

Dr. Linda Aiken, right, stands next to the bust of Dorothy M. Smith, founding dean of the University of Florida College of Nursing, in front of the wall dedicated in Smith's honor at the UF College of Nursing. Dr. Aiken is pictured with Dr. Kathleen Ann Long, dean of the UF College of Nursing.

ter, Sam Martin, became her mentors as well. They all contributed greatly to her career trajectory even after she left the university. She was exposed to the thinking of great leaders who took the time to prepare the next generation. From this experience, Linda learned that preparing tomorrow's leaders to surpass one's own accomplishments is the mark of a professional.

THE REALITY OF NURSING PRACTICE

In 1964, Linda became a staff nurse on the general and thoracic surgery unit at the J. Hillis Miller Health Center (Shands Teaching Hospital) in Gainesville, Florida. She worked for a year in this highly challenging unit prior to returning to the University of Florida College of Nursing for a graduate degree as a clinical nurse specialist (CNS) in heart surgery.

In 1967, the Aikens moved to Missouri. On July 28th of that year, their second child, Alan James Aiken, joined the family. The family was ready for a new adventure, and Linda was ready to spread her professional wings beyond Florida.

Linda became the first CNS at the University of Missouri in Columbia. She was excited about taking her skills to new frontiers, but she soon discovered that she was quite alone in her progressive ideas. The CNS role was new to the profession, and it initially created considerable tension within nursing—primarily due to lack of role clarity. Moreover, nurse managers and physicians were not sure how best to use the CNS. Linda had received a forward-thinking education and was teeming with ideas; however, she found her new environment dampened rather than exploited her capabilities. Linda also felt unprepared to direct colleagues who were twice her age with much more experience.

The CNS role required her to work diligently at building effective relationships. She describes this time as a period of professional isolation. She discovered that as a new generation nurse, there were plenty of op-

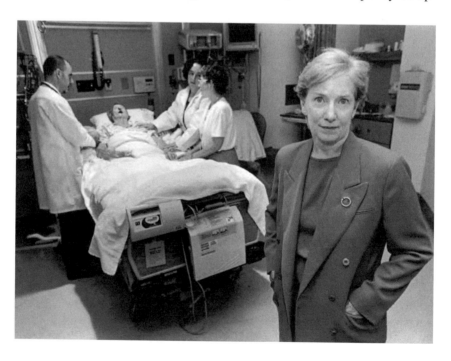

portunities to create an evidence-based practice, and subsequently, her interest in research blossomed.

Her first research study was conducted at the University of Missouri Medical Center in collaboration with Theodore Hendricks, an experienced researcher and clinical psychologist. Linda had observed a clinical phenomenon of postoperative psychosis in heart surgery patients. She noted these heart-surgery patients were psychologically normal preoperatively and consistently psychotic postoperatively. She hypothesized that a nursing intervention, such as systematic relaxation, could potentially reduce the incidence of psychosis.

Linda and Hendricks published their findings, documenting the statistically significant positive effect of the intervention in *Nursing Research* in 1971. This article launched Linda's prolific publishing career—the first of many publications that extol the impact of the nurse's role on patient outcomes.

Linda remembers the late 1960s as a time of expansive development in clinical advancements in the area of heart surgery. Intensive care units (ICUs) were nonexistent; nursing assistants were frequently clinically managing intubated patients, and cardiovascular surgeons were performing open-heart surgery in the laboratory on dogs on some days and on people other days.

It was a time of technological advancement in which the rules were being developed along the way. Observation and anecdotal responses were commonly the foundation of practice. Linda was the CNS heart surgery expert in a field with a paucity of research to guide practice. Everyone was learning together. As a leader, Linda was forced to fall back on what she knew was right, and that was seeking an evidence-based practice.

Linda recalls a physician-recommended change in practice secondary to recurrent tracheal necrosis hypothesized to be caused by sustained endotracheal tube cuff inflation. The cardiovascular surgeons concurred that the inflated cuff was logically diminishing tracheal capillary blood flow and thereby creating pressure ulcerations and tracheal necrosis. The surgeons suggested deflating the endotracheal tube cuff for 5-10 minutes per hour and removing the patient from the ventilator, thereby theoretically reducing the incidence of tracheal necrosis—this is similar to the practice of repositioning patients to avoid decubitus ulcers (bed sores). It made conceptual sense, yet Linda was observing a different outcome.

Soon after the recommended change in practice, several patients died unexpectedly. This significant and unexpected increase in mortality did not make sense. In response, Linda determined that the clinical outcome warranted scientific evaluation. She queried the physiological changes caused by cuff deflation and removal from the ventilator. Her concern was that the deaths may have been iatrogenic. What she discovered was that these ventilator patients were experiencing reduced carbon dioxide blood levels secondary to pulmonary hyperinflation resulting in a turning off of the patient's drive to breathe. The outcome was increased mortality. This was an unexpected chain of events, and one that had defied anticipated logic. The lesson learned was to assume nothing, question everything, and collect evidence along the way.

Linda loved working in hospitals but found the culture frequently made it difficult to institute fundamental change. She could impact individual patient outcomes by working long hours but felt incapable of correcting processes. Moreover, innovations that had been incorporated into practice were commonly lost due to a lack of institutional memory, something that is symptomatic of a high turnover of nurses and recurrent nursing shortages.

Linda believed the healthcare system was not working for patients or nurses. Patients were frequently left out of the care process and were vulnerable to poor outcomes. Accountability for patient outcomes appeared lost in dysfunctional systems. Nurses were paid a meager salary, and their work schedules were horrendous.

Linda concluded the healthcare system was broken, and it would take broad sweeping measures emanating from public policy to create the needed change. She had the vision to see beyond the daily minutia and to identify a more global healthcare infrastructure dysfunction. Linda was committed to be part of the solution, and she realized a doctoral education was an essential first step.

In pursuit of her doctoral degree, Linda had received a National Institutes of Health (NIH) Nurse Scientist Award. This award resulted in her admission to several top nursing schools, but she ultimately chose the University of Texas at Austin because her husband had been offered a position there as a counseling psychologist. Linda entered the sociology PhD program and specialized in demography.

Linda says she learned from her doctoral studies how to ask a question, answer the question in a rigorous manner, and report the findings in a meaningful format. Although the University of Texas at Austin had not been her first choice, it proved to be instrumental in providing the necessary tools and networking for her future career.

THE THINKING YEARS

In 1973, Linda moved to the University of Wisconsin to pursue a postdoctoral research fellowship in medical sociology with David Mechanic. She believes it was David Mechanic who taught her how to think about problems. He was a mentor who fueled her already inquisitive nature.

She learned soon after her arrival that the postdoctoral fellowship was sponsored by the Robert Wood Johnson Foundation (RWJF), and her grant was one of the first that had been awarded. The RWJF was in its infancy. By the time she had completed her postdoctoral education, the position of program officer for research and program evaluation at RWJF had been developed.

In 1974, as a result of her work and her relationship with the RWJF, Linda was invited to the RWJF office in Princeton, New Jersey, to interview for the program officer position with Robert Blendon, policy analyst researcher and vice president, and David Rogers, internist and president of RWJF. She was hired on the spot, and this was without a doubt a career-defining moment.

As a result of this role, she had the opportunity to work with some of the brightest minds in the country on research, public policy, and health-care issues. With the foundation being so new, it was very small in size and

Linda Aiken, with David Rogers (to her right), Secretary of Health and Human Services Dr. Otis R. Bowen (to her left), and Robert Blendon during the 1980s.

had no power structure. Thus, says Linda, "Anybody [on RWJF staff] could develop a $20 million program if they had a good idea and they could defend it to the chairman of the board and the rest of the staff."

Linda was the only nurse on the RWJF staff; this proved to be a double-edged sword. The foundation was dominated by a medical perspective, thus requiring her to establish a level of legitimacy beyond nursing. On the other hand, she was able to proffer and defend nursing ideas that otherwise would not have been considered by the foundation. As a result, this was an extraordinary period for Linda and nursing because she had found a perfect platform for developing nursing ideas and for following the quest of evidence-based practice.

Linda acknowledges that the RWJF environment was initially intimidating, but she was able to negotiate the enormity of the role thanks to several mentors who invested in her career. Margaret Mahoney, who was a senior vice president for RWJF and, later, president of The Commonwealth Fund, was influential as a role model for how women could effectively lead in a predominantly male world. Linda recalls that she studied Margaret Mahoney's decorum and timing in public forums. Margaret advised Linda to always be prepared and to know her facts. She always advised Linda to speak early in the meeting because the ability to add to the creativity and innovation diminishes as the conversation progresses. Margaret was masterful in knowing how to lead from a minority position, and she taught Linda the art of eluding gender bias.

Robert Blendon and David Rogers not only hired Linda but invested significantly in her career growth and development. They carefully groomed her to understand and debate the merits of ideas. Moreover, they acted as her sounding board and practice audience before she presented to the board. Robert and David coached her to think outside of the box and to draw from established knowledge in order to create new versions of old ideas.

Two examples of new versions of an old idea were the Clinical Nurse Scholars Program and the Teaching Nursing Home Program. The Clinical Nurse Scholars Program, initiated in the early 1980s, was a result of Linda taking a lesson from medicine and applying it to nursing.

Linda had observed that nationally the most influential physicians had a strong academically based clinical or research background. The power in medicine seemed less related to academic-based administrative success and more related to academic-based research or clinical success.

She noted that the most influential nurses tended to gain power through administrative positions. Nursing research was in the early stages of developing a scientific foundation. Linda argued that nursing needed a program that would prepare nurse scholars. She believed such a program would be a win-win for nurses and healthcare. Nurses, being the largest group of healthcare providers, had the potential to offer a unique perspective that was being lost due to a lack of scholarly preparation. According to Rheba de Tornyay, RN, PhD, FAAN, one of the directors of the program, this was Aiken's brain child, and "she was a great inspiration for the scholars."

Linda designed the program to provide nurses with a unique exposure to clinical, research, and leadership development experiences. The program was highly successful, and approximately 90 nurse scholars were infused into healthcare as national leaders and public policy participants. Most RWJF programs are funded for approximately five years, but the value of the Clinical Nurse Scholar led to program support for nearly a decade.

In the early 1980s, Linda also originated the Teaching Nursing Home Program. It was a time of highly publicized scandals portraying substandard quality of care in nursing homes. Linda believed strongly that poor outcomes were a result of a paucity of professional care in the setting. The missing link was too few nurses in nursing homes.

Linda also believed the growing elderly population and the poorly staffed nursing homes were on a collision course for even worse future outcomes. Her vision was to link nursing homes to nursing schools, creating a link between education and the delivery of quality care. This approach is analogous to the link between teaching hospitals and medical schools.

In the 1960s, the Veterans Administration (VA) was in a similar, high-profile state of disrepair. They had successfully corrected the quality of care by affiliating with medical schools and by infusing physician residency programs into the system. Nursing homes, Linda believed, needed a similar professional infusion.

The Teaching Nursing Home Program was instrumental in establishing the positive outcomes of geriatric nurse practitioners. This, in turn, contributed to the first direct reimbursement by Medicare for services provided by advanced practice nurses. This was a remarkable victory for nurse-practitioner recognition, and it paved the road for future reimbursement practices. The program raised the public's consciousness that nurses can be integral in solving seemingly hopeless healthcare challenges.

During the RWJF years, Robert Blendon and David Rogers molded Linda into a healthcare public policy professional with expert knowledge in nursing issues. By broadening her public policy knowledge and savviness, Linda enhanced her depth of respect from other disciplines. This respect further enabled her to develop greater influence, allowing her to impact fundamental change in healthcare and in nursing.

Referring to the RWJF years, Linda says they were "mind broadening," and that "it was at this time that I started developing into a real thinking person." Linda is quick to credit much of her success to her mentor relationships—it was their experience and savvy that facilitated her in developing her own brand of leadership.

THE IMPORTANCE OF ONE IDEA

Linda was president of the American Academy of Nurses (AAN) from 1979-1980 when the academy formulated the idea for perhaps its most important contribution to nursing—the magnet hospital study. As the AAN president, Linda was convinced the time had arrived for the academy to become relevant. According to Linda, the AAN had, up to that point, not made unique and influential contributions to healthcare. In her presidential address, Linda spoke about the future of hospitals and nursing homes as being a priority for nursing. She wanted to direct the AAN back to a clinical agenda. At this time, the nation was facing a nursing shortage that was having a crippling effect on hospital operations.

The Governing Council of the AAN put together a task force on nursing practice in 1981 in order to evaluate hospital organizational differences that either enhanced or impeded professional nursing practice. It was the leadership of the AAN members and national nurse leaders Margaret McClure, Muriel Poulin, Margaret Sovie, and Mabel Wandelt that drove this historic study. They noted that during a time of a nursing shortage, certain hospitals possessed "magnet-like" capabilities that helped to attract and retain quality nurses. Nurses at these institutions were simply more satisfied with the work environment.

The AAN hospital study established that these magnet-like organizations had a practice model that was different, but it was Linda who then asked the critical question—did these organizations have different outcomes? When Linda first started to study the magnet outcomes, she says, "We didn't get it right—we were studying the wrong things."

Linda initially used the American Hospital Association Nursing Personnel Annual Survey (discontinued in 1993) database to conduct an item review of such things as clinical ladders, tuition benefits, and vacancy rates to explain the outcome differences. The single-item review didn't work because, as individual variables, it didn't explain the lower mortality rate that she had discovered in the magnet hospitals. Linda and her group went back to the drawing board and reasoned that there had to be something more

fundamental here. She then experienced the "ah-ha" moment, thinking that perhaps the magnet concept was a more complex proposition. It was not one innovation but the presence of a common set of organizational characteristics in concert that explained the magnet outcomes. Linda explains they hit pay dirt by stepping back and examining the question from a slightly different perspective.

In her search for a global approach, she contacted Marlene Kramer. Marlene had done a significant amount of empirical work on the organizational characteristics of magnet hospitals. She had developed a quality-of-care-to-nurse-satisfaction instrument called the Nurse Work Index. This index was used to evaluate professional nursing practice.

Linda knew Marlene had a treasure-trove of data, and Marlene agreed to allow Linda to use her data to unscramble the magnet success puzzle. Linda believes her entire research program owes an enormous debt to Marlene. It was her data and instrument, with some modifications, that formed the basis for all of Linda's organizational studies. Linda feels strongly that this successful collaboration should be a leadership lesson for nursing: Sharing data could help to facilitate building bigger and better research programs.

When Linda began to study the impact of organizational attributes on patient outcomes, she strategically chose her study population. Many of her early magnet outcomes studies involved patients with acquired immune deficiency syndrome (AIDS). She states that she was not really interested in researching AIDS as a disease, but rather she used AIDS as a vehicle to study what she was interested in—the relationship of organizational structure and innovation to professional nursing practice.

Early in the acute-care treatment of AIDS, Linda observed that nurses were receiving an unusual amount of latitude to reorganize units because they were concerned about the ability to care for AIDS patients. Linda had the remarkable vision to focus her attention on this patient population as a natural experiment in hospital reform.

In 1994, Linda, Herbert Smith, a sociologist at the University of Pennsylvania, and Eileen Lake, currently one of the core faculty at the Center for Health Outcomes and Policy Research at the University of Pennsylvania, published a landmark study showing lower Medicare mortality in patients cared for by magnet hospitals. It was the strength of evidence generated by Linda's research that prompted the ANCC in 1994 to formally designate these nursing organizations as centers of excellence.

To appreciate the enormity of her contribution to legitimizing the magnet concept, all one needs to do is open the 2002 ANCC magnet manual and note that the entire page of research citations for magnet references is the same first author—Linda Aiken.

It was the work of Linda and her research team that has changed the world view of the relationship of work environment and patient outcomes. The United States is currently experiencing a tremendous upsurge in interest and support for magnet programs, and nurses owe Linda and her research team a great debt because this initiative has resulted in improved outcomes for patients and for nurses. Linda has also changed the nature of the debate on the nursing shortage to include evaluation of the nurse work environment.

This shift is a significant accomplishment. For years, hospital administrators have blamed insurance reimbursement, managed care, and patient acuities for nurse turnover and nurse vacancy rates. Linda has concluded the problem is not that there is a shortage of nurses—there are more nurses today than ever before. The real problem, Linda concludes, is that there is a shortage of hospitals where nurse want to work. Linda, through her thoughts and actions, reminds us to never doubt that the power of one idea or observation can generate innovative and creative research that can dramatically change the world view of practice.

HEALTH OUTCOMES AND POLICY RESEARCH

In 1987, David Rogers retired from the presidency at the RWJF, and Robert Blendon Blendon took a position at Harvard. Linda had spent 13 years at the RWJF as a research administrator and felt the time was right to make a change. She explored several different options, including deputy assistant secretary of the U.S. Department of Health and Human Services and various academic positions including deanships. Ultimately, she was drawn to the University of Pennsylvania because of Claire Fagin, dean of the School of Nursing, and Sam Preston, chair of sociology.

The University of Pennsylvania had aggressively recruited Linda and offered her an endowed professorship in both nursing and sociology. This provided the opportunity to operationalize a center that could support her vision for healthcare research. In January 1988, Linda developed the Center for Health Outcomes and Policy Research at the School of Nursing at the University of Pennsylvania.

Creating and sustaining the center is without a doubt the most difficult challenge of her career. She finds it amusing that today she is a professor, and she never wanted to be a teacher. She had never really paid attention to the fabulous platform or enabling force that academics could provide for catalyzing change. As her career progressed, she discovered that all change needs a platform to mobilize the concepts and extend influence beyond what an individual can do. As Linda matured and looked at the various platforms such as foundations, politics and public policy, private consulting, or academics, she decided that the university setting provided creative freedom, professional legitimacy, and invaluable networking and interdisciplinary resources.

As Linda began to assemble the center, she received great support from Claire Fagin, who was instrumental in assisting her in securing a grant from Smith Kline, a multinational corporation based in Philadelphia. This grant facilitated the recruitment of outside scholars (such as Eileen Lake) to the research team and expert consultation for quantitative methods and survey research. By 1990, the center had obtained NIH funding, and Linda was on her way to building a large interdisciplinary research program. Today, the center is one of the pre-eminent clinical research healthcare outcomes and public policy programs in the nation, if not the world.

As healthcare floundered, and nurses exited the profession because of unsafe work conditions, hospital administrators threw their hands in the air and blamed the Balanced Budget Act of 1997, reductions in reimbursement, and the penetration of managed-care plans as reasons why hospital budgets were cut or restrained. Linda refused to throw up her hands. The evidence was pointing to the importance of internal organizational decision making, and she wanted to specifically define what this meant without the burden of the U.S. healthcare system confounders.

She reasoned that an international study of countries—those that were not constrained by the Balanced Budget Act and U.S.-style managed-care plans—had the potential to illustrate that the problem of nurse retention was due to poor decision making within hospitals. If this question could be resolved, then perhaps problems could be addressed by intra-institutional changes.

Linda took a risk. She had been told over and over again by many people that an international study of this magnitude could not be conducted. Linda disagreed. She recruited seven influential interdisciplinary research teams from around the world, including hers at the University of

L-to-R, Linda Aiken, Christine Hancock, Jan Heinrich, and Marla Salmon in Bellagio, Italy, planning the international study on nursing retention.

Pennsylvania, to conduct a five-country study. The United States, Canada, the United Kingdom, Germany, and New Zealand would participate in the study. Each team would include a world-renowned scientist and a nurse researcher.

In 1996, Linda used a planning meeting at the Rockefeller Conference Center in Bellagio, Italy, to launch the study concept. She utilized an NIH grant to study U.S. hospitals in order to leverage additional funding for all seven teams. The University of Pennsylvania research protocol was used by all teams. Linda and her team of researchers worked side by side with the international researchers. This group of researchers conducting the study became known as the International Hospital Outcomes Consortium. She successfully acted as ambassador for the administrative differences inherent in the merging of five different and complex healthcare systems.

Linda recalls a critical juncture wherein the time had come for the United Kingdom to demonstrate "in-country" financial support to leverage

The International Hospital Outcomes Research Consortium in London, England, in July of 1999.

additional funding from the NIH. A decision on a pending proposal before a United Kingdom foundation had not yet been made. Christine Hancock, the general secretary of the Royal College of Nursing (RCN), stepped forward and provided a signature of assurance through the RCN to guarantee the in-country funding if the foundation did not provide funding. Ultimately, the Nuffield Trust of London did grant a portion of the funding, but the confidence and collegiality demonstrated by the RCN validated the consortium's shared research vision.

Linda was able to coordinate the disparate approaches into one focused study design that surveyed 43,000 nurses and 700 hospitals to evaluate quality of care, nurse satisfaction, and the overall state of healthcare in countries with distinctly different delivery systems. The study successfully demonstrated that in each of the five countries, the factors within the control of the hospital management, such as staffing adequacy, good physician-nurse relationships, administrative support of nurses, and career support of nurses, defined successful hospitals in their ability to attract and retain nurses and to produce superior outcomes.

The international data confirmed previous U.S. findings and thus bolstered the legitimacy and influence of other seminal studies. Linda believes the impossible was accomplished because of the strength of the team at the Center for Health Outcomes and Policy Research at the University of Pennsylvania. It was the leadership of the individual scholars and their ability to work as international team members that supported the success.

Leaders must be able to select a team that can individually and collectively execute a vision. Linda is gifted at building the team and driving the concepts, and the International Hospital Outcomes Consortium is a perfect example of this. Linda is particularly pleased that in addition to the important scientific papers from the project, they were also successful in strengthening the nursing research infrastructure in each of the participating countries. This will have a lasting effect on nursing research around the world.

Linda's research through the center has been bold and relevant. She has studied nurse staffing levels and nurse educational preparation related to patient mortality outcomes. Both topics are controversial and commonly generate heated debate. Being the quintessential researcher, Linda is focused on providing the evidence and generating the debate without picking sides. Nursing research, bedside nurses, healthcare providers, administrators, and, most importantly, patients owe Linda and her research team a huge debt of gratitude for their vision, courage, and persistence in creating an evidence-based practice—it has shown the United States and the world how to make the right things happen.

OPPORTUNITIES FOR NURSES

Linda feels one of the weaknesses of nursing is that nurses are not well read. She indicates there is richness in the literature that never gets discovered because nurses do not take the time to use the knowledge that could guide clinical practice and enhance professional communication. Linda suggests that the commonalities across different examples of clinical practice have the potential to empower the profession, and nurses simply have not taken advantage of this.

She states that nurses have made it an unfortunate habit of, as she says, "reproducing everything over and over and over and over again without realizing someone else has already completed the work." Nursing, in her opinion, needs to learn to expand on the work of other researchers and expert clinicians rather than continually reinventing the wheel. Moreover, nurses do not publish often enough or seek interdisciplinary journals for publication, something that would help to influence the development of science more broadly. According to Linda, it is a professional responsibility to disseminate findings so others can build on the work.

Linda is without a doubt one of the most prolific writers in nursing; however, she sympathizes with the angst nurses have with writing. She has a love/hate relationship with it and states that writing is hard work. However, she indicates the outcome is simple—no pain, no gain. Linda is adamant that if it is important enough to do, it is important enough to write about.

By publishing, the researcher puts a nugget of knowledge out for the world to critique and improve on so that the scientific base might expand. She believes fervently that writing is a skill set that must be learned. Unfortunately, most nurses do not learn to write in a scholarly manner until they pursue graduate education and, even then, few publish.

Linda's publications have captured the attention of medical journals such as the *Journal of the American Medical Association, Medical Care, Health Affairs, International Journal for Quality in Healthcare, Work and Occupations,* and *Health Services Research,* thereby taking nursing research and issues to the next level of legitimacy.

Linda has observed that nursing leadership has missed numerous opportunities. Some nurse leaders have neglected to make their voices heard because they either don't invest their time or they don't think strategically about how to use their leadership in the proper context. Linda has been instrumental in promoting nurse leaders to be considered for election to the Institute of Medicine (IOM), and often they forfeit leadership opportunities because they do not attend meetings or volunteer for committees, thereby missing opportunities to have their voices heard.

When nurse leaders do speak, too often they speak only about nursing. Nursing is crippled by the inability of nurses to speak to the broader context of the healthcare discussion, which is the purpose of the IOM. Nurses in these forums need to be utility players, says Linda, capable of contributing to all discussions by being informed and prepared. She also feels strongly that nurse leaders have a responsibility to mentor, develop, and convince future leaders that they can do things they hadn't considered possible.

According to Linda, Claire Fagin is the best example of this in nursing leadership. She muses that "after spending five seconds with Claire, you are convinced you can do something you never dreamed that you could do." Under this kind of leadership, anything is possible, and barriers become unexpected opportunities for creative solutions.

As a faculty member, Linda has a perfect setting to find and build future leaders. She loves this part of her job. Commonly, she will expose students to "big ideas and even conflicting ideas about how to solve them" by presenting contemporary problems. She is devoted to developing analytic thinking capacity and vision in the next generation.

According to Linda, education is not about knowledge, because knowledge changes too quickly; rather, education is about the process of thinking. This was the gift given to her by Dorothy Smith, David Mechanic, Robert Blendon, and David Rogers, and she is committed to passing this insight on to the next generation through her work and mentorship.

Linda believes some of the dysfunction in healthcare today emanates from significant inefficiency. Nurses should be at the bedside, but instead they spend too much of their time doing things over and over again in order to find solutions for issues or problems they should not have to solve. From her perspective, this is the unnecessary hunting and gathering in nursing practice that results in nurses being overworked and underutilized.

She states with concern that it is very difficult to be a bedside nurse today, and she believes that this is because nurse labor is cheap compared to its relative value. Hospital administrators have yet to feel pressured to adopt labor saving and information technologies that would increase efficiency and free nurses to get back to the bedside where they are of greatest value.

The good news is that in countries with modern healthcare systems, there is no alternative to nurses. So, nurses can't help but become more and more important. The bad news is that if we do not have enough people who are willing to be nurses, we are in a constant state of shortage that undermines everything that we want to achieve. Linda is concerned that the PhD in nursing has "slowed down the advancement of nursing research."

She is concerned that there are too many different kinds of doctoral programs, not enough faculty to support all the doctoral programs, and underutilization of interdisciplinary faculty. In addition, she feels that the standards for nursing PhD programs are not high enough. If not addressed, Linda believes, these issues present a real threat to the integrity of nursing PhD programs. She further believes that in some cases, PhD programs from other disciplines may better prepare nurse researchers. Nursing, she feels, will also remain sequestered if publishing is restricted to nursing journals.

SUMMARY

Linda is a troublemaker who has set the world of public policy on fire for nurses. Healthcare decision makers have been unable to avoid hearing the voice that constantly reminds them of the perspective from the largest healthcare provider in the United States—nurses. She has gone to international markets to seek solutions and continues to provide evidence that generates great and necessary debate. Her leadership has been grounded in education, risk-taking, courage, patience, rigor, and, most prominently, vision.

Linda Aiken with the Baxter Episteme Research Award from Sigma Theta Tau International in 2001.

Linda Aiken has a long list of recognition for her outcomes research, public policy initiatives, and leadership. In 2001, she received the Episteme Award from Sigma Theta Tau International. This award is the most prestigious award in nursing research. Equally impressive has been the interdisciplinary recognition of being named the individual winner of the Ernest A. Codman Award from the Joint Commission on Accreditation of Healthcare Organizations in November 2003 for her research on staffing levels and patient mortality. However, the true recipient of recognition in Linda's research is nurses and patients. The profession has an enhanced understanding of the value of nurses to the healthcare process, and patients have the potential of improved outcomes by using evidence to direct organizational decision making.

The vision she offers is so forward reaching that when you ask what is left to be done she responds with, "I have so many things I want to do. ... Specifically, I want to elevate nursing to a position where it can have greater influence because there is so much to offer." Influence, in Linda's world, is *evidence.*

Nurse leaders have often been criticized for getting farther away from understanding the challenges of those they lead as they move higher in the ranks as leaders. This could never be said of Linda. She is passionate about remaining relevant to those with the most knowledge for healthcare solutions—bedside nurses.

APPENDIX A

Leadership Challenges

CHAPTER I: LORETTA FORD

1. Loretta Ford was a leader who was known to be focused on the mission even in the face of criticism and isolation by peers. Can you identify a situation where you had an idea for innovation and creativity that went against the grain of the culture? How do you prepare and execute proposed change in the face of resistance or hostility?

2. In her journey, which changed the face of healthcare delivery, Loretta encountered numerous unexpected curves in the road that she could not have predicted. She indicated she dealt with the situations by defending her decisions utilizing data. Can you identify a situation you were involved in where the outcome may have been improved by the support of data? Can you give an example of how evidence-based practice has changed the direction of healthcare?

3. Loretta was driven by her focus on the question "What is best for the patients and how can nurses best meet the need?" She forced healthcare providers to respond to patients' needs rather than patients' responding to the healthcare capability. In today's multitude of healthcare crises, how can nurses contribute to the solution?

CHAPTER 2: SHIRLEY CHATER

1. As demonstrated in Shirley Chater's chapter, successful leaders do not have good fortune handed to them but demonstrate incredible levels of perseverance in order to accomplish their goals. Reflect upon a time in your career when it was your ability to really break down barriers through perseverance and determination that allowed you to be successful. How do you use these past successes for inspiration and strength in your new endeavors and challenges?

2. As a leader, Shirley mentioned numerous times throughout her chapter that, when faced with crises, the tool she relied on most was effective communication, both through active listening and her ability to articulate her vision. As a leader, how have you used communication to help "steady the waters" within your organization? Were you effective or ineffective? What did you learn from those experiences?

3. Shirley acknowledges one of the keys to her success as a leader has been her ability to surround herself with some of the best and brightest people in her arena. This quality of leadership made her a more effective leader because she could focus on the overall mission and vision of the organization, while not having to re-learn knowledge already possessed by members of her staff. This created a participatory work environment versus a controlling work environment. In the role of employee,

have you experienced either or both of these models of leadership within your company? How did you respond?

CHAPTER 3: JOYCE CLIFFORD

1. Joyce's brand of leadership was grounded in doing the "right thing" because it supported the professional growth of nursing and created a work environment that was only limited by imagination. If you had to sell a new nursing innovation that had no previous track record to hospital administrators or medical or nursing staff, how would you create the buy in? What aspects of your vision would you be willing to compromise? What would you refuse to compromise and why?

2. Under Joyce's leadership, the Beth Israel Hospital staff incorporated the talents of the "troublemakers" to get out of trouble. Can you give some examples in your education or career where troublemakers identified significant system or infrastructure problems that were then ignored by leadership? How would you utilize the troublemakers in your organization? What would it take to develop their leadership?

3. Joyce was a master at building the leadership skills of her staff. She believed all staff members were potential leaders. Joyce built the vision and then got out of the way so that her colleagues could turn the vision into a reality. How would you define the leadership team of your organization? Describe how your organization mirrors or deviates from the professional practice model created at the Beth Israel Hospital.

CHAPTER 4: LUTHER CHRISTMAN

1.   Throughout this chapter, Luther cites numerous occasions when he courageously spoke his mind against popular opinion. Have you ever been in this position professionally where you had the opportunity to speak your mind and be different, or you went so far as to seek popular opinion against your better judgment?

2.   Luther took steps early in his career to demonstrate his abilities as a successful visionary. Some of his ideas were accepted and used, while others were not so widespread. Regardless, he demonstrated repeatedly the mind of a visionary and how it works. What cutting-edge ideas do you think would improve the profession? What stops you from implementing them, even at a lower level?

CHAPTER 5: VERNICE FERGUSON

1.   Vernice best illustrates how she persevered career and life challenges by having a mantra that reminded her "to never take the back seat" and "never accept no for an answer." Reflect on what key internal motivator you use to remind yourself during tough times that you will not give up the battle.

2.   The majority of Vernice's leadership demonstrates that her primary focus was on empowering nurses and moving them out of the shadow of organized medicine. She kept a perspective that if it was good enough for the physicians, then she would seek it for nurses. Reflect on how many of your decisions as a leader parallel the servant leadership model of moving the agenda of other individuals forward without direct reward to you.

3. Vernice worked hard in her career and achieved great success as a leader but always remained a "nurse's nurse." There never was a doubt who or what Vernice was fighting for throughout her career. Many times, as leaders advance, they are criticized for forgetting what it was like earlier in their careers. Reflect upon the decisions you make as a leader and the "battles" you choose to take on. What is most important to you as a leader? Is it evident to those around you?

CHAPTER 6: ADA SUE HINSHAW

1. Ada Sue knew as a nurse researcher that language would be central to her success. This meant careful selection of words for their inclusion or exclusion into her writing and communication. She had to be crisp, clear, and convincing in her dialogue to move her research agenda forward. Give an example of how your choice of language has either helped or hurt your leadership outcome. Describe instances where "nursing language" has isolated the profession or, conversely, invited interdisciplinary participation.

2. Leadership requires an element of knowing what you do *not* know. When Ada Sue became a director at the NIH, she had limited experience with large government agencies and limited interactions with congressional members. Think about the times you found yourself in an unfamiliar situation. What did you do to learn more about the situation? What strategies did you use to move forward?

CHAPTER 7: FAYE G. ABDELLAH

1. Faye G. Abdellah illustrates for leaders how she successfully critiqued her own leadership style in order to be more effective in making change. Realizing she was not getting the results she wanted by one style, she became more politically correct and diplomatic, without changing the essence of who she was or what she believed was worth fighting for in nursing. Reflect on your own leadership style and ask yourself how effective you are in getting things accomplished. What would your subordinates/colleagues say about your leadership style? Is there anything you would like to change about your style of leadership? What could you do to initiate that change?

2. Faye described through trial and error how important it is to "know your audience" in order for change to occur. Whether working with the nationals in Africa or teenage girls in the states, Faye had to assess what was viewed as important to each group of individuals and provide that before her message could be heard. Describe times in your career or times in a leader's career you respect when creative thinking and ingenuity were used to accomplish a goal that had initially failed.

CHAPTER 8: SUE DONALDSON

1. Sue's leadership developed in two very different worlds—nursing and physiology. When she completed doctoral study, she discovered the art and science of both worlds were engrained in her work. Give an example of how differing and sometimes competing influences have impacted your work either positively or negatively. Can you describe a circumstance when you had to change your world view to achieve your goals?

2. One of the benefits of Sue's relationship with Dorothy Crowley was the opportunity to debate the subject of nursing research. She and Dorothy pushed each other to think about what contributed to the debate and how they could apply the concepts differently. How could you develop opportunities for this kind of intellectual exercise in your work environment? What could you do to create more freedom of thought and enhance creative contribution?

CHAPTER 9: GRETTA STYLES

1. One of the keys to Gretta Styles' successful career as a leader is her ability to become an expert in a niche area, while continuing to further her education. As a leader, what niche area would you most like to be known for? What is your plan for distinguishing yourself from all other leaders in that niche area?

2. Gretta has demonstrated the ability to leave a profound and lasting legacy for the profession. What legacy would you most like to be remembered for as a leader? Are you on the path to making it happen? If not, why?

CHAPTER 10: RHEBA DE TORNYAY

1. Rheba is a leader who was ignited by an academic system she believed was counterproductive to attracting and retaining the best students. She was committed to changing the face of academics. Rheba wrote a book that facilitated the art and science of teaching. If you were about to embark on a professional passion, what would the title of your book be?

How would you attract and retain the best and brightest in your area of practice?

2. As colleagues discuss Rheba's talents, it is clear she knew how to get the best out of the group. Her diplomacy and ambassadorship contributed to consensus leadership. Rheba understood, through experience, the value of the "greater good" for the future of nursing. Can you describe a "greater good" situation that may have resulted in a personal sacrifice for a professional gain?

CHAPTER 11: CLAIRE FAGIN

1. Early in Claire's career she learned a valuable lesson that offered her inspiration and perseverance for the challenging times that were yet to occur. The lesson was about how nurses can actually make a difference in healthcare. Claire was able to witness firsthand the impact her dissertation had on pediatric units across the country, and this in turn gave her strength to continue pursuing the advancement of nursing and the improvement of patient care. As a leader, what opportunities have you taken to institute change where you are employed or for the profession? How successful were you in making a lasting impact?

2. Claire highlights in her chapter how courage and risk-taking are linked for a leader. After accepting the position of president at the University of Pennsylvania, Claire knew this would be the capstone of her career, no matter how it ended. A savvy and strong leader will generally embrace challenge instead of shying away, even when the risk might be quite high. Ask yourself, when was the last time you took a risk in your career? How

did it feel internally as you were going through the journey? Did you finish a stronger leader because of the risk?

3. Claire offered a challenge to the reader at the end of her chapter. While positive change is good, how does a leader ensure the change is institutionalized and remains in place long after the leader is no longer at the organization?

CHAPTER 12: LINDA AIKEN

1. Linda was exposed to mentors early in her career who contributed to her belief that she was expected to change the face of healthcare. Dorothy Smith, from day one, let her know she was a member of a new generation of nurse leaders. Describe how expectations impact actions in your work environment. Can you give an example of where the outcome was positively or negatively impacted by the stated or unstated expectation of performance? How would you enhance vision when your colleagues are mired in the moment?

2. One of Linda's gifts is to create opportunity when others could not see the possibility. She is an example of someone who has executed major ideas and has been able to do so by creating a foundation of credibility. Define what professional credibility means to you and how you could use your professional reputation to accomplish a multilevel project. Who would you need on your team to bolster your credibility?

3. Linda has had a remarkable publishing career. She was not satisfied unless she was sure nurses were practicing according to the strongest evidence. Linda always came back to the outcome question—did it make a difference? Can you think of a topic that you should have had published because you experienced something different and important in your practice that should be shared with the public and other healthcare professionals? What does evidence-based practice mean to your practice? How can you contribute to creating this level of excellence?

APPENDIX B

Biographical Summaries

FAYE GLENN ABDELLAH

Faye Glenn Abdellah, RN, EdD, ScD, FAAN, is recognized internationally for her public service in nursing, education, and healthcare. She holds Bachelor of Science, Master of Arts, and Doctor of Education degrees from Columbia University, New York, and has done graduate work in the sciences at Rutgers University, New Jersey. Dr. Abdellah is the recipient of 12 honorary degrees from universities that have recognized her pioneering work in nursing research, in the development of the first nurse scientist program, as an international expert in health policies, and for making invaluable contributions to the health of the nation. She was the chief nurse officer and deputy surgeon general with the U.S. Public Health Service, where she retired with the rank of rear admiral. She was the first nurse to hold the rank of rear admiral, two stars, and the first nurse to hold the title of deputy surgeon general for the United States.

She is a national pioneer in nursing research in the areas of long-term care policy, mental retardation, the developmentally disabled, home health services, aging, hospice, and AIDS. She managed and coordinated these activities in health-based and nonhealth-based agencies, directing efforts to improve the overall quality of health for all Americans. Abdellah was actively involved in working with the U.S. surgeon general in the formation of national health policies related to AIDS, drug addiction, violence, smoking, and alcoholism.

As part of her international health outreach role as a nurse and health services consultant, she has been a member of official U.S. delegations on exchange missions to the former Soviet Union, Yugoslavia, and France, and she was designated as coordinator for nursing for the U.S.-Argentina Cooperation in Health and Medical Research Project. In 1974, she served as a World Health Organization research consultant for the Multinational Study on the International Migration of Physicians and Nurses, and she was a member of the 1976, 1979, and 1983 U.S. delegations to the World Health Assembly in Geneva, Switzerland.

In 1976, at the request of the American ambassador, Abdellah provided consultation to the Portuguese government in the development of programs for the care of the elderly and disabled. Also in 1976, Abdellah provided consultation to the faculty of Tel Aviv University in Israel on long-term care and nursing research. In 1977, 1992, and 1996, Abdellah provided consultation to the Japanese Nursing Association on nursing education and research.

In 1978, she served as a member of theNational Council of Health Care Services on a visit to the People's Republic of China to study the care of the elderly and mentally retarded. In 1982, by invitation of the health ministers for New Zealand and Australia, Abdellah participated in a seminar series for nursing home leaders in Australia, and she participated in nursing education and research meetings in New Zealand.

In Tel Aviv, Israel, in 1985, Abdellah met with 94 chief nursing leaders from member countries who belong to the International Council of Nurses. The purpose of this first-time meeting was to develop a strategy for working with the director general of the World Health Organization to provide nursing leadership in achieving improved health for all by the year 2000.

She has authored or co-authored more than 153 publications, some of which have been translated into six languages. Abdellah is the recipient of 90 professional and academic honors. In 1994, she received the Living Legend Award from the American Academy of Nursing; in 2000, she was inducted into the National Women's Hall of Fame; and in 2002, she was awarded the G.V. Montgomery Award. She has the unique honor of being elected as a charter fellow of the American Academy of Nursing where she later served as vice president and president. Her Sigma Theta Tau International awards include the Excellence in Nursing award and the first Presidential Award. In 1989, she was recognized with the prestigious Allied Signal Award for her pioneering research in aging. The Institute of Medicine recognized her contributions to the environment and healthier lifestyles in 1992, with the Gustav O. Lienhard Award. Her military awards include the Surgeon General's Medallion and Medal, two Distinguished Service Medals, the Uniformed Services University of the Health

Sciences Distinguished Service Medal, the Meritorious Service Medal, the Secretary of the Department of Health Education and Welfare Distinguished Service Award, and two Founders Medals from the Association of Military Surgeons of the United States.

LINDA AIKEN

Linda H. Aiken, RN, PhD, FAAN, FRCN, is director of the Center for Health Outcomes and Policy Research. She is also the Claire M. Fagin Leadership Professor of Nursing, professor of sociology, and senior fellow at the Leonard Davis Institute for Health Economics at the University of Pennsylvania. Dr. Aiken is the individual winner of the 2003 Ernest A. Codman Award from the Joint Commission on Accreditation of Healthcare Organizations (JCAHO) for her leadership in utilizing performance measures to demonstrate relationships between nursing care and patient outcomes. She and her co-authors were honored in 2003 with the Health Services Research Article of the Year Award by AcademyHealth for their paper in the *Journal of the American Medical Association* documenting the effect of nurse staffing on surgical mortality. Aiken leads the International Hospital Outcomes Consortium, which studies the impact of nursing on patient outcomes in eight countries.

Aiken is a member of the Institute of Medicine of the National Academy of Sciences, the American Academy of Arts and Sciences and the National Academy of Social Insurance, and she is a Woodrow Wilson Fellow of the American Academy of Political and Social Science. Aiken is a fellow and former president of the American Academy of Nursing and an honorary fellow of the Royal College of Nursing of the United Kingdom. Prior to coming to the University of Pennsylvania in 1988, she was vice president of the Robert Wood Johnson Foundation. Aiken received her bachelor and master degrees in nursing from the University of Florida, Gainesville, and her PhD in sociology and demography from the University of Texas at Austin. She was a postdoctoral research fellow in medical sociology at the University of Wisconsin, Madison.

SHIRLEY SEARS CHATER

Shirley Sears Chater, RN, PhD, FAAN, a native of Pennsylvania, received a diploma in nursing from the Hospital of the University of Pennsylvania, a Bachelor of Science degree in nursing from the University of Pennsylvania, a Master of Science degree in nursing from the University of California, San Francisco, a PhD in education from the University of California, Berkeley, and a certificate from the Massachusetts Institute of Technology, Sloan School of Management. Chater has been elected to the American Academy of Nursing, Institute of Medicine of the National Academy of Sciences, the National Academy of Public Administration, and the National Academy of Social Insurance.

From 1993 until February 1997, Chater served as commissioner of the United States Social Security Administration where she launched a "Put customers first strategy" and successfully implemented redesign efforts to increase efficiency. She served as the country's 12th commissioner of the Social Security Administration where she oversaw more than 1,500 district offices across the country while administering one of the largest and most complex of the U.S. federal programs. Among her other positions, Chater served as an associate with the American Council on Education, Division of Academic Affairs and Institutional Relations in 1983-1984 and as senior associate of the Association of Governing Boards of Universities and Colleges from 1984-1986. She was vice chancellor for academic affairs at the University of California, San Francisco from 1977-1982, and she was the first woman to hold a high-level administrative position in the system. She held faculty appointments from 1964-1986 in the Department of Social and Behavioral Sciences, School of Nursing, at the University of California, San Francisco and in the School of Education at the University of California, Berkeley.

Chater is currently adjunct professor for the Institute for Health and Aging at the University of California, San Francisco, School of Nursing. From 1986-1993, she was president of Texas Woman's University (TWU) in Denton, Dallas, and Houston, and she initiated major restructuring there, resulting in increased enrollment and fiscal stability. Texas Woman's University is a public university with 10,000 students, four campuses, and 600 faculty members. Chater instituted a strategic planning process that involved faculty, staff, students, and administrators, leading to a restructuring and streamlining of operations so that student enrollment increased from 7,000 to 10,000 with no corresponding increase in budget. Under her leadership, TWU maintained one of the highest minority enrollments (20%) in the Texas state system.

In 1991, Chater was appointed by Governor Ann Richards as chair of a 29-member state health task force to address the urgent need for dependable, accessible, and affordable healthcare for Texans. Many of the more than 100 recommendations the task force presented to the governor and legislature (including an immunization initiative and insurance reform) have been written into law. She currently serves as chair of the national advisory committee for the Robert Wood Johnson Foundation Executive Nurse Fellow Program and is an independent lecturer and consultant. Chater lectures on public policy and on economic and social issues concerning the aging population in the United States. She has published extensively in the fields of management theory, health sciences, academic administration, and research methodology. Chater has numerous honors and awards to her credit. She holds 12 honorary doctoral degrees, remains a longstanding member of Sigma Theta Tau International, and was honored in 2000 as a Living Legend by the American Academy of Nursing.

LUTHER CHRISTMAN

Luther Christman, RN, PhD, FAAN, is recognized internationally as a leader, innovator, and consultant to nursing schools, healthcare agencies, and professional organizations in nursing and medicine. Dr. Christman holds a Bachelor of Science in Nursing, Master of Science in Clinical Psychology, and a doctorate in sociology and anthropology. He is the recipient of two honorary doctorate degrees, one from Thomas Jefferson University (1980) and the other from Grand Valley State University (1998). Christman has consulted nationally to more than 14 countries in the area of nursing education and healthcare and has won numerous recognition awards. He has been a visiting fellow in New Zealand for the Nurses' Education and Research Foundation. In 1991, Christman received the Lifetime Achievement Award from Sigma Theta Tau International, and, in 1996, he was awarded the Living Legend Award by the American Academy of Nursing.

Christman was the first male dean for a U.S. nursing school. He was appointed dean of Vanderbilt School of Nursing in 1967 and served in that capacity through 1972. During those same years, he also held the position of director of nursing for Vanderbilt University Hospital. Christman was also the first to employ African-American women as faculty members at Vanderbilt University. He was the founding dean of Rush University in Chicago (1972) and is dean emeritus of the College of Nursing at Rush University. While Christman was dean at Rush University, he also held the position of vice president of nursing affairs, Rush-Presbyterian-St. Luke's Medical Center. He introduced the nationally recognized Rush Model for Nursing, which stresses a faculty comprised of expert clinical nurses, the use of a physician-nurse team, quality assurance, and research.

The Rush Model covers all aspects of nursing, from the presence of an all-registered nurse staff to the system of compensating nurses. It includes decentralized decision making about patients' needs and centralized allocation of nursing personnel. While at Rush University, Christman also held the position of professor of sociology in the Rush School of Medicine (1972-1978).

Christman was named a distinguished alumnus by Temple University in 1996, by Rush University in 1997, and by Michigan State University in 1999. He received the Lifetime Achievement Award from Sigma Theta Tau International for his contributions and superior achievement in nursing practice, research, education, creativity, leadership, and high professional standards. In addition, the American Association for Men in Nursing, an organization founded by Christman, presents the Luther Christman Award annually. The first recipient of this award was President Gerald Ford in 1975. Christman is a leading expert in nursing education, has worked in the field since 1939, and has been the subject of numerous news and magazine articles.

Christman was president of Christman-Cornesty and Associates from 1990-1997; he chaired the White House Committee on Children and Youth, Forum 10, in August 1970; and he was a fellow with the National League for Nursing, American Academy of Arts and Science from 1950-1960. Other accolades include the Jesse M. Scott Award in 1998; honorary lifetime membership with the American Association of Critical-Care Nurses was bestowed on him in 1997; the Elinor Frances Reed Distinguished Visiting Professorship at the University of Tennessee was awarded to him in 2000; the Marguerite Rodgers Kinney Award for a distinguished career was given to him in 2002; and the Lifetime Achievement Award from the Tennessee Nurses Association was presented in 2002.

Christman has written numerous articles and books on nursing and healthcare, and he is recognized as a distinguished international speaker. Two doctoral dissertations have been written on the subject of Christman's contributions and his future visions for the profession of nursing.

JOYCE C. CLIFFORD

Joyce C. Clifford, RN, PhD, FAAN, is the former senior vice president for nursing programs at CareGroup in Boston. Prior to the merger of the Beth Israel and Deaconess hospitals, she was the vice president and nurse-in-chief at Beth Israel Hospital in Boston, a position she held for more than 25 years before she established The Institute for Nursing Healthcare Leadership, an affiliate of The Carl J. Shapiro Institute for Education and Research at Harvard Medical School and Beth Israel Deaconess Medical Center. Clifford serves as the executive director of this institute. A graduate of St. Anselm College, she received her master's in nursing from the University of Alabama and a doctorate in the field of health planning and policy analysis at the Heller School of Brandeis University. She is a fellow of the American Academy of Nursing, a member of multiple professional organizations, and a former president of the American Organization of Nurse Executives. She was a member of the board of trustees of the American Hospital Association from 1991 to 1994. In addition, she is a trustee for her alma mater, St. Anselm College, and was the first nurse to be a member of Harvard Medical School's Admissions Committee. Clifford also serves on the editorial advisory boards of several nursing journals.

Clifford is an established author and consultant on the subject of organizational restructuring and the development of a professional practice model. She has spoken both nationally and internationally in countries such as Norway, Finland, Japan, New Zealand, Australia, Israel, and the Netherlands. Her past nursing experiences include multiple nursing positions and active and reserve duty in the U.S. Air Force Nurse Corps where she achieved the rank of major. She has served on the faculty of several nursing schools including the University of Alabama in Birmingham and Indiana University in Indianapolis. She currently holds a visiting scholar appointment at Boston College School of Nursing and is a lecturer in medicine at Harvard Medical School in Boston.

Clifford has been recognized for her contributions by receiving the American Hospital Association's Award of Honor in 1990; she has received honorary doctorate degrees from St. Anselm College, Simmons College, and Indiana University; she has received numerous awards, including the national Sigma Theta Tau International Dorothy Garrigus Adams Founders Award for Excellence in Fostering Professional Standards and the Massachusetts Organization of Nurse Executives Award for Excellence in Nursing Administration. In 1996, she received the American Organization of Nurse Executives (AONE) Leadership Award. In 2003, she received the AONE Lifetime Achievement Award. She was a member of the charter class of the Johnson & Johnson-Wharton Fellows Program in Management for Nurse Executives; she served as a commissioner for U.S. Health and Human Services Secretary Otis R. Bowen's National

Commission on Nursing in 1988; and, in 1995, she was a member of the committee on the Adequacy of Nurse Staffing of the Institute of Medicine. She has served on the Robert Wood Johnson Foundation (RWJF)-sponsored Council on Economic Impact of Health System Change, and she is currently a member of the National Advisory Committee of the RWJF Executive Nurse Fellows Program.

RHEBA DE TORNYAY

Rheba de Tornyay is professor and dean emeritus at the School of Nursing, University of Washington. A graduate of Mount Zion Medical Center School of Nursing in San Francisco, California, she received her bachelor's degree in nursing and her master's degree in education from San Francisco State University. In addition to her earned doctoral degree from Stanford University, she holds three honorary doctorates.

Prior to joining the faculty at the University of Washington, she was dean and professor at the University of California, Los Angeles, School of Nursing, a Professor at the University of California, San Francisco, School of Nursing, and professor and chair of the Department of Nursing at San Francisco State University. She has held positions in hospitals and community health agencies.

She was the first president of the American Academy of Nursing, and her professional associations include being a member of the Institute of Medicine, National Academy of Sciences. She has been a member or an officer of the board of directors of a number of nursing and health organizations. Her honors include the 1982 Woman of Achievement, Women in Communications, Seattle Chapter, the Distinguished Nursing Alumna Award from Mount Zion Hospital and Medical Center, the Sr. Bernadette Armiger Award from the American Association of Colleges of Nursing, the Isabel Stewart Award for Excellence in Nursing Education from the National League for Nursing, and the Second Century Award from Columbia University, and she has been designated as a "Living Legend" by the American Academy of Nursing.

She is a trustee emeritus of the Robert Wood Johnson Foundation having served for 10 years as the first woman trustee. She has authored two books and more than 100 book chapters, articles, and editorials. Her primary interest is in aging and long-term care. She was a member of the San Francisco Institute on Aging for many years, and currently serves on the Regional Advisory Board of the Northwest Geriatric Education Center.

SUE KAREN DONALDSON

Since 1994, Sue Karen Donaldson, RN, PhD, FAAN, has held a dual roll at Johns Hopkins University in Baltimore, Maryland. She is professor of nursing for the School of Nursing, and she is professor of physiology for the School of Medicine. She also holds a joint appointment in oncology for the School of Medicine and for the Johns Hopkins Hospital. From 1994-2001, she was dean of the Johns Hopkins University School of Nursing. During her tenure, $32 million was raised for nursing, and the first building dedicated to the Hopkins School of Nursing was designed and built.

Dr. Donaldson received her Bachelor of Science in 1965 and her Master of Science in Nursing in 1966. Both degrees were from Wayne State University, Detroit, Michigan. She earned her PhD in physiology and biophysics in 1973 from the University of Washington, Seattle. Prior to moving to Johns Hopkins, Donaldson was a faculty member at the University of Washington, Seattle from 1973-1978 and at Rush University, Chicago, Illinois, from 1978-1984. She was with the University of Minnesota in Minneapolis, Minnesota, from 1984-1994, where she held the dual roles of professor of physiology for the School of Medicine and professor of nursing for the School of Nursing. While at the University of Minnesota, she was the Cora Meidl Siehl Chair for Nursing Research and the founding director of the Center for Long-Term Care of the Elderly.

Donaldson is a pioneer in the development of nursing research and is known internationally for her basic science research in cellular skeletal and cardiac muscle physiology. She has held leadership positions in the Biophysical Society and the American Heart Association. Donaldson served on the advisory committee of the Robert Wood Johnson Foundation Clinical Nurse Scholars Program from 1986-1991. During the period from 1998-2003, she served as a member of the advisory council for the National Institute of Arthritis and Musculoskeletal and Skin Diseases (NIAMS) at the National Institutes of Health.

In 1992, Donaldson was inducted as a fellow in the American Academy of Nursing (FAAN). In 1993, she was elected to the Institute of Medicine (IOM) of the National Academies.

She currently serves as a member of the Special Medical Advisory Group (SMAG), U.S. Department of Veteran Affairs. Donaldson continues to serve as the American Academy of Nursing (AAN) representative to the National Coalition for Health Professional Education in Genetics (NCHPEG) and as a member of the AAN Expert Panel on Genetics, a group that she chaired in 2001-2002. Donaldson is currently chair of the Genetics

Committee, Council on Collegiate Education in Nursing, Southern Regional Education Board. She serves as a consultant to the NIH, the National Research Council, and other research organizations and academic institutions.

CLAIRE FAGIN

The career of Claire Fagin, RN, PhD, FAAN, has blended an interest in consumer health issues with professional health and nursing issues. She is known for her efforts with consumers and health professionals for creating new paradigms for access and quality. Dr. Fagin is a consultant to foundations, national programs, and educational institutions. Currently, she is director of the John A. Hartford Foundation National Program, Building Academic Geriatric Nursing Capacity. She served as dean of the School of Nursing at the University of Pennsylvania from January 1977 to January 1992. During her tenure as dean, the school developed landmark education and research programs, a privately funded research center, and a PhD program; had the most faculty members of any nursing school in the American Academy of Nursing and the Institute of Medicine; and was ranked number one by *U.S. News and World Report*. Fagin served as the interim president of the University of Pennsylvania from July 1, 1993, to June 30, 1994. Fagin assumed the latter position at a time of great turbulence in the university. At the conclusion of her term, the university climate was extremely positive, it was at higher rank than at any time in its history, and had its best-ever results in fund raising. Fagin was the first woman to serve as chief executive officer of the university and the first woman to serve a term as interim president of any Ivy League university. Presently she is Leadership Professor Emerita and Dean Emerita at Penn.

Fagin has extensive and progressive experience in nursing, healthcare, and educational administration, including teaching, practicing, and consulting, and in the forming of health policy, both in public and private sectors. Her doctoral thesis, published in 1966, was a study of the relationship between the recovery of hospitalized children and their parents "rooming in." This research received national attention, and combined with subsequent work, it helped to permanently change attitudes and rules about parental visitation in pediatric facilities. Later research surveyed changes in hospital visiting, studied cost-effectiveness of nursing research and nurse practitioners, and investigated nursing home reform.

Fagin has served on three corporate boards (Provident Mutual, Salomon, Inc., and Radian Guarantee, Inc.) and has been in elected and appointed positions with many professional organizations. Currently she is a member of the board of the Van Ameringen Foundation, the Visiting Nurse Service of New York, the New York Academy of Medicine, the American Academy of Nursing (fellow), the Institute of Medicine, National Academy of Sciences, the Expert Panel on Nursing of the World Health Organization, and the American Academy of Arts and Sciences.

Fagin has received 12 honorary doctoral degrees and numerous alumni, civic, and professional awards. In recognition of her contribution to nursing education and leadership and her influence on healthcare policy, Fagin received the Honorary Recognition Award of the American Nurses Association, the most prestigious honor awarded in the nursing profession. Among her other awards are the first Distinguished Scholar Award given by the American Nurses Foundation and the Hildegard E. Peplau Award (for her work in psychiatric nursing) from the American Nurses Association. In 1990, she was named a "Woman of Courage" by Philadelphia's Women's Way, and in 1992, she received the Caring Award from the Visiting Nurses Association of Philadelphia—the first nurse to receive this award. In 1994, she received the Lillian D. Wald Spirit of Nursing Award from the New York Visiting Nurses Association and was named a Distinguished Daughter of Pennsylvania. In 1998, Fagin was made a Living Legend by the American Academy of Nursing and received the President's Medal from New York University. In 2001, she was awarded the Nightingale Award from the American Nurses Foundation, and she was named an honorary fellow of the Royal College of Nursing in 2002.

She received the Bachelor of Science degree from Wagner College, the Master of Arts degree from Teachers College, Columbia University, and the PhD from New York University. Fagin has published 12 books and monographs and more than 90 articles.

VERNICE D. FERGUSON

Vernice Ferguson was a senior fellow in the School of Nursing at the University of Pennsylvania holding the Fagin Family Chair in Cultural Diversity. For more than 20 years, she served as a top nurse executive in federal service and was the chief nurse at two VA medical centers affiliated with academic health science centers in Madison, Wisconsin, and Chicago, Illinois. For 12 years, she was the nurse leader for the Department of Veterans Affairs, the largest organized nursing service in the world with more than 60,000 nursing personnel. Prior to the VA assignment, she served as chief of the Nursing Department of the Clinical Center, the National Institutes of Health.

Ferguson is an honorary fellow of the Royal College of Nursing of the United Kingdom, the second American nurse so honored, following the late Virginia Henderson, and is a fellow and past president of the American Academy of Nursing. She is a past president of Sigma Theta Tau, nursing's international honor society, and served as the chair of the Friends of the Virginia Henderson Library Advisory Committee. She is a past president of the International Society of Nurses in Cancer Care.

Her awards and honors are numerous, including eight honorary doctorates. She was the recipient of two fellowships, one in physics at the University of Maryland and the other in alcohol studies at Yale University, and was a scholar-in-residence at the Catholic University of America. She was the Potter-Brinton Distinguished Professor for 1994 at the School of Nursing, the University of Missouri at Columbia.

In 1995, she spent nine weeks in South Africa serving as visiting associate professor in the Department of Nursing Science at the University of the North West. While in South Africa in her capacity as president of the International Society of Nurses in Cancer Care, she toured the country extensively, meeting with healthcare providers in university nursing programs, voluntary associations, hospitals, and homes in townships and squatter camps. She conducted workshops and offered presentations in a variety of settings throughout South Africa, most of which were geared to cancer care and health policy issues.

Ferguson serves on the board of directors of the Bon Secours Health Care System's Assurance Company, the Independence Foundation's Advisory Committee on the Nurse Managed Primary Health Care Initiative, the Robert Wood Johnson Foundation Executive Nurse Fellows Advisory Committee, and the board of overseers, School of Nursing, the University of Pennsylvania. She is the immediate past chairman of NOVA Foundation of the Nurses Organization of the Department of Veterans Affairs. She was appointed to the Program Committee of the American College of Physicians-American Society of Internal Medicine's Foundation and served on the Nominating Committee of the Catholic Hospital Association, the board of trustees of BISA (Black Women in Sisterhood for Action), and the Washington Home's Hospice and Palliative Care Committee.

At the 25th anniversary celebration of the American Academy of Nursing in 1998, she was honored as a "Living Legend," an exemplary role model whose contributions continue to make an impact on the provision of healthcare services in the United States and in all regions of the world. In 2000, Indiana University's School of Nursing conferred upon her the Emily Holmquist Lifetime Achievement in Nursing Award.

LORETTA C. FORD

Dr. Loretta C. Ford, dean and professor emerita, School of Nursing, University of Rochester, is an internationally known nursing leader. She has devoted her career to practice, education, research, consultation, and influencing health service delivery and inquiry. Her practice of nursing has spanned inpatient and outpatient services, community health, and military nursing. Ford's studies on the nurse's expanded scope of practice in public health nursing, her specialty, led to the creation of the first pediatric nurse practitioner model of advanced practice at the University of Colorado Medical Center. Later, convinced of the need to meld nursing education, practice, and research, she provided administrative leadership for a unification model in nursing at the University of Rochester Medical Center in the position of the dean of the School of Nursing and the director of nursing in the university's Strong Memorial Hospital. Her interest in global healthcare issues has resulted in foreign assignments including educational tours to the USSR and China, as well as a three-month teaching assignment in Japan.

Ford's advanced degrees were earned at the University of Colorado Schools of Nursing and Education. She holds honorary doctorates from six prestigious universities and a myriad of awards, including the Gustav Leinhard Medal from the Institute of Medicine, National Academy of Sciences, the Living Legend Award from the American Academy of Nursing, the Trailblazer's Award from the American College of Nurse Practitioners, the Elizabeth Blackwell Award, and many others. She has authored over 100 publications on the history of the nurse practitioner, unification of practice, education and research, and issues in advanced nursing practice.

Currently, Ford consults and lectures on the historical development of the nurse practitioner and on policy issues in the advanced practice of nursing.

ADA SUE HINSHAW

Ada Sue Hinshaw, RN, PhD, FAAN, a nationally and internationally recognized contributor to nursing research, has been dean and professor at the University of Michigan School of Nursing since July 1, 1994.

Before coming to the University of Michigan, Dr. Hinshaw was the first permanent director of the National Institute of Nursing Research (NINR) at the National Institutes of Health in Bethesda, Maryland. Hinshaw led the institute in its support of valuable research and training in many areas of nursing science, such as disease prevention, health promotion, acute and chronic illness, and the environments that enhance nursing care patient outcomes. From 1975 to 1987, Hinshaw served as director of research and professor at the University of Arizona College of Nursing in Tucson, and as director of nursing research at the University of Arizona Medical Center's Department of Nursing. She has also held faculty positions at the University of California, San Francisco, and the University of Kansas.

Throughout her career, Hinshaw has conducted nursing research, including projects on the quality of patient care giving and nursing staff turnover. She has given hundreds of presentations, and her findings have been widely published in more than 300 journal articles, books, and abstracts. In addition, she has served on numerous scientific advisory committees and task forces and has been a visiting professor and lecturer at various schools of nursing. Currently she serves as vice-chair of the Institute of Medicine's Work Environment for Nurses and Patient Safety Committee

Hinshaw has received many awards and honorary doctorates, including the MNRS;(Midwest Nursing Research Society)Midwest Nursing Research Society (MNRS) Lifetime Achievement Award, Health Leader of the Year Award from the Public Health Service and the Nurse Scientist of the Year Award from the Council of Nurse Researchers of the American Nurses Association. She has received alumni awards from Yale University and the Universities of Kansas and Arizona, as well as the Elizabeth McWilliams Miller Award for Excellence in Nursing Research, extended by Sigma Theta Tau International. Hinshaw has also received honorary Doctor of Science degrees from the Mount Sinai Medical Center, University of Maryland, Medical College of Ohio, Marquette University, University of Nebraska, University of Medicine & Dentistry of New Jersey, University of Toronto, Grand Valley State University, St. Louis University, and Georgetown University. Her professional organization memberships include the American Nurses Association, Sigma Theta Tau International, the National Academies of Practice, the Maryland Nurses Association, and Sigma Xi. She is also a member of the Institute of Medicine, a member of the Institute of Medicine Council, and past president of the American Academy of Nursing.

Hinshaw received her PhD and MA in sociology from the University of Arizona, an MSN from Yale University, and a BS from the University of Kansas. Her major fields of study included maternal-newborn health, clinical nursing and nursing administration, and instrument development and testing.

MARGRETTA MADDEN STYLES

Margretta Madden Styles, RN, EdD, FAAN, is recognized internationally for her contributions in academic nursing, credentialing, and professional organizations. Styles is past president of the American Nurses Association (ANA) from 1986-1988, the American Nurses Credentialing Center (ANCC) from 1996-1998, and the International Council of Nurses (ICN) from 1993-1997. ICN, headquartered in Geneva, Switzerland, is a federation of the national nursing associations of more than 120 countries, including the ANA as representative of the United States, and is the global voice for nursing.

Styles has served as professor and dean of the schools of nursing at the University of California, San Francisco; Wayne State University in Michigan; and the University of Texas Health Science Center at San Antonio. She was Fulbright fellow at the University of Athens, Greece, in 1990.

She was a member of the National Commission on Nursing (1980-1983) and subsequently chaired the Governing Council of the National Commission on Nursing Implementation Project. She chaired the Commission on Organizational Assessment and Renewal (1987-1989), which stimulated several structural changes within ANA. She has been keynote speaker to and is honorary member of a number of nursing specialty organizations.

Styles is recognized worldwide for her special expertise in professional issues, particularly regulation and credentialing. Within the United States: She chaired the national study of credentialing in nursing, a project involving all of the organizations engaged in setting professional standards and the certification of nurses; From 1984-1988, as the first distinguished scholar of the American Nurses Foundation, she conducted an extensive survey of nursing specialties and published a monograph on the subject,

and thereby evolved the model for the American Board of Nursing Specialties, established in 1991. From 1989-1991, she co-chaired the ANA Task
Force on Nursing Practice Standards.

In the international arena, Styles directed the 1983 ICN worldwide project on the regulation of the profession. Two publications resulted, including
the ICN's official position paper on this subject, comprised of principles of
professional regulation, policy objectives for nursing regulation, and guidelines for national regulatory models. Both are circulated and used widely
throughout the world. As a result of this project, involving consultation with
more than 80 nations, the nursing laws in many countries were first enacted
or improved. Subsequently, as chairperson of the ICN Professional Services
Committee, Styles co-authored the international guidelines on the designation of nursing specialties and the regulation of nurse specialists. As a consultant for ICN, she completed in 1997 a feasibility study called The Role of
ICN in Credentialing: Answering the Global Need for Quality Assurance.
She chaired the World Health Organization (WHO) Study Commission on
Nursing Regulation in 1985. She was first director of Credentialing Interna-
tional for the American Nurses Credentialing Center, providing leadership
and direction during the initial phase of the global expansion of services.
She was a U.S. delegate and/or ICN representative to a number of World
Health Assemblies and participated in the Fourth World Conference on
Women in Beijing in 1995.

Styles was nurse consultant to the surgeon general for the Air Force for
a term of two years and was a member of the Defense Advisory Council on
Women in the Services from 1972-1974. Also, within the government arena,
she was a member of the Secretary's Commission on Nursing of the then-
U.S. Department of Health, Education, and Welfare (HEW), 1988-1990.

Styles earned her Bachelor of Science degree in biology and chemistry
at Juniata College, her Master of Nursing degree at Yale University, and her
doctorate in education at the University of Florida. She holds a number of
honorary doctorates and awards from universities in the United States,
Canada, and Greece. She was awarded the 2005 Christiane Reimann Prize,
nursing's most prestigious international award, for her remarkable achievements and contributions to the nursing profession internationally. She has
been admitted to the ANA Hall of Fame and recognized as a Living Legend
by the American Academy of Nursing. She is an elected fellow of the American Academy of Nursing, the Institute of Medicine, and the Royal College
of Nursing of the United Kingdom.

Styles was married for 47 years to the late Douglas Frederick Styles
and is the mother of three children and two grandchildren.

APPENDIX C

Resources

Abdellah, G., (1960). *Patient-centered approaches to nursing,* New York: Macmillan.

Aiken, L., Clarke, S., Cheung, R., Sloane, D., and Silber, J. (2003). Educational levels of hospital nurses and surgical patient mortality. *JAMA.* 290,12.

Avery, C. *A conversation with Luther: The opinions & predictions of Dr. Luther Christman,* videotaped interview.

Christman, L., (1982). Opinion. *American Nursing News,* 3, 9, p. 13.

Christman, L., (1997). Advanced practice nursing: Is the physician's assistant an accident of history or a failure to act. *Clinical Excellence for Nurse Practitioners,* 1, 5.

Christman, L., (1996). Democratic administration. *Journal of Nursing Administration,* 26, 1, p. 7-8.

Donaldson, S.K.B., & Crowley, D.M. (1978). The discipline of nursing. *Nursing Outlook,* 26 (2), 113-120. Reprinted from Nursing Outlook, V26, 1978, with permission from Elsevier.

Gamma Phi Chapter, Sigma Theta Tau International (2000). *The future of nursing: An interview with Luther Christman,* videotaped interview.

Hinshaw & Merritt, (1988). *Perspectives in Nursing 1987-1989.* New York: National League for Nursing Press. 94-95.

Fagin, C., (2000). *Essays on nursing leadership,* New York: Springer-Verlag.

Schorr, T. & Zimmerman, A., (1988). *Making choices taking chances.* St. Louis, MO: Mosby.

Sullivan, E. (2002). In a woman's world. *Reflections on Nursing Leadership,* 28, 3, p. 10-17.

Tomey, A. & Alligood, M., (2001). *Nursing theorists and their work.* St. Louis, MO: Mosby

INDEX

A

AAMN (American Assembly for Men in Nursing), 85
Aamodt, Agnes, 110
AAN (American Academy of Nurses), 196, 236-239, 203
Abdellah, Faye Glenn, 129-145
  advocacy for baccalaureate level education, 142
  awards, Surgeon General's Medallion and Medal, 139
  development of the first federally tested coronary care unit, 135
  education
    Fitkin Memorial Hospital School of Nursing, 131
    Rutgers University, 131
    Teachers College at Columbia University, 131
  employment
    Office of Long-Term Care (DHHS), 135-136
    Yale University faculty position, 131
  formation of Cadet Nurse Corps, 132
  gender discrimination, 138
  Hindenburg crash, effect on career choice, 130
  leadership opportunities
    collaboration with World Health Organization in Kenya, 142-143
    exchange programs, 144
    Graduate School of Nursing (founder), 140, 142
  mentor relationships, 139
    Donnelly, Sister Rosemary, 140
    Henderson, Virginia, 140
    Leone, Lucile Petry, 140
  military service, 132
    proposed reorganization of nursing research, 132
  mission-oriented program, 130, 138-139
  mock disaster exercises, 130
  nursing research, 133
    evidence-based documentation, 137-138
    seminal research during house arrest, 134
    Typology of 21 Nursing Problems, 135
  retirement, 144-145
  USUHS/GSN (founding dean), 130
  writing, National Library of Medicine, 137
ACE (American Council on Education), 30
Acquired immune deficiency syndrome. *See* AIDS
actualization of nursing, 98
Advanced practice nurses. *See* APNs

Affirmative action programs, 29, 83-84
AIDS (acquired immune deficiency syndrome), 238
Aiken, James, 227
Aiken, Linda H., 225-247
  award, education
    University of Texas, doctoral degree, 232
    University of Wisconsin, postdoctoral research fellowship, 233
    RWJF program officer, 233-236
      Episteme Award (Sigma Theta Tau International), 247
      Ernest A. Codman Award, 247
      NIH Nurse Scientist Award, 232
  Center for Health Outcomes and Policy Research, 239-243
  Clinical Nurse Scholars program, 235
  education, 227-229
  employment
    AAN presidency, 236-239
    J. Hillis Miller Health Center, 229
    University of Missouri, CNS, 230
    University of Pennsylvania, endowed professorship, 239-243
  healthcare public policy, 225, 232
  importance of publication, 243-244
  international study on nurse retention, 240-241
    International Hospital Outcomes Consortium, 241-243
    Rockefeller Conference Center planning meeting, 241
  magnet organization research, 225, 236-239
    outcomes focus, 238
    work environment, 239
  mentor relationships
    Blendon, Robert, 234
    Kramer, Marlene, 238
    Mahoney, Margaret, 234
    Martin, Sam, 229
    Mechanic, David, 233
    Rogers, David, 234
    Smith, Dorothy, 228
  outcomes vision, 226
  parental influence, 226
  recognition of nursing's leadership opportunities, 244-245

research
    focus on evidence-based practice, 231-232
    University of Missouri Medical Center, 231
    Teaching Nursing Home Program, 235-236
Air Force (Clifford, Joyce), 51-53
Alta Bates Hospital Obstetrics and Gynecology unit, 108
AMA, (American Medical Association) resistance to
    nurse practitioner movement, 15
American Academy of Nurses. *See* AAN
American Assembly for Men in Nursing. *See* AAMN
American Council on Education. *See* ACE
American Hospital Association
    McMahon, Alex, 65
    Nursing Personnel Annual Survey, 237
American Journal of Nursing AJN (American Journal of
    Nursing), 92
American Medical Association. *See* AMA
American Nurses Association. *See* ANA
American Nurses Credentialing Center. *See* ANCC
American Nurses Foundation Distinguished Scholar
    Award, 223
ANA (American Nurses Association), 24, 196
    AAN (American Academy of Nurses), 196
    Cabinet on Nursing Research
        Hinshaw, Ada Sue, 112, 116-118
        Pender, Nola, 113
    Christman's presidential candidacy, 84
    global nursing credentialing study, 178
    international exchange programs, 24
    Styles, Gretta Madden, 182-183
    white paper on nursing shortage, 184
ANCC (American Nurses Credentialing Center), 170,
    183, 225
    Magnet Hospitals, 225
    Styles, Gretta, 183
APNs (advanced practice nurses), 140
    uniformed services, 140
Armed Forces, rejection of Luther Christman, 72
Army Air Force, Ford, Loretta C., 4
Army Nurse Corps, rejection of Luther Christman, 72
Assistant vice chancellor (UCSF), Chater, Shirley Sears,
    28
Associate degree programs
    Broward Community College, 172-174
    UTHSC, 173
Atwood, Jan, 109

B

Baccalaureate level education, advocacy by Abdellah,
    142
Balanced Budget Act of 1997, 240
Barrett, Jean, as mentor to Joyce Clifford, 51
Batey, Marjorie, 161
Bay Area Student Nurses Association, 189-190
behavior changes, strategies of Abdellah, 142-144
Beland, Irene, 150
Bellevue Hospital, Fagin, Claire
    interaction with adolescents, 209
    interaction with children with tuberculosis, 208
Beth Israel Deaconess Medical Center, 63
Beth Israel Hospital
    Clifford, Joyce, 45

chief nursing officer, 60, 63
    Seminars in Nursing, 50
    Rabkin, Mitch, CEO, 59
Black Student League, 219
Black, Ann, 58
Black, Dorothy Mary, 68
Blendon, Robert, 234
Boehle, Carole, 51
Born to Rebel (Sulloway), 169
Bowen, Otis R, 118
Broward Community College, development of associate
    degree program, 172-174
Buckley, William F., *Firing Line*, 219
Busse, Ewald W., 80

C

Cabinet on Nursing Research (ANA)
    Hinshaw, Ada Sue
        healthcare initiative proposed by Congressman
            Madigan, 112
        policy paper directing future of nursing research,
            112
        second round for proposed NIN, 116-118
    Pender, Nola, 113
Cadet Nurse Corps, 132
Calcium metabolism research, 92
California Nursing Students' Association, 189
Campbell, James, MD, 81
Care Group, Beth Israel Deaconess Medical Center, 63
Carter, Michael, 15
Catholic University of America, 94
Center for Health Outcomes and Policy Research
    development by Linda H. Aiken, 239-243
    Lake, Eileen, 238
Chairship, National Advisory Committee (Robert Wood
    Johnson Executive Nurse Leadership Program),
    42
Chater, Shirley Sears, 23-43
    children, 27
    consultant capacities, 42
    education, 24
        international exchange program, 24
        UCSF (University of California at San Francisco),
            26-28
        University of Pennsylvania Hospital School of
            Nursing, 24-26
    family history, 23
    leadership
        ACE commissions, 30
        assistant vice chancellor (UCSF), 28
        commissioner SSA, 34-41
        head of Functional Division (UCSF), 28
        presidency TWU (Texas Woman's University), 30,
            32-34
        Robert Wood Johnson Executive Nurse Leadership
            Program, 42
        vice chancellor (UCSF), 29
    professorships, UCSF (University of California at San
        Francisco), 28
    views on workplace culture, 41-42
Cherry Ames series on nursing, 227
Cherryvale High School, 107

childhood separation anxiety, Fagin, Claire
doctoral thesis, 211-212
roots at Seaview Hospital, 208
Children's Hospital, Washington, D.C., 211
Christman, Luther, 67-87
affirmative action programs, 83-84
education
Michigan State University, 77
Pennsylvania Hospital School of Nursing, 68
Temple University School of Nursing, 70
family history, 68
founding of AAMN (American Assembly for Men in Nursing), 85
founding of Rush University and Rush University School of Nursing, 81-83
presidential candidacy for ANA, 84
retirement, 85
reverse discrimination, 69-74, 84-85
unification model, 80-83
vision for minimum standard education to enter nursing, 78-79
Cleland, Virginia, 150
Clifford, Joyce, 45-65
Air Force, 51-53
awards, 65
education
St. Anselm's College, BSN, 47
St. Raphael's Hospital School of Nursing program, 46
University of Alabama, 57
employment
Beth Israel Deaconess Medical Center, 63
Beth Israel Hospital, 45, 60, 63
St. Anselm's College, BSN, 47
St. Raphael's Hospital, 46-47
University of Alabama Hospital, 54-58
mentor relationships
Barrett, Jean, 51
Hall, Lydia, 49-50
Kennelly, Evelyn, 48-49
Reiter, Frances, 50-51
professional growth, 48-49
professional practice model, 60-65
Clifford, Larry, 54
Clinical Center (NIH)
Fagin, Claire, 210-211
Ferguson, Vernice, 97-102
Clinical Nurse Scholars Program, 234-235
Clinical nurse specialist. *See* CNS
clinical research
Hinshaw, Ada Sue
ANA Cabinet on Nursing Research, 112, 116-118
NCNR directorship, 119-124
return to education after establishment of NINR, 124
support for NIH to include NIN, 113-116
University of Arizona Medical Center, 109-112
Clinton, President William, NIH Revitalization Act of 1993, 124
CNS (clinical nurse specialist), 230-232
Cole, Eunice, 118
Commission on Organizational Assessment and Renewal (ANA), 183

Communicating Nursing Research, 161
Cooper Hospital School of Nursing, 74
Coulter, Pearl Parvin, 5
credentialing, global nursing, 178
Credentialing International (ANCC), 183
Crowley, Dorothy
defining the discipline of nursing, 153-155
collaboration with Sue Donaldson, 155-159
end result, 165
formulation of PhD programs for nursing, 163-165
as mentor to Sue Karen Donaldson, 151

D

Daily Pennsylvanian, 219
Davis, F.A., publication of Fagin's work on childhood separation anxiety, 212
De Madras De Madras (from mother to mother) program, 33
De Tornyay Center for Healthy Aging (UW School of Nursing), 191
de Tornyay, Rheba, 183-203
AAN role, 196
awards, 203
Clinical Nurse Scholars program, 235
education
Mount Zion Hospital School of Nursing, 188-190
San Francisco State College, 191
San Francisco State University, 192
Stanford University, 192
employment
Langley Porter Neuropsychiatric Hospital, 190
Maimonides Rehabilitation Center, 191
Mount Zion Hospital School of Nursing, 192
SFSU faculty member, 192
UCLA deanship, 194-195
UCSF faculty, 192-193
University of Washington deanship, 194-199
family history, 188
IOM membership, 195-196
leadership skills, 199-203
Making a Good Move to a Retirement Community, 191
mentor relationships
McDonald, Fred, 192
Nahm, Helen, 193-194
response to WICHEN paper of Donaldson and Crowley, 162
Strategies for Teaching Nursing, 187, 193
Department of Health and Human Services. *See* DHHS
Department of Physiological Nursing (UW), 155
Department of Physiology and Biophysics at the School of Medicine (UW), 151-155
Department of Veterans Affairs, 102
DHHS (Department of Health and Human Services), 135-136
Dickoff, James, 107
Discipline of nursing, Donaldson, Sue Karen, 153-159, 163-165
Discovery learning, 108
discrimination, experience of Luther Christman, 69-74, 84-85
dissertations, laws of behavior, 77

Distinguished Health Leader of the Year award, 105, 126
Distinguished Scholar Award, 223
Division of Nursing (HRSA), 114
DNSc doctoral degree (Doctor of Nursing Science), 163
Doctor of Nursing Science. *See* DNSc doctoral degree
Donaldson, Sue Karen, 147-167
  education
    University of Washington, 150-153
    Wayne State University School of Nursing,
      149-150
  employment, 155
  leadership opportunities
    defining the discipline of nursing, 153-159
    formulation of PhD programs for nursing,
      163-165
    influence on nursing as a discipline, 165
  mentor relationships, 150-151
Donnelly, Sister Rosemary, 140
Duke University, School of Nursing, 174
Dumas, Rhetaugh, 107

E

education
  Abdellah, Faye Glenn, 131
  Aiken, Linda H.
    University of Florida College of Nursing, 227-229
    University of Texas, doctoral degree, 232
    University of Wisconsin, postdoctoral research
      fellowship, 233
  Chater, Shirley Sears
    international exchange program, 24
    UCFS (University of California at San Francisco),
      26-28
    University of Pennsylvania Hospital School of
      Nursing, 24-26
  Christman, Luther
    Michigan State University, 77
    Pennsylvania Hospital School of Nursing, 68
    Temple University School of Nursing, 70
  Clifford, Joyce
    St. Anselm's College, BSN, 47
    St. Raphael's Hospital School of Nursing
      program, 46
  de Tornyay, Rheba
    Mount Zion Hospital School of Nursing, 188-190
    San Francisco State College, 191
    San Francisco State University, 192
    Stanford University, 192
  Donaldson, Sue Karen
    University of Washington, 150-153
    Wayne State University School of Nursing,
      149-150
  Fagin, Claire
    Hunter College, 207
    NYU, 211-212
    Teachers College in New York, 209
    Wagner College, 207-208
  Ferguson, Vernice, 90
  Ford, Loretta C.
    Middlesex General Hospital nursing program, 3
    University of Colorado, 4
    University of Colorado, 5

Hinshaw, Ada Sue
  Cherryvale High School, 107
  University of Arizona, 108-109
  University of Kansas, 106-107
  Yale University, 107
Styles, Gretta Madden
  Juniata College, 170
  University of Florida in Gainesville, 174
  Yale University, 171-172
Eisenhower, General Dwight D., support for male nurses
  in Nurse Corps, 72
Elizabeth Blackwell Award, 21
Episteme Award (Sigma Theta Tau International), 247
Ernest A. Codman Award, 247
erosion of care study (Fagin), 222
evidence-based documentation, 137-138
evidence-based practice
  Aiken, Linda H., 231-232
  contributions of Abdellah, 135
exchange programs, 144

F

faculty positions. *See* teaching opportunities
Fagin, Claire, 205-223
  awards, Distinguished Scholar Award, 223
  chair of their board of advisors, Hartford Institute for
    Geriatric Nursing at NYU, 222
  desire to change entry level of nursing to
    baccalaureate level, 222
  education
    Hunter College, 207
    New York University (NYU) doctoral program,
      211-212
    Teachers College in New York, 209
    Wagner College, 207-208
  employment
    Bellevue Hospital, 208-209
    Children's Hospital, Washington D.C., 211
    faculty position at NYU, 211
    Lehman College nursing department chair,
      213-215
    NIH (National Institutes of Health), 210-211
    NLN (National League for Nursing), 209-210
    Seaview Hospital, 208
    UCSF, presidential chair, nursing home reform,
      216
    University of Pennsylvania, dean of School of
      Nursing, 215
    University of Pennsylvania, Leadership Professor,
      216
    University of Pennsylvania, presidency, 216-222
    University of Pennsylvania, retirement, 222
    Honorary Fellow of the Royal College of Nursing,
      223
  Institute of Medicine, scholar in residence, 216
  John A. Hartford Foundation, Building Academic
    Geriatric Nursing Capacity program, 222
  leadership, graduate programs at NYU, 213
  Living Legend honor (ANA), 223
  Milbank Memorial Fund, study of erosion of care,
    222
  support for Linda Aiken's Center for Health
    Outcomes and Policy Research, 240

Felton, Geraldine, 114
Ferguson, Vernice, 89-103
    awards, Lavinia Dock prize, 91
    education, NYU (New York University), 90
    employment
        Montefiore Hospital, 92
        NIH Clinical Center, 97-102
        VA (Veterans Affairs) health system, 92-96, 100
    leadership opportunities
        actualization of nursing, 98
        International Society of Nurses in Cancer Care
            (presidency), 95
        Sigma Theta Tau International Honor Society of
            Nursing (presidency), 95
    mentor relationships, 90
    research opportunities, Montefiore Hospital, 92
    retirement, 102
    sabbatical at Catholic University of America, long-
        term care focus, 94
Firing Line, 219
Fitkin Memorial Hospital School of Nursing, Abdellah,
    Faye Glenn, 131
Florence Nightingale award, Chater, Shirley Sears, 24
Ford, Loretta C., 1-21
    awards, Elizabeth Blackwell Award, 21
    education
        Middlesex General Hospital nursing program, 3
        University of Colorado, baccalaureate degree, 4
        University of Colorado, MSN, 5
    employment
        Army Air Force, 4
        public health nursing, Boulder County, Colorado,
            5-6
        Visiting Nurse Service (New Brunswick), 4
    family history, 3
    mentor relationships, 3, 5
    nurse practitioner movement, 1-17
        demonstration project, 8-10
        faculty concerns, 10-11
        gaining national acceptance, 12-14
        legislative battles, 15
        Missouri profile case, 16-17
        political implications, 14
        public health nursing experience, 6
        relationship with Henry K. Silver, 7
        relationship with Henry Kempe, 7
        social implications and resistance to change, 14
        VNS site, 12
        WCHEN influence, 7
    retirement, 21
    work ethic, 19, 21
Functional Division (UCFS), administrative leadership of
    Shirley Sears Chater, 28
funding, NCNR, efforts of Ada Sue Hinshaw, 121-123

G

Gehringer, Gerald (Missouri profile case), nurse
    practitioner movement, 16
gender discrimination
    Abdellah, Faye Glenn, 138
    Christman, Luther 69-72, 84-85

Geriatric nursing
    John A. Hartford Foundation, Building Academic
        Geriatric Nursing Capacity program, 222
    Teaching Nursing Home Program, 235-236
Gibbons, Trish, 61
Gibbs, Jack, model construction, influence on Ada Sue
    Hinshaw, 108
Global nursing, Styles, Gretta Madden, 178-182
Gottdank, Mildred, 209
Governing Council (AAN), magnet research study, 236
Governing Council (IOM), Hinshaw, Ada Sue, 126
Graduate Record Exam. See GRE
Graduate School of Nursing. See USUHS/GSN
GRE (Graduate Record Exam), 211

H

Hall, Lydia, as mentor to Joyce Clifford, 49-50
Hamblin, Bob, social behavioral measurement, 108
Harrell, George, 228
Harrison's Textbook on Internal Medicine, 56
Harrison, Tinsley, 56
Hartford Institute for Geriatric Nursing at NYU, Fagin,
    Claire (chairship), 222
Hatfield, Mark, support for proposed NIN, 117
The Head Nurse (Barrett), 51
Health and Human Services, Shalala, Donna, 34
Health Research Extension Act of 1985, 118
Health Resources and Services Administration. See
    HRSA
Healthcare public policy, Aiken's influence, 225, 232
Healy, Bernadine, transitioning the NCNR to NINR, 123
Heinrich, Jan, transition of NCNR to an institution, 123
Henderson, Virginia, 8, 140
Hendricks, Theodore, University of Missouri Medical
    Center research study, 231
Hill, Jean, 107
Hinshaw, Ada Sue, 105-127
    ANA Cabinet on Nursing Research
        healthcare initiative proposed by Congressman
            Madigan, 112
        policy paper directing future of nursing research,
            112
        second round for proposed NIN, 116-118
    awards
        Distinguished Health Leader of the Year, 105, 126
        Nurse Scientist of the Year, 105, 126
        President of the American Academy of Nurses,
            105
    education
        Cherryvale High School, 107
        University of Arizona, 108-109
        University of Kansas, 106-107
        Yale University, 107
    employment
        Alta Bates Hospital, 108
        UCSF, School of Nursing, 108
        University of Arizona Medical Center, clinical
            researcher, 109-112
        University of Arizona, associate professor, 109-112
        University of Michigan, Dean, 126
    family history, 106-107
    Institute of Medicine Governing Council, 105, 126

mentor relationships
 Hill, Jean, 107
 Kramer, Marlene, 108
 Merritt, Doris, 121
 Williams, Frank, 121
National Institute of Nursing Research, 105
NCNR directorship, 119-124
 efforts to increase funding, 121-123
 transition of NCNR to NINR, 123-124
presidency of the American Academy of Nurses, 126
return to education after establishment of NINR, 124
support for NIH to include NIN, 113-116
 benefits of becoming an NIH institute, 114
 IOM study, 116
 NIH Task Force on Nursing Research study, 116
 Republican Party resistance, 115
 resistance from nurse leaders, 114
 veto by Reagan, 115
Hogness, John, 197
Honor Society of Nursing (Sigma Theta Tau
 International), presidency of Vernice Ferguson,
 95
Honorary Fellow of the Royal College of Nursing, Fagin,
 Claire, 223
Hospital diploma programs, Clifford, Joyce, 47
Hoyt, Raymond Martin, 46
HRSA (Health Resources and Services Administration),
 114
Human resource challenges, Hinshaw's development of
 clinical research program, 110
Hunter College, Fagin, Claire, 207
Hunter, Robert, nurse practitioner movement, 14

I

ICN (International Council of Nurses), 170, 177-178
Inouye, Senator Donald K., 117, 140
Institute of Medicine. See IOM
Institute of Nursing. See NIN (National Institute of
 Nursing)
Integration of races, Christman, Luther, 79
International Council of Nurses. See ICN
International exchange program, Chater, Shirley Sears,
 24-26
International Hospital Outcomes Consortium, 241-243
International Society of Nurses in Cancer Care,
 presidency of Vernice Ferguson, 95
International study on nurse retention, Aiken, Linda H.,
 240-241
 International Hospital Outcomes Consortium,
 241-243
 Rockefeller Conference Center planning meeting, 241
Intramural research program (NCNR), 123
IOM (Institute of Medicine), 112
 Fagin, Claire, scholar in residence, 216
 Hinshaw, Ada Sue, 105
 de Tornyay, Rheba 195-196
 *Nursing and Nursing Education: Public Policy and
 Private Actions* study, 112, 116

J

J. Hillis Miller Health Center, Aiken, Linda H. (staff
 nurse), 229

James, Patricia, 107
JCAHO (Joint Commission for the Accreditation of
 Healthcare Organization), Ernest A. Codman
 Award, 247
John A. Hartford Foundation, Building Academic
 Geriatric Nursing Capacity program, 222
JONA (*Journal of Nursing Administration*), 58
Journal of Clinical Investigation, 92
Journal of Clinical Nutrition, 92
Journal of Nursing Administration. See JONA, 58

K

Kellogg Foundation, 172
Kelly, Katherine, 5
Kempe, Henry, establishing roots for nurse practitioner
 movement, 7
Kennedy, Edward, support for proposed NIN, 117
Kennelly, Evelyn, 48-49
Kerrick, W. Glenn, 151
Keyhoe, James, Missouri profile case, 16
Kirschstein, Ruth (Director of the National Institute of
 General Medical Sciences), 120
Klingensmith, Anne, Donaldson-Crowley framework for
 discipline of nursing, 158-159
Koop, Surgeon General C. Everett, formation of national
 health policies, 138
Kramer, Marlene
 discovery learning, 108
 magnet hospital research, 238
 Reality Shock, 228
Krueger, Janelle, 110

L

Lake, Eileen, magnet hospital research, 238
Langley Porter Neuropsychiatric Hospital, de Tornyay,
 Rheba, 190
LASER (Light Amplification by Stimulated Emission of
 Radiation) research, 165
Lavinia Dock prize, Ferguson, Vernice, 91
Laws of behavior, Christman, Luther, 77
Leadership Professor (University of Pennsylvania),
 Fagin, Claire, 216
Lee, Dr, Phillip, 34
Legislative battles, nurse practitioner movement, 15
Lehman College, Fagin, Claire (nursing department
 chair), 213-215
Leonard, Robert, 107
Leone, Lucile Petry, 140
Light Amplification by Stimulated Emission of
 Radiation. See LASER research
Living Legend award (AAN)
 de Tornyay, Rheba, 203
 Fagin, Claire, 223
Livingston Chair (UCSF), Styles, Gretta, 176
Loeb's Center for Nursing Rehabilitation Center, 50
Long-term care
 de Tornyay, Rheba, Maimonides Rehabilitation
 Center, 191
 policies, Abdellah, Faye, 135-136
Longman, Alice, 110
Loughran, Henrietta, 5

Luther Christman Center, 86
Lynch, Theresa, 26

M

Madigan, Congressman Edward, 112
Magnet Hospitals, research by Aiken, 225, 236-239
Magnet Recognition Program, Styles, Gretta, 183
Mahoney, Margaret, 234
Maimonides Rehabilitation Center, de Tornyay, Rheba, 191
Making a Good Move to a Retirement Community (de Tornyay), 191
Martin, Sam, 229
Mary Edding Nutting Award, Clifford, Joyce, 65
Mason, Jim, 123
Mayo, Colonel, support for male nurses in Nurse Corps, 72
McClure, Margaret, magnet hospital study, 236
McDonald, Fred, 192
McMahon, Alex, American Hospital Association, 65
Mechanic, David, 233
Mentoring programs, VA (Veterans Affairs) health system, 94
Merchison, Irene, 5
Mereness, Dorothy, 211
Merritt, Doris
    as mentor to Ada Sue Hinshaw, 121
    interim director of NCNR, 119
Mezey, Mathy, 222
Microteaching technique, de Tornyay, Rheba, 192-193
Middlesex General Hospital nursing program, Ford, Loretta C., 3
Milbank Memorial Fund, Fagin's study of erosion of care, 222
Mission-oriented program, Abdellah, Faye Glenn, 130, 138-139
Missionary work, Styles, Gretta, 171
Missouri profile case, nurse practitioner movement, 16-17
Mock disaster exercises, Abdellah, Faye Glenn, 130
Montague, Mildred, 48
Murdaugh, Caroline (NCNR Director of Intramural Programs), 123
Murrah Federal Building bombing, response of Shirley Sears Chater, 38-40

N

Nahm, Helen
    mentorship to Rheba de Tornyay, 193-194
    mentorship to Shirley Sears Chater, 28
    UCSF (University of California at San Francisco) deanship, 26
National Advisory Committee (Robert Wood Johnson Executive Nurse Leadership Program), 42
National Center for Nursing Research. *See* NCNR
National health policies, Abdellah's contributions, 138
National Institute for Mental Health. *See* NIMH
National Institute of Arthritis and Musculoskeletal and Skin Diseases. *See* NIAMS
National Institute of Nursing Research. *See* NINR
National Institute of Nursing. *See* NIN

National Institutes of Health. *See* NIH
National League for Nursing Education. *See* NLN
National League for Nursing. *See* NLN
National Library of Medicine, 137
National nursing program (VA), Ferguson, Vernice, 96
NCNR (National Center for Nursing Research), 118
    directorship of Ada Sue Hinshaw, 119-123
        efforts to increase funding, 121-123
        transition of NCNR to NINR, 123-124
    establishment at the NIH, 118
    interim directorship of Doris Merritt, 119
Nelson, Katherine, 48
New York State Nurses Association. *See* NYSNA
New York University. *See* NYU
NIAMS (National Institute of Arthritis and Musculoskeletal and Skin Diseases), 113
NIH (National Institutes of Health), 105, 210
    Clinical Center, Ferguson, Vernice, 97-102
    Fagin, Claire, 210-211
    Nurse Scientist Award, Aiken, Linda H., 232
    nursing research, proposal for NIN, 113-116
NIH Revitalization Act of 1993, 124
NIMH (National Institute for Mental Health), 209
NIN (National Institute of Nursing), push for acceptance in NIH, 113-118
    authorization of NCNR to NIH, 118
    benefits of becoming an NIH institute, 114
    evidence supporting the legislation, 117
    IOM study, 116
    NIH Task Force on Nursing Research study, 116
    nursing Tri-Council, 117
    renaming to NCNR (National Center for Nursing Research), 118
    Republican Party resistance, 115
    resistance from nurse leaders, 114
    unification of professional organizations, 117
    veto by Reagan, 115
NINR (National Institute of Nursing Research), 105, 123
NLN (National League for Nursing), 65, 209
    Fagin, Claire, 209-210
    Mary Edding Nutting Award, Clifford, Joyce, 65
    rejection of advanced clinical nursing role, 81
Nurse actualization, Ferguson, Vernice, 98
The Nurse Practitioner Journal, 6
Nurse practitioner movement, Ford, Loretta C., 1-17
    demonstration project, 8-10
    faculty concerns, 10-11
    gaining national acceptance, 12-14
    legislative battles, 15
    Missouri profile case, 16-17
    political implications, 14
    public health nursing experience, 6
    relationship with Henry K. Silver, 7
    relationship with Henry Kempe, 7
    roots in public health nursing position, 5-6
    social implications and resistance to change, 14
    VNS site, 12
    WCHEN influence, 7
Nurse Scientist Award (NIH), Aiken, Linda H., 232
Nurse Scientist of the Year, Hinshaw, Ada Sue, 105, 126
Nurse Scientist Program, Wayne State University, 149-150

Nurse Work Index, professional nursing practice evaluation, 238
Nursing and Nursing Education: Public Policy and Private Actions study (IOM) 112, 116
Nursing home reform, Fagin, Claire, 216
Nursing Outlook, 161
Nursing research
  Abdellah, Faye Glenn, 133
    development of the first federally tested coronary care unit, 135
    evidence-based documentation, 137-138
    proposed reorganization of nursing research, 132
    seminal research during house arrest, 134
    Typology of 21 Nursing Problems, 135
  Aiken, Linda H.
    focus on evidence-based practice, 231-232
    magnet hospital study, 238-239
    University of Missouri Medical Center, 231
  Ferguson, Vernice, Montefiore Hospital, 92
  Hinshaw, Ada Sue
    ANA Cabinet on Nursing Research, 112, 116-118
    influence of Yale professors, 107
    NCNR directorship, 119-124
    return to education after establishment of NINR, 124
    support for NIH to include NIN, 113-116
    University of Arizona Medical Center, clinical researcher, 109-112
    University of Arizona, associate professor, 109-112
Nursing shortages, affirmative action programs, 83-84
NYSNA (New York State Nurses Association), 182
NYU (New York University), 211
  Fagin, Claire
    doctoral education, 211-212
    faculty position, 211
    leadership of graduate programs, 213
  Ferguson, Vernice, 90

O

Office of Long-Term Care (DHHS), Abdellah, Faye Glenn (director), 135-136
Optimizing Environments for Health: Nursing's Unique Perspective (WICHEN), 157-158
Outcome-based model (nursing research), Abdellah, Faye Glenn, 135
Outcomes focus, Aiken, Linda H., magnet hospital research, 238

P

PAs (Physician Assistants), 13
Patient-care focus, Clifford, Joyce
  Beth Israel Hospital, 60, 63
  University of Alabama Hospital, 56-57
PAVLA (Pope's Appeal for Volunteers in Latin America), 51
Pearson, Linda, 6
Pediatric care, Silver, Henry K., MD, 7
Pediatric Nurse Practitioner model, Ford and Silver, 7
  demonstration project, 8-10
  faculty concerns, 10-11

gaining national acceptance, 12-14
legislative battles, 15
Missouri profile case, 16-17
political implications, 14
social implications and resistance to change, 14
VNS site, 12
Pender, Nola, 113
Pennsylvania Hospital School of Nursing, Christman, Luther, 68
Peplau, Hildegard, 209
Peregrin, Jesse, 110
PhD nursing programs
  Donaldson-Crowley framework for discipline of nursing, 163-165
  versus DNSc doctoral degree, 163
Philadelphia Inquirer, 221
Physician Assistant program, application of unification model, 81
Physician Assistants. *See* PAs
Physician-nurse team approach to patient care, Rush Unification Model, 82-83
Pope's Appeal for Volunteers in Latin America. *See* PAVLA
Poulin, Muriel, magnet hospital study, 236
Problem-solving model (nursing research), Abdellah, Faye Glenn, Typology of 21 Nursing Problems, 135
Professional practice model, Clifford, Joyce, 63-65
Professional Services Committee (ICN), Styles, Gretta, 178
Professorships. *See* teaching opportunities
Programs Committee of the American College of Physicians, American Society and Internal Medicine Foundation, 102
Psychiatric nursing
  de Tornyay, Rheba, Langley Porter Neuropsychiatric Hospital, 190
  Fagin, Claire
    Children's Hospital, Washington D.C., 211
    faculty position at NYU, 211
    leadership of graduate programs at NYU, 213
    Lehman College nursing department chair, 213-215
    NIH (National Institutes of Health), 210-211
    NLN (National League for Nursing), 209-210
Public health nursing, Loretta C. Ford, 5-6
Public Law 99-158, 118
Public policies program, Aiken, Linda H., 225, 232, 239-240
Pursell, Carl, support for proposed NIN, 117

R

Rabkin, Mitch, CEO, Beth Israel Hospital, 59
Racial integration, Christman, Luther, 79
Rawlinson, Mary, as chairperson of WICHEN conference, 160
Reality Shock (Kramer), 228
Recruitment and retention model for minorities, Fagin, Claire, 213
Regents Professorship (UCSF), Chater, Shirley Sears, 41
Regulatory model for global nursing, 177-179, 182

Reiker, Ellen, 113
Reiter, Frances, 50-51
Republican Party, resistance to establishment of NIN in
    NIH, 115
Research. *See* Nursing research
Reverse discrimination, Christman, Luther, 69-74, 84-85
Richards, Ann, 34
RO1 funding (externally funded research grants), 197
Robert Wood Johnson Executive Nurse Leadership
    Program, 42
Robert Wood Johnson Foundation. *See* RWJF
Robertson, James, *A Two Year Old Goes to the Hospital,*
    211
Rockefeller Conference Center planning meeting
    (nursing retention study), 241
Rogers, David, 234
Rogers, Martha, 211
Rooming in concept, dissertation on childhood
    separation anxiety (Fagin), 212
Rush Unification Model, physician-nurse team approach
    to patient care (Christman), 82-83
Rush University/Rush University School of Nursing,
    81-83
Rutgers University, Abdellah, Faye Glenn, 131
RWJF (Robert Wood Johnson Foundation), 233

S

Salary initiative, Beth Israel Hospital (Clifford), 63
San Francisco State College, de Tornyay, Rheba
    (bachelors degree), 191
San Francisco State University, de Tornyay, Rheba
    (masters degree), 192
Schlotfeldt, Rozella, 162
Scholarships, NIMH (National Institute for Mental
    Health), 209
Seaview Hospital, Fagin, Claire, 208
Seminars in Nursing (Beth Israel), 50
Separation anxiety (children), Fagin, Claire
    doctoral thesis based on personal experience, 211-212
    roots at Seaview Hospital, 208
SFSU (San Francisco State University), de Tornyay,
    Rheba (faculty position), 192
Shalala, Donna
    Federal Register notice, 124
    secretary of Health and Human Services, 34
Shortage of nurses, affirmative action programs, 83-84
Sigma Theta Tau International Honor Society of Nursing
    Episteme Award, Aiken, Linda H., 247
    presidency of Vernice Ferguson, 95
Silver, Henry K., MD, nurse practitioner movement, 7-17
Smith, Dorothy, 228
Smith, Herbert, magnet hospital research, 238
Social Security Administration. *See* SSA
Sooy, Frank, 29
Sorenson, Gladys, WNRS (Western Nursing Research
    Society Conference), 108
Southern Regional Education Board, 79
Sovie, Margaret, magnet hospital study, 236
SSA (Social Security Administration), 34
    Chater, Shirley Sears (commissioner), 34-41
    conversion from governmental agency to individual
        agency, 38

St. Anselm's College, Clifford, Joyce, BSN, 47
St. Bartholomew's Hospital, international exchange
    program (ANA), 26
Standard education, Christman's vision, 78-79
Stearly, Sue, 9
Stevenson, Joanne, 112
Stokes, Gertrude, 209
Strategies for Teaching Nursing (de Tornyay), 187, 193
Strickland, Ora, 112
Styles, Gretta Madden, 169-181
    ANA presidency, 182-183
    education
        Juniata College, 170
        University of Florida in Gainesville, 174
        Yale University, 171-172
    employment
        associate director of nursing at community hospital
            (Pompano, Florida), 172
        Broward Community College, 172-174
        instructor in school of nursing (Tampa, Florida),
            172
        School of Nursing at Duke University, 174
        UCSF deanship, 176
        University of Texas Systemwide School of
            Nursing, 174-175
        UTHSC, 173
        Wayne State University, 175
    family history, 169-170
    global nursing, 178-182
        credentialing, 178
        regulatory models, 177
    professionalism, 184
    religious influence, 170
    specialty areas, 184
Sullivan, Lewis, 123
Sulloway, Frank, *Born to Rebel,* 169
Surgeon General's Medallion and Medal, Abdellah, Faye
    Glenn, 139
Systematic relaxation, 231

T

Task Force on Nursing Research study (NIH), 116
Teaching Nursing Home Program, 234-236
Team nursing, Rush Unification Model, 82-83
Temple University School of Nursing, Christman, Luther,
    70
Texas Woman's University. *See* TWU
Tri-Council, 117
Tudor, Gwen, 210
A Two Year Old Goes to the Hospital, 211
TWU (Texas Woman's University), presidency of Shirley
    Sears Chater, 30-34
Typology of 21 Nursing Problems, 135

U

UCLA, deanship of Rheba de Tornyay, 194-195
UCSF (University of California at San Francisco)
    Chater, Shirley Sears, 26
        assistant vice chancellor, 28
        doctoral education, 28
        head of Functional Division, 28

professorship, 28
vice chancellor, 29
de Tornyay, Rheba, microteaching technique, 192-193
Fagin, Claire (presidential chair), 216
Hinshaw, Ada Sue, 108
Styles, Gretta, 176
Unification model, Christman, Luther, 80-81
   clinical master's degree program, 80-81
   focus on clinical setting, 80
   Rush Unification Model, 82-83
Unification of practice, research and education, Ford,
   Loretta C., 18-19
Uniformed Services University of the Health Sciences,
   Graduate School of Nursing. *See* USUHS/GSN
United States Public Health Service. *See* USPHS
University Medal (UCSF), Chater, Shirley Sears, 41
University of Arizona, Hinshaw, Ada Sue, 108-112
University of Colorado, Ford, Loretta C., 4-5
University of Florida College of Nursing, Aiken, Linda
   H., 227-229
University of Kansas, Hinshaw, Ada Sue (BSN), 106-107
University of Michigan, Hinshaw, Ada Sue (Deanship),
   126
University of Michigan School of Nursing, Christman,
   Luther (professorship) 79
University of Missouri, Aiken, Linda H., 230-231
University of Pennsylvania
   Aiken, Linda H., endowed professorship, 239-243
   Center for Health Outcomes and Policy, Lake, Eileen,
     238
   Fagin, Claire
     dean of School of Nursing, 215
     Leadership Professor, 216
     presidency, 216-222
     retirement, 222
University of Texas Health Science Center at San
   Antonio. *See* UTHSC
University of Texas Systemwide School of Nursing,
   Styles, Gretta, 174-175
University of Washington
   de Tornyay Center for Healthy Aging, 191
   de Tornyay, Rheba (deanship) 194-199
   Donaldson, Sue Karen
     assistant professor position, 155
     nurse scientist traineeship, 150-153
University of Wisconsin, Aiken, Linda H., postdoctoral
   research fellowship, 233
USPHS (United States Public Health Service), 129
   mission-oriented program, 138-139
   traineeships, 27
USUHS/GSN (Uniformed Services University of the
   Health Sciences, Graduate School of Nursing),
   130, 140-142
UTHSC (University of Texas Health Science Center at
   San Antonio), 173

V

VA (Veterans Affairs) health system, Ferguson, Vernice,
   92-96, 100
Visiting Nurse Service (New Brunswick), 4
VNS (Visiting Nurse Services), 12

W

Wagner College, nursing program design, 207-208
Wandelt, Mabel, 236
Water buffalo incident, University of Pennsylvania,
   218-219
Wayne State University School of Nursing, 149-150
Western Interstate Commission for Higher Education,
   See WICHE
Western Interstate Council for Higher Education for
   Nursing. *See* WICHEN
Western Nursing Research Society Conference. *See*
   WNRS
Wheeler, Dorothy, 207
When Care Becomes a Burden (Milbank Memorial
   Fund), 222
WICHE (Western Interstate Commission for Higher
   Education), 132
WICHEN (Western Interstate Council for Higher
   Education for Nursing), 157
   Donaldson's biological consultant role, 157-158
   Donaldson-Crowley framework for discipline of
     nursing presentation
     formulation of PhD programs for nursing, 163-165
     influence on nursing as a discipline, 165
William J. Ford and Loretta C. Ford Chair, 4
Williams, Frank (director of the NIA), 121
Willman, Marilyn, 174
WNRS (Western Nursing Research Society Conference),
   108
Wood, Nancy, 112
Work environment research, 239
work ethic, 19-21
workplace culture, 41-42
writings, National Library of Medicine, 137
WSU (Wayne State University), 175
Wyngaarden, Jim (Director for NIH), 120

Y

Yale University
   Abdellah's faculty position, 131
   Hinshaw, Ada Sue, MSN, 107
   Styles, Gretta, 171-172
Yankton State Hospital, employment of Luther
   Christman
   hiring of objectors and Native Americans, 74-75
   local support, 77